# Lettering

## a reference manual of techniques

Andrew Haslam

# Lettering
## a reference

K LAURENCE KING

Published in 2011 by
Laurence King Publishing Ltd

361–373 City Road, London EC1V 1LR
Tel +44 20 7841 6900
Fax +44 20 7841 6910
e-mail: enquiries@laurenceking.com
www.laurenceking.com

Copyright © 2011 Central Saint Martins
College of Art & Design, The University of
the Arts London

Published in 2011 by Laurence King Publishing
in Association with Central Saint Martins
College of Art & Design

This book has been produced by Central Saint
Martins Book Creation, Southampton Row,
London, WC1B 4AP, UK

A catalogue record for this book is available
from the British Library.

ISBN 978-1-85669-686-9

Design and diagrams by the author
Jacket design: Jason Ribeiro based on
an idea by Andrew Haslam
Senior editor: Peter Jones
Picture research: Suzanne Doolin
and the author
Printed in China

# manual of techniques

Andrew Haslam

with photographs by Daniel Alexander

Laurence King Publishing

# 4
Cut, engraved and etched three-dimensional lettering

# 5
Moulded and cast three-dimensional lettering

# 6
Lettering in textiles

# 7
Illumination, animation and motion graphics

# ...0.0 Introduction

Lettering is everywhere. It labels the physical environment: road signs, shop façades, fairgrounds, advertising hoardings, underground diagrams, estate agents' boards, manhole covers. It provides information, prophecy, poetry, stories, humour and tokens of value. It forms printed matter: posters, books, newspapers, magazines, maps, banknotes, cheques, licences and certificates. It identifies and promotes: brands, products, packaging, clothing, bags and shoes. It is both illuminated and animated on film, television, the internet, laptops, Blackberrys, phones, iPods, Game Boys and a plethora of electronic devices. Yet at its simplest it is utilitarian handwriting at the tip of a pencil, as we jot down a phone number. From the first minutes of life, when a label stating our name is clipped around a tiny wrist, to our final resting place, a headstone or memorial book, it is lettering that quite literally scores the alpha and omega of our lives.

But how are letters made? Who is it that makes them? Where are they produced? These are the questions that have prompted this book. I have attempted to visually document, record and explain the many processes by which lettering is produced today. I hope the reader will visually experience the process, and not merely read about it. That understanding will be gleaned through seeing, for this is a book of visual explanation: pictures carry the narrative; and digital photography was the medium for over 1,100 images. I made a decision that this had to be a book about real places and that Daniel Alexander – the principal photographer – and I would visit all the locations and record what went on in studios, workshops, and factories. The photography was difficult: machines, acid baths, over-friendly dogs, wobbly ladders, intense heat, freezing conditions and health and safety regulations that restricted the use of tripods and flash, have all presented a considerable challenge.

The range of processes featured is broad and eclectic, covering both design and manufacture, gathering into a single book the expertise of those for whom lettering is a profession and others who merely reproduce letters as an element of manufacture. It brings together craftspeople steeped in years of apprenticeship with those unskilled operators who push a button, relying on precise technology for an excellent reproduction. It has taken Daniel and I on a fascinating journey of discovery, we have travelled over 10,000 miles in two years, visiting designers, artists, craftspeople, manufacturers, technologists, scientists, academics and librarians, all of whom have generously shared their expertise, knowledge and, crucially, granted us permission to photograph on their premises. Nearly every visit has produced a new lead; the more we photographed, the longer our itinerary grew. It is unlikely that such an undertaking is ever really complete, (certainly the impression of my long-suffering editors) as the vagaries of economics, fashion and emerging technology are in constant flux. Some crafts are fading away, clinging to an ever-diminishing client base, others are being revived, while new technologies are continually making processes and even industries obsolete. The photography can only freeze a moment in time and so the book can only really claim to record ways of making letters at the beginning of the twenty-first century and does not include the many others that have already been consigned to history. This is not a book that seeks to record the historical development of lettering, yet it seemed appropriate to identify the origins of a process where possible.

I have pondered long on how to organize and classify the processes for the reader, alphabetically? chronologically? into two-dimensional/three-dimensional lettering? or by material? The book's seven chapters group common processes together: Hand-drawn and painted lettering; Type casting, composition and design; Printing; Cut, engraved and etched three-dimensional lettering; Moulded and cast three-dimensional lettering, Lettering in textiles, Illumination, animation and motion graphics. I have been intrigued how certain approaches to lettering within one discipline have triggered developments in another and I have tried to cross-reference common features.

The word lettering in the book's title loosely includes all letterforms both calligraphic and typographic. Lettering in its strictest sense is a one-off – no two letterforms being identical – while typography is the mechanical, consistent repetition of characters of a particular font or fonts.

There have been many writers of articles and books who have dealt more extensively with specific crafts, techniques and processes involved in the design and reproduction of lettering but some in particular have provided an enduring source of inspiration throughout the writing of this book: Phil Baines and Catherine Dixon, Alan Bartram, Robert Bringhurst, Michelle P. Brown and Patricia Lovett, Glen U. Cleeton and Charles W. Pitkin, Ken Garland, Geoffrey Ashall Glaister, Nicolete Gray, Bob Gordon, Michael Harvey, David Kindersley, Jock Kinnear, Robin Kinross, Tony Lewery, Rick Poyner, Fred Smeijers, Herbert Spencer, Michael Twymann, Richard Ward and Geoff Weedon.

As well as photographically documenting the various processes by which lettering is made, I have attempted to feature some inspirational examples, some produced by the manufacturers we visited, others merely illustrative of the process. This book is not a how-to, encouraging the reader to recreate the processes, but I hope it will provide an informed insight for graphic designers, calligraphers, typographers, architects, academics, craftspeople and artists who share an interest in, or seek to commission, lettering in a range of media. I have attempted to explain any unfamiliar technical terms and supported this with a glossary. A list of further reading and the contact details of those companies and individuals who allowed us to photograph processes is found at the back of the book.

Andrew Haslam

# The anatomy of a letterform

Specific technical names for the various parts of a letterform are used throughout this book. Familiarity with these basic terms will support an understanding of the descriptions of processes that follow. Although the letterforms below are type – the example shows Monotype Bembo at 396 points – many of the terms used are derived from calligraphy. Over the page these terms have been applied to a complete alphabet, together with

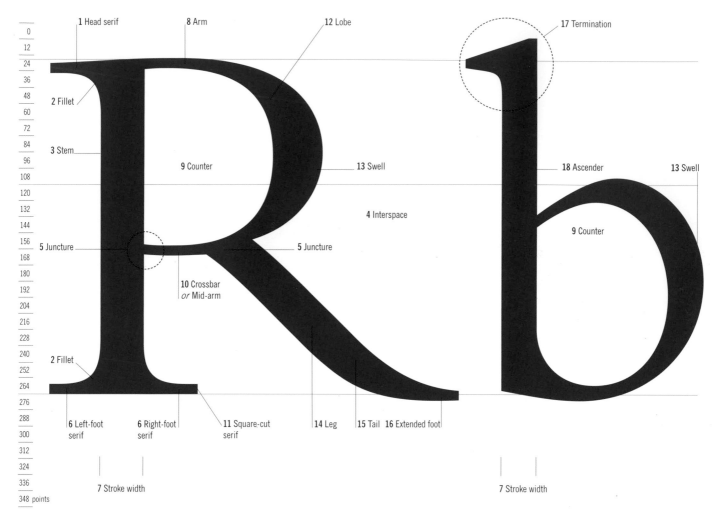

**1 Head serif** A projection at the top of the stem of a roman letterform. Believed to have been developed by painting on stone with a brush. Progressively inscribed within lettercutting in stone.

**2 Fillet or bracket** The small quadrant that infills between the serif and the stem.

**3 Stem** The vertical stroke of a letterform, upper or lowercase from which crossbars, arms or bowls hang.

**4 Interspace** The ground as opposed to the figure (character) between the parts of a letterform, falling to the left and right.

**5 Juncture or Node** The point at which strokes converge or from which they emanate.

**6 Foot serif** A serif at the bottom of the stem of a roman letterform.

**7 Stroke width** The breadth of a stroke. Strokes may be consistent in width, mono width or taper. Bowls and swashes may include many logarithmic variations in stroke width.

**8 Arm** A horizontal stroke emanating from the vertical stem.

**9 Counter** The enclosed, negative space contained within a series of strokes and junctures. Some letterforms, such as stencil forms, have open counters where the negative space is not entirely enclosed.

**10 Crossbar or Mid-arm** A horizontal stroke which emanates from the stem in either

majuscule or minuscules, approximately at the centrepoint of the stem between baseline and cap line.

**11 Square-cut serif** A serif that ends with a truncated geometric form. Slab serif is a broad, square serif in which a stroke and serif width are similar. A filleted or bracketed square serif is a wedge-shaped serif with flared terminals where the stroke progressively broadens. A tapered serif, where the converging lines run to a point, is often seen in stone cutting. A Tuscan or fishtail (bifurcating) serif is a vestigial serif with a tiny broadening of the stroke which visibly affirms the baseline. A sans serif is a letterform without a serif.

**12 Lobe** A rounded stroke broadening or tapering from the vertical stem.

**13 Swell** A term used by some calligraphers and signwriters to describe the broadest point of a rounded stroke. Also used by some signwriters to describe the relative proportion of a letterform, its height to width. A form with swell is broad or expanded.

**14 Leg** A diagonal stroke emanating from a junction which is often tapering and may not terminate in a serif but a tail.

**15 Tail** A stroke termination which tapers and resembles a tail.

**16 Extended foot** The foot is the final element of the leg and sits on the baseline.

**17 Termination** A generic term for the endings of strokes.

additional terminology relating to typography. Further technical terms relating to letterpress printing and metal type production and composition derived from casting techniques are then explained. This introduction concludes on page 12 with terms relating to the design and drawing of digital type forms.

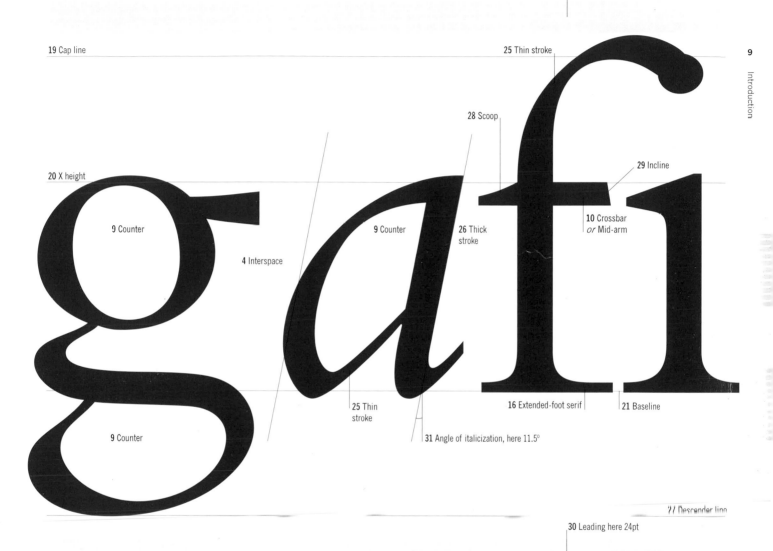

30 Leading here 24pt

19 Cap line

25 Thin stroke

28 Scoop

29 Incline

20 X height

9 Counter

9 Counter

26 Thick stroke

10 Crossbar *or* Mid-arm

4 Interspace

16 Extended-foot serif

21 Baseline

25 Thin stroke

9 Counter

31 Angle of italicization, here 11.5°

27 Descender line

30 Leading here 24pt

**18 Ascender** The stroke of a lower-case letter that extends beyond the x height.

**19 Cap line** An imaginary line that establishes a common height for the capital letters in an alphabet

**20 X height** An imaginary line that establishes a common height from the baseline for the lower-case letters without the ascenders or descenders and is derived from the height of the lower-case x.

**21 Baseline** An imaginary line on which cap and lower-case letters sit.

**22 Descender** Stroke of a lower-case letter which extends below the baseline.

**23 Italic** Letters which slope forward and may be linked by connectives so that the letters flow into one another. See the 'a' above.

**24 Ligature** A pair of letters combined in a new form as a special character in a font or drawn as a pair in calligraphy.

**25 Thin (stroke)** A stroke made with a pen characteristically held at a consistent angle in which the full breadth of the nib is not exploited.

**26 Thick (stroke)** A stroke made with a pen characteristically held at a consistent angle in which the full breadth of the nib is exploited.

**27 Descender line** An imaginary line that marks the extent of the lower-case descenders.

**28 Scoop** A curved line that visually lightens the appearance of a stroke.

**29 Incline** The angled termination of a stroke.

**30 Interline space and leading** The space between lines of calligraphy is called interline space, in type this is referred to as leading.

The term comes from the strips of lead inserted between lines of metal type to create white space between the lines of print on the page.

**31 Angle of italicization** The degree of slope in italicized lettering.

## Upper- and lower-case letterforms

Below is the anatomy of a letterform applied to a single alphabet. Leading can be established by measuring from one baseline to the next. In this example, 60pt Bembo is set on a 72pt baseline, there are therefore 12 points of leading marked in 5 per cent cyan.

Type aligned here is ranged left.

Type aligned here is centred.

Type aligned here is ranged right.

10

**Below:** Non-aligning numerals have ascenders and descenders and relate to the x height in lower-case characters, aligning numerals stand between baseline and cap height and relate to upper-case forms.

| 1 Head serif | ○ 9 Counter | 17 Ascender | 25 Incline |
|---|---|---|---|
| ◆ 2 Fillet or Bracket | — 10 Crossbar or Mid-arm | 18 Cap line | 26 Descender line |
| 3 Stem | 11 Square-cut serif | 19 X height | |
| 4 Interspace | ╱ 12 Lobe | 20 Baseline | |
| ◯ 5 Juncture or Node | ········ 13 Swell | 21 Descender | |
| 6 Foot serif | 14 Leg | 22 Thin | |
| ‖ 7 Stroke width | 15 Tail | 23 Thick | |
| 8 Arm | 16 Extended foot | 24 Scoop | |

# The anatomy of metal type

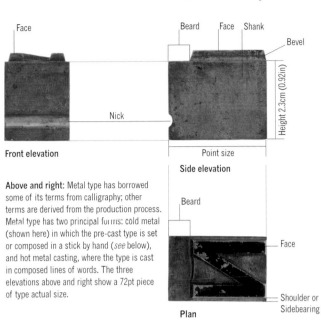

Face

Beard  Face  Shank

Bevel

Nick

Height 2.3cm (0.92in)

Front elevation

Point size

Side elevation

Beard

Face

Shoulder or
Sidebearing

Plan

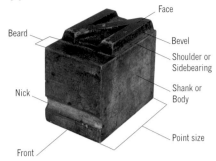

Face

Beard

Bevel

Shoulder or
Sidebearing

Shank or
Body

Nick

Point size

Front

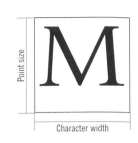

Point size

Character width

**Above and right:** Metal type has borrowed some of its terms from calligraphy; other terms are derived from the production process. Metal type has two principal forms: cold metal (shown here) in which the pre-cast type is set or composed in a stick by hand (*see* below), and hot metal casting, where the type is cast in composed lines of words. The three elevations above and right show a 72pt piece of type actual size.

**Above:** The body of the type has a raised relief letterform cast wrong-reading on its surface. The face of the type is inked before printing and pressed into the paper. The bevel tapers away from the letterform to the body. The beard of the type is the space between the baseline and the edge of the body and creates space between lines. The nick is an aid to the compositor, that ensures all the characters are correctly orientated in the stick. The point size is the measure of the cast body, not the printed baseline to cap height.

**Above:** Metal type of a single size has two fixed dimensions: the body or point size and the type height (the depth of the type between the press bed and paper). The last dimension is determined by the character width. Upper-case M or W are generally the widest characters, the narrowest, the lower-case i. A square of the same point size is referred to as an em and is used as the basis for metal spacing units: en (half em), thick (a third), mid (a quarter), a thin (a fifth) and a hair (either a sixth or a twelfth).

## Type sizes

**Below:** Metal type is cast in standard sizes, points were standardized in 1886. The standard sizes are factorially related,

non-standard sizes, such as 13 point are referred to as 'bastard' sizes.

M 6pt  M 7pt  M 8pt  M 9pt  M 10pt  M 12pt  M 14pt  M 18pt  M 24pt  M 36pt  M 48pt  M 60pt  M 72pt

## Type width

**Below:** All standard numerals are the same width to support the correct alignment of columns of figures.

**Right:** Some special characters extend the letterform beyond the body, those combining several letterforms are referred to as ligatures.

Tracking is the equal adjustment of space between letters in a line

36 points

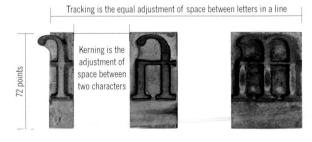

72 points

Kerning is the adjustment of space between two characters

## The stick, measure and column width

**Below:** Cold metal type is set in a holder called a stick calibrated in picas (12pts), and used to set the measure or column width. The stick shown here is carrying 72pt Bembo type and is reproduced actual size; the column width is set to the book's grid. Type characters in the stick vary in width but align on a common baseline.

Measure or column width

Character widths

CORNERSTONE

# Digital letterforms and type

Many terms used to describe digital type have been appropriated from calligraphy and metal type. Digital type can be output through laser- and ink-jet printers, photographic processes, and used as a keyline to guide computer-aided manufacture (CAM) processes. It is planar (flat) but can be imported into three-dimensional drawing programs that enable designers to extrude and visualize three-dimensional type forms linked to milling or rapid prototype machines, which can produce three-dimensional lettering used for casting processes. A number of key terms that relate to digital letterform construction and digital type production and composition are defined below. Like so much of the digital world, many of the terms relate to production systems not all of which have a visible form.

**Right** Digital technology provides a common platform for drawing both calligraphic letterforms or designing type. The calligraphic forms (right) were originally hand-drawn on paper, scanned, before being traced as outlines and adapted. The lower-case b (far right) drawn by Andy Benedek of Fine Fonts shows a similar approach in relation to type. Here shoulders or side bearings of the type are shown as vertical strokes either side of the character.

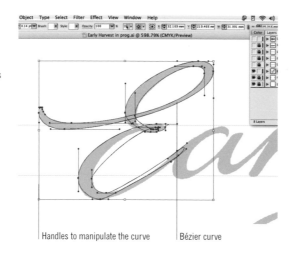

Handles to manipulate the curve | Bézier curve

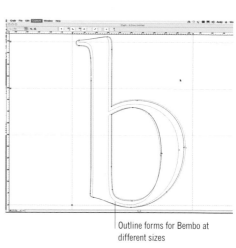

Outline forms for Bembo at different sizes

## Digital type sizes
Digital type has no standard sizes, type can be scaled by percentage or specified by hundredths of a decimal point.

## Encoding
The outline of a letterform can be stored in a computer in different ways.
**Pixel encoding** works on simple binary principals: pixels that make up the letterform are encoded and saved as black, while those that make up the ground and counters are stored as white.
**Run-length coding** is a more efficient way of storing the letterform. It is made up of vertical lines that terminate at a point where they define the character outline, only the start and end point are stored.
**Vector encoding** is even more economical with memory as the curved outline of a letterform are stored as facets. Only points at either end of each facet are stored.

## Hinting
Process undertaken by the designer either automatically or manually to make the best fit between outline and the screen pixel presentation to improve character recognition.

## Interpolation
Process of adjusting the form of a character's presentation at different type sizes within a font family by moderating between two selected sizes to create a third weight. Designers can then manually adjust stroke widths and counters in the new form.

## ISO Latin set 1
The basic set of 256 characters held in a matrix that links through OpenType to the QWERTY keyboard.

## OpenType
Launched in 1997 Open Type supports both PostScript and TrueType formats and was developed by Adobe and Microsoft for both Macintosh and PC operating platforms. TrueType fonts have the suffix .ttf while PostScript fonts have the suffix .otf.

## Pixels and Bitmaps
Short for picture elements, pixels are the smallest unit of digital storage and can be rectilinear or square. Bitmap characters are stored by area through pixel encoding and are heavy on memory.

## PostScript
A cross-platform PC and Macintosh computer language independent of specific software packages which enables users to combine typefaces from different designers and manufacturers. The universality of PostScript has overcome some of the inherent problems associated with its predecessors hot metal and photosetting, where many fonts could only be composed by a particular company's equipment. The shift has democratized font production and availability. Individual type designers using relatively cheap software are now able to single-handedly develop fonts which they can sell directly to the public or to digital founderies without calling upon the specialist abilities or production processes of tracers, pantograph reduction, engravers, specialist lettercutters, tooling or matrix manufacture.

## Resolution
The quality of the digital letterform both on screen and in printed form: the more pixels per inch, the higher the resolution. The print clarity and crispness of a letterform is determined by the refinement of the outputting printer. Domestic laserwriters may output at 300–600dpi (dots per inch) while image-exposing systems for plate-making, film or paper outputs are capable of running 2,500lpi (lines per inch).

## Set width and digital spacing
The complete characters set in metal type is based on the em square, characteristically divided into eighteen units. Each character has a body calibrated in these unit widths, referred to as set width. Digital type divides the em into 1,000 units, supporting characters with individual digital bodies. Consequently intercharacter and interword spacing can be adjusted by these tiny tolerances.

## TrueType
A format invented by Apple to support typesetting. It makes use of quadratic curves as opposed to the Bézier curves used for PostScript.

## Unicode
A character language that accommodates 95,156 characters and is therefore capable of supporting alphabets, scripts and associated symbol and glyph sets for the majority of the major world languages. Alternative characters can be carried, for example, roman Q, swash Q, small caps and lower case. This universality was clearly advantageous during the development of the internet in the early 1990s.

## Vectors
Vectors describe shapes by outline, using straight and curved lines and link specific points on a plane. They are light on memory.

234567**1**

Hand-drawn and painted lettering

Calligraphy literally means beautiful writing, from the Greek *kalligraphia,* and *kallos,* meaning beauty. Unlike type design, calligraphy does not rely on construction or drafting, drawing and redrawing. Each calligraphic letter is individual, described by H. Jenkins as: 'a freehand in which the freedom is so nicely reconciled with order that the understanding eye is pleased to contemplate it'.

The origins of calligraphy stretch back into ancient times. From 3200 BCE, Egyptian scribes are known to have written hieroglyphs on papyrus and calligraphy was practised in China, Japan and Korea as early as 2000 BCE. The Western or Latin alphabet used today was primarily developed during Imperial Roman times in the first few centuries CE. The formal, square capital letters used for Roman inscriptions were derived from earlier Greek characters and are referred to as majuscules. Early Roman handwritten letterforms (in contrast to inscribed letterforms) were also majuscules – all the letters shared a common cap line and baseline – but these rustic forms (condensed capitals with pronounced thick and thin strokes) were quicker to write than formal, square caps.

**Above:** Carolingian minuscules from the *Gospels of Metz* (early ninth century). These early calligraphic minuscules inform our modern perception of lower-case characters.

## The development of minuscules

The desire of scribes to write quickly led to the development of informal handwriting and the use of minuscules (small letters). The simplest minuscules were scribed using a bronze stylus (writing implement for scratching letters) on a small wax tablet contained in a wooden frame. Once the words had been read, the wax could be melted and the tablet used again. The pointed stylus produced a scratched, single-width line and, as a consequence, the letterforms were functional but crude. Important documents were written with a reed dip pen on papyrus, vellum or parchment (a two-sided skin stretched on a frame, dried, whitened with chalk and smoothed flat with a pumice stone). The dip pen was held at a consistent angle so that the letters were made up of the thick and thin strokes characteristically associated with calligraphy.

From the fourth century CE, Roman uncials – 2.5-cm-(1-in-) high letters – were popular. The forms had large, round counters, very short ascenders and descenders and minimal interword spacing. Referred to as insular uncials, they were initiated by monasteries at the edge of the Roman Empire – Kells in Ireland and Lindisfarne in Northumberland, England.

## A combined alphabet

At the end of the ninth century, the Holy Roman emperor Charlemagne (742–814) sought to unify the disparate script styles of the various monastic orders by imposing a new form known as the Carolingian minuscule, developed by Alcuin of York (c.735–804 CE) in the monastery at Tours in France. It was written with a pen held at an angle and used round, open forms and formalized the idea of a twin alphabet, both upper- and lower-case letters were the products of a single-dip pen. Charlemagne's hope that the Carolingian minuscule would unify the lettering style of his empire was initially realized, but over the next five centuries a range of hands or lettering styles evolved throughout Europe from the original forms. The principle of holding the dip pen at a common angle, and producing consistent thick and thin stroke widths, was retained.

In parts of northern Europe, letterforms were condensed, the nodes and transition points emphasized and descenders and ascenders were compacted to produce angular forms (*see* p.17) – later termed blackletter because of their colour, gothic after the period, or broken script after their appearance. In fifteenth-century southern Europe, the Carolingian minuscule was used as a basis for the development of humanist bookhand which had wide, open forms, generous ascenders and descenders and significant interline space. Both broken script and humanist bookhand featured paired alphabets in which upper- and lower-case letters were integrated on a single line, as in handwriting today.

The development of calligraphic letterforms from the rustics, Roman uncials, insular uncials, Carolingian minuscules and broken script, was based on the hands or lettering styles not of individuals but of a particular monastic order. Each scribe in a monastery learned his craft in a scriptorium (the room where manuscripts were copied) as an apprentice copying the work of a master. Several scribes would work on different pages of a psalter that was bound into a single codex (ancient manuscript text in book form). Such was the conformity of the letterforms that to the untrained eye they appear to be the work of a single hand. Calligraphy was the principal form of reproducing writing, and the craft skills of the scribe were highly prized.

## The invention of movable type

After Johannes Gutenberg (1400–68) discovery of movable type (in the West) and letterpress printing in around 1454, the pre-eminence of the scribe diminished. Gutenberg's type was often referred to as mechanical writing as the letterforms used in the Mainz indulgences of 1454–55 were modelled on the informal calligraphic broken script Bastarda, while his more famous *42-line Bible* of 1455 used the more formal broken script Textura. With letterpress printing, a literate middle class emerged in fifteenth- and sixteenth-century Europe whose interest in literature, poetry, scientific investigation, mathematics, exploration, trade and banking was enabled by their ability to write and to read in both Latin and their own language. The purpose of writing had expanded beyond the domain of the specialist calligraphic scribe, who copied precious ecclesiastical books. Handwriting had become detached from the calligraphy of the Church and began to carry a plethora of secular messages.

In early sixteenth century Italy the forms of the Carolingian minuscule were adapted into Chancery script by the calligrapher Ludovico Arrighi (1475–1527). Austere in form and inclined for speed, this script was ideally suited to legal documentation. It also had a range of alternative decorative majuscules that were used to open paragraphs. Arrighi published his new calligraphic letterforms in *La Operina* (1522). Chancery script was widely adopted by Renaissance diplomats, scholars and artists.

## Engraved lettering

In the mid-eighteenth century, the use of lettering engraved into a copper plate with a burin – a hand-held steel tool – led to the development of a new calligraphic hand: copperplate (*see* p.19). Engravers devised lettering with flowing forms ideally suited to chasing the burin away from the hand. As a result many of the characters in a single word were linked through connectives. Calligraphers of the time, impressed by the style's fine lines and flourishes, sought to imitate it by cutting very fine points to their quill pens and italicizing the lettering. This form of handwriting was adopted by the fashionable middle classes throughout Europe in the late eighteenth century. Countries developed national characteristics in proportions, connectives and the lavishness of the flourishes. Distinct versions of copperplate roundhand were developed in the Netherlands, Italy, France, Spain and England. For much of the nineteenth century, copperplate formed the pattern for the formal hand used for teaching schoolchildren. It remained the predominant letter-writing style until the early twentieth century.

Calligraphic teaching, as opposed to functional handwriting, was often formalized and linked with heraldic illustration and illumination. During the nineteenth century calligraphy was taught in art and design schools as both an independent study and as part of a typography course. A revival of calligraphy occurred under the influence of William Morris (1834–96) and the Arts and Crafts Movement in England and coincided with similar revivals in Germany and France. At the beginning of the twentieth century the English calligrapher Edward Johnston (1872–1944), who sympathized with the craft traditions so treasured by Morris, inspired a generation of students, teachers, calligraphers and type designers to reconsider the importance of penned letterforms. Today, most graphic design courses include the study of letterform and some organize introductory workshops in calligraphy.

## Calligraphic drawing tools

**Below:** Drawing tools used by Rachel Yallop and Carol Kemp, professional calligraphers and lettering artists. Kemp works both by hand, using drawing instruments, and also by adapting or redrawing characters digitally. She develops lettering specifically for brands, logos, straplines and insignia, for many commercial clients. Yallop tends to work with a freer approach and uses a wide range of drawing tools: commercial ruling pens, ruling pens made from old aluminium cans, pointed dip pens, square chisel-edged and round brushes, reed and calligraphic felt pens. Each tool produces a different type of mark and a stroke with an individual character.

**Below:** Flat-tipped, brass poster pens, are so called because they are designed for drawing large lettering. The pen is dipped into the ink or loaded with the aid of a brush. The ink is held between the two brass plates in a reservoir. When the pen is pressed on the paper a small gap between both plates opens allowing the ink to flow smoothly on to the page; the breadth of the pen determines the maximum width of the stroke. Thicks and thins are formed by the pen being held at a consistent angle as the letters are drawn.

Ruling pens were originally designed to draw lines of even thickness for orthographic drawing but have been appropriated by calligraphers for drawing. The pen has a rounded point made up of two flat plates, the distance between which is determined by turning a screw. When the pen is drawn along a ruler, the stroke width is consistent but held at an angle it produces a splattering of ink. Some ruling pens have multiple nibs which draw lines in parallel.

Yallop made these pens using old aluminium cans. The right side of the pen, which forms the top, is enclosed by a single sheet of metal. The tip is pointed and bellies out to form the ink reservoir, while the left edge of the pen opens to release the ink when pressed on the page. Unlike commercially produced ruling pens, the gap between the edges is irregular and consequently the stroke created is clean on one side and roughly scratched on the other (see p.23).

Pointed dip pens have two basic forms: copperplate pens (left) and nibs with a reservoir (right). The brass nib has a small metal clip on the reverse which forms an ink reservoir. The pen nib is split vertically down the centre. The stroke width in copperplate is controlled by the amount of pressure applied, not by the angle at which the pen is held. The greater the pressure, the wider the nib splits and the more ink flows.

Brushes are used to load ink on to a pen and as drawing tools in their own right. Most calligraphers build up a collection which includes round, square, and chisel-ended brushes, long-haired brushes used by signwriters, and Chinese calligraphic brushes.

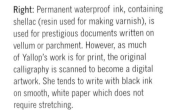

**Right:** Permanent waterproof ink, containing shellac (resin used for making varnish), is used for prestigious documents written on vellum or parchment. However, as much of Yallop's work is for print, the original calligraphy is scanned to become a digital artwork. She tends to write with black ink on smooth, white paper which does not require stretching.

# Gothic hands

Calligraphers have developed many hands which today are grouped together as Gothic. These scripts have historical names such as Textura, Bastarda, Rotunda, Schwabacher and Fraktur. Some of them retain both their form and name, but over time calligraphers have adapted letterforms and renamed hands so that today there are inconsistencies between the terms used by historians to describe the development of writing and those used by modern calligraphers in professional practice. The phrase modern Gothic is frequently used to describe a hand developed in the twentieth century from an older Gothic pattern. Many of these modern hands are based on those developed by the German calligrapher Rudolf Koch (1876–1934). They are characterized by full-width principal pen strokes and curved, vertical strokes that create an elliptical lozenge between the characters. It is this form of modern Gothic that Rachel Yallop has drawn below.

## Writing in a gothic hand

**1** A broad ruling pen is held at an angle of 45 degrees, although many calligraphers prefer to use a shallower angle of 40 degrees. The vertical stroke is drawn first as a bow and then the top of the 'g' is formed with a thin upstroke and a thick down. Calligraphers who use nib widths to determine the height of the letter are likely to base the letter on nine – three for ascenders, five for the x height and one for descenders.

**2** Gothic scripts are characterized by the consistent figure and ground relationship – the stroke widths, the character's counters and the intercharacter spacing are virtually identical. The harsh contrast between the black strokes and the white spaces accentuated in Quadrant Gothic is marginally alleviated by the bows, which create elliptical intercharacter spaces.

**3** The proportions of Gothic letters do not relate to the skeleton alphabet which underpins so many calligraphic hands. The breadth of the majority of minuscule letters – 'a', 'b', 'd', 'f', 'h', 'k', 'n', 'o', 'p', 'q', 'u', 'v', 'x' and 'z' – is based on three stroke widths. The letters 'i', 'j' and 'l' are one and a half stroke widths; 'c', 'e', 'r' and 't' are perhaps two and a half stroke widths; 'g', 's' and 'y' are three and a half stroke widths; 'm' and 'w' are five stroke widths.

**Left:** The basic calligraphic principle of maintaining a common pen angle is often broken by frequent pen lifts and returns. Compare the return on the 'g' (approximately 30 degrees) with the pen lift on the dot of the 'i' (45 degrees) and the pen lift on the 'c' (60 degrees). Some cap Gothic letters make use of 40 degrees for thick, vertical strokes, 30 degrees for returns and 50 degrees for pen lifts.

## Letter proportions and nib widths

Some calligraphers approach their work in a very mannered way, and always use the same process of preparation. A calligrapher decides on the style of hand, majuscules or minuscules, the lettering size and the stroke width. These decisions affect the x height and the length of the ascenders and descenders. A set of nib widths is drawn up the side of the page to serve as a guide for the x height and the proportions of the ascenders and descenders. For example, uncials might be drawn with an x height of six nib widths, while half uncials may have only five and Carolingian minuscules only four nib widths. The relationship between the x height and the nib width determines the apparent weight of the letter on the page. A tall x height with a narrow nib will create a letterform that appears light, while a thick nib will produce a bold form.

## Writing in an italic hand

**1** Most calligraphic hands rely on the pen being held at a consistent angle (here 45 degrees). The thick strokes are drawn down from the top of the letter.

**2** The thin stroke is made by retaining the common pen angle and writing from the baseline up. In this letterform the thick and thin strokes forming the bowl of the 'a' have been made without the pen being lifted from the page.

**3** The height of the ascender of the 'b' is estimated and the vertical thick stroke is written. The bowl of the 'b' is formed as a separate stroke. The pen is pushed up to form a thin stroke and pulled back down to the baseline to produce a tapered, thick stroke.

**4** The 'c' is drawn down from the top. In this hand the curve is steeper in the top quarter than in the bottom three-quarters.

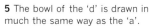

**5** The bowl of the 'd' is drawn in much the same way as the 'a'.

**6** The broad stroke is added last. All the characters are independent, without ligatures (two letters connected with a stroke or combined into a single type form) or connectives, but visually they hold together. Unifying the whole design visually is very important to the calligrapher, who carefully considers how letters will combine when positioned next to one another. Calligraphers who work in this free way may adapt the position of each letterform and on occasion the letterform itself, adding ligatures and swashes (extended flowing strokes).

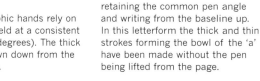

**Above:** Calligraphic, non-aligning numerals drawn by Yallop with a broad-nib dip pen, held at an angle of 45 degrees. The shapes of the numerals are considered in relation to one another, and some butt up to, or overlap, others. Unlike type there is no common baseline.

## Copperplate hand

Copperplate hand is one of the hardest to master as it relies on a dexterity that is very different from that required by other letterforms. The stroke width is determined by the pressure on the page and not the angle at which the pen is held. Copperplate has several variations which were developed in the Netherlands, Italy, France, Spain and England. English copperplate is often referred to as English roundhand or even London script as it was popularized by academics and lawyers in London. Although the hand was designed for everyday writing most professional calligraphers are meticulous about the preparation of the page, drawing up fine pencil lines for the baseline, x height, ascenders, descenders and cap heights. To ensure the angle of the pen is maintained, nearly all calligraphers draw a series of diagonal pencil guidelines at either 40 degrees or, as here, 54 degrees.

**Above:** English copperplate, also known as London script.

### Writing in a copperplate hand

**1** It is the consistency of angle coupled with the smooth transition from a thin to a thick stroke that gives copperplate its precise nature. Here the progressive increase in pressure on the nib broadens the stroke, while simultaneously realizing the curve of a minuscule.

**2** Unlike most other calligraphic hands, copperplate is not made up of a series of strokes. It is a single line shaped into letters emphasized by variations in line weight and thick vertical and fine looping connectives. The pen is often only lifted from the page at the end of a word or to be reloaded with ink.

**3** The pressure on the nib is increased as the pen is moved down the page and progressively released as the loop of the connective is formed.

**4** The same letterform drawn at two very different sizes with the same pen. The right-hand edge of the vertical is at 54 degrees, while the left-hand edge has soft, flowing curves. The stroke of the larger letterform shows how the consistent release of pressure on the nib of the pen tapers the line width.

**Right:** Variations in styles of copperplate are both national and individual to the calligrapher. The looping forms of the 'f' and 'k' are found in many copperplate hands but the flourishes on the 'd' are particular to Yallop.

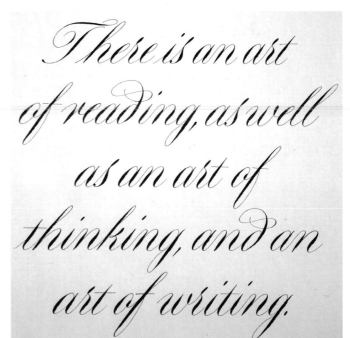

## Formal drawing with French curves

French curves are plastic drawing instruments, the edges of which form a perfect Bézier curve (a logarithmic spiral). They come in sets with different proportions and form the perfect edge against which to draw. Carol Kemp is able to refine hand–drawn lettering styles using French curves and, more recently, digital calligraphy.

### Writing with French curves

**1** The lettering here has not been drawn with a copperplate pen, as the artwork is A3 and the letter would be too broad in proportion to the paper size. A rough is first drawn in pencil on paper and, once approved by the client, it is redrawn on a ceramic-faced board using French curves and a blue propelling pencil.

**2** The plastic curve is shifted and rotated slightly until it finds the line of best possible fit with the drawing on the base board.

**3** The curve is held firmly in place with one hand while the pen is drawn around its edge.

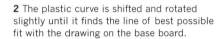
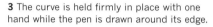

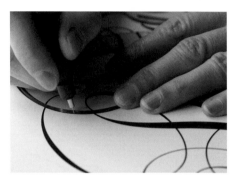

**4** The advantage of drawing on a ceramic-faced board is that any tiny mistakes can be corrected and lines removed or redrawn. Here Kemp uses a 10a scalpel blade to scrape away a minor blemish.

**5** The design stage may take far longer than the artwork. The latter – which has taken about a day to draw and ink in using French curves, Rotoring pen and waterproof ink – shows beautifully controlled flourishes and swirls.

1

2

3

4

**This page:**
Working with French curves and other traditional drawing instruments enables Kemp to rework ideas and progressively refine a word or individual letterform, and ensure consistent letter proportions, common line and stroke widths, and an exceptionally precise finish.

**1** The complexity of this decorative initial 'C' would make it almost impossible to draw it freehand as the letterform has many internal patterns, which rely on consistent stroke widths to create the clarity between the figure and ground effect.

**2** This script lettering is beautifully even and exhibits the flourish and swash forms made by drawing around a French curve.

**3** The secondary line, which mimics the connectives of the broader strokes, appears to lift the lettering for this wine label. The capital forms have been drawn to fit the curve of the baseline.

**4** Like the previous example, the form of the lettering here is significantly determined by the variable space between cap line and baseline. The connectives are almost continuous. The phrase or strapline visually expresses the pleasure of drinking chocolate.

**5** The ligature between the 'H' and 'O' gives the name of a manufacturer of chocolate drinks a unique visual identity.

**6** The forms of the upper- and lower-case characters are drawn in outline so that they appear to run into one another in this logo for an American hip hop group.

5

6

## Ruling pens and free lettering

Most professional calligraphers develop a range of conventional hands – Gothic, italic and copperplate, etc. – and like Rachel Yallop begin to adapt styles in a way that is personal and expressive. This looser approach to calligraphy is generically referred to as 'freehand' as it encompasses a wide range of styles and tools. Yallop has developed her own set of pens (*see* p.16), cut from aluminium beer cans.

The visual consistency of all calligraphic hands relies on even stroke widths, pen angles and common letter proportions. These principles are generally practised through conventional hands before being developed in expressive freehands. Most calligraphers are formally taught a set of horizontal letter proportions based on a skeleton alphabet. While the styles of the majority of angled pen hands a calligrapher develops differ greatly, the relative proportions remain the same. This establishes in the mind of the craftsperson a set of consistent proportions shared with signwriters (*see* pp.30–41) and lettercutters (*see* pp.132–39), although how common letters are grouped varies. Many calligraphers have been taught on a skeleton alphabet based on a square which is generally divided into 9, 11, 13, or 15 units; odd numbers support the symmetrical letters by centring them on the square. The letters are learned as separate groups of majuscule and minuscule. There are variations but a typical scheme for the majuscule, based on 15 units, groups together: M, O and Q occupying the full-square 15 units; C, D and G occupying 13 units; A, H, N, T, U, V, W, X, Y and Z occupying 11 units; J, K, R and S occupying eight units; B, E and L occupying seven units; F and P occupying six units; I occupying one unit; W breaks with the square and occupies 19 units.

### Writing using a home-made ruling pen

1

2

3

4

**1–4** The home-made ruling pen has a reservoir of ink that is delivered to the nib. One side of the nib creates a smooth line while the other splatters the ink unevenly. Here the ruling pen is used very freely, producing ebullient strokes; the pen remains in contact with the paper and the letters are linked with connectives. The x height is very low and the ascenders and descenders are exaggerated.

**Above:** Part of an alphabet Yallop drew using her home-made ruling pen and white ink on black paper.

## Writing in freehand

**1** The home-made ruling pen can be used with many hands but is perhaps best suited to free, expressive letterforms. The angle of the pen remains the same (here approximately 30 degrees). The outer edge of the stroke is clean but due to the irregularity of the inkflow on the inner edge, the line becomes scratched and uneven.

**2** The letterforms are drawn quickly with confidence and the ink forms accidental patterns, blots and scratches.

**3** The strokes are vibrant and the letterforms have a strident quality. The letter proportions and hand are similar to those on p.18 but the quality of the stroke is more varied.

**4** By extending the length of the vertical strokes and accentuating the swashes with lavish, curved forms, the scratched edge is exaggerated. The letters do not have flowing connectives like copperplate or the example opposite, but the strokes overlap one another to link, making sharp contrasts between the counter forms and character space.

## Brush scripts

Brush scripts can be painted with either a chisel-ended or round brush and tend to be loose in character. They were much favoured by American cartoonists, comic book artists and animators from the 1930s to 1960s. Brushes come in a variety of widths which determine the size of the stroke within the letterform. The strokes are usually made at a consistent angle and the brush is allowed to run free of ink before being dipped and reloaded with ink. This repeated process of dipping and stroke-making creates a smooth stroke edge (here on the left of the vertical stroke) with the tip, while the edge of the stroke made with the hairs nearest the grip is broken (here on the right).

### Writing in freehand

**1** Here Yallop uses a pointed brush which is heavily loaded with black ink. By pushing the brush down on to the paper and progressively lifting it from the sheet the stroke is tapered.

**2** The angle at which the brush is held, usually between 30 degrees and 45 degrees, affects the nature of the stroke. Each letter is generally completed before the brush is dipped again.

**3** Here the letters are drawn with exaggerated tails and just touch one another.

**4** As the ink on the brush is released, the even stroke breaks down into a tracery of fine lines, which gives variations in tone to different parts of each letter.

**5** Capitals in brush scripts are often butted, the strokes continually taper from the touch point (where the brush initially touches the paper) to the brush lift (where it is lifted from the paper). Although the appearance is loose and free, the lettering remains consistent. Note the common elements to the upper bowl of the B and R, and the tail flourish of the B and S.

**Left:** Loose, expressive letters can be drawn with a square-top brush. Yallop separates the hairs of the brush and dilutes the ink with water to produce a tone made up of many parallel lines before drawing over the form with a soft, black felt pen.

# 1.2 Digital calligraphy

Carol Kemp is commissioned by design groups to create lettering for specific purposes. This may involve developing specific letters based on existing patterns to exemplify a product name. The nature of the brief varies. Some designers and advertisers provide the wording and a very free brief that describes the product, its associated values, market and customer, and allow her to develop roughs that visually encapsulate these ideas. Others are more prescriptive in their briefing strategy. They define the proportions of a logotype and present typographic roughs using fonts that approximate to the letterforms they wish to commission, arranged and printed out in a rough layout. With this type of brief Kemp is responsible for redrawing and reconsidering the forms and spaces created by a word, making it work emblematically as a whole. Kemp's professional career has spanned the transition from hand-drawn artwork to digital files, and she still tends to begin most jobs by drawing on paper. Here she draws letters by hand and adapts them digitally. The final design reveals flourishes related to copperplate hand (*see* p.19).

## Calligraphic forms on screen

**1** Most digital calligraphers draw on graphics tablets rather than using a mouse. Some draw directly on to the computer but Carol, like many calligraphers trained with a pen, prefers to make the letters on paper first. She feels that the paper provides instant feedback and is intrinsically less mechanical.

**2** Carol scans hand-drawn sheets usually up to A3 then imports them into digital drawing programs, such as Illustrator and FontLab. Here the scanned, hand-drawn lettering is shown on screen. Two blue guidelines have been drawn to mark the x height.

**3** Drawing on the graphics tablet, Carol creates Bézier curves, which she attempts to match to the forms of the hand-drawn lettering shown in grey.

**4** Kemp creates the outline of the letters by progressively adding handles and pulling the black lines into shapes that match the base drawing.

**5** Complex curves may require more points, and redrawing the letterform may take almost as long as making a hand-drawn artwork. The designer constantly checks the effect of minor movements in one direction and how these affect the balance and weight of line in another. The computer allows the designer to review the curves which are often far larger than they will ever be reproduced in print.

**6** When all the letters have been digitally traced the outline can be filled in. Here the original drawing is shown in grey and the infilled tracing in black. The lettering can be further refined and, unlike ink-based artwork, can be rekerned without being redrawn.

# 1.3 Graffiti

Graffiti, meaning writing on walls, is derived from the Italian *graffito*, a little scratch and has been used to describe the cave paintings of prehistory and to identify political slogans scratched illegally on walls in ancient Roman cities. Today the term is characteristically associated with styles of lettering made with a stencil, a canister of spray paint or an indelible marker pen.

The first aerosol can was patented by the Norwegian engineer Erik Rotheim (1898–1938) in 1927. Today specialist firms such as Belton Molotow, Montana Colors and Monster Colors have developed metallic and fluorescent paints with more intense colours specifically for use by street artists. Advanced nozzle technology and a range of actuators (caps that atomize the paint) are available in different widths from skinny to fat. These control how the paint droplets disperse and create crisp or soft lines.

The marker pen, the graffiti artist's secondary tool, was invented by Sidney Rosenthal in 1953 when he attached a felt-tip pen to the lid of a bottle of ink and found he could write smoothly as the flow was even, and the mark permanent. He founded Speedry Chemical Products in New York to make the pens but renamed the company the more familiar Magic Marker in 1966. According to graffiti folklore it was Rosenthal's Magic Marker pens, with their distinctive slim, aluminium tubes that were first used to write on walls in Philadelphia during that same year. This is thought to be the origin of modern graffiti. The writers signed themselves Cornbread and Cool Earl, their decorative signatures were referred to as tags, probably after the aluminium identity tags worn by soldiers. Illegal writing on walls and trains had similar military associations and was known as bombing.

The trend was soon picked up on by taggers in the Washington Heights district of New York, while the term graffiti was first used to describe this new art form in a *New York Times* article of 1971 featuring a tagger – TAKI 183 – who had begun to leave his distinctive mark on buildings and subway trains. Coverage given to the New York tags and lettering by magazines and photographic books, and in films, inspired youngsters in other American cities to imitate the styles. Very quickly tagging spread to the metro and rail networks of European cities. Taggers began to personalize their lettering styles and, as they attempted to distinguish their work from one another, the scale of the lettering grew. As the artists became more ambitious, crews (several artists working together) such as POG, 3yb and BYB, collaborated to paint entire subway carriages.

Since the 1970s, independent styles of lettering have continued to develop. Some are associated with particular cities – New York, Los Angeles, Berlin, Paris, London, São Paolo, Mumbai – others are linked to an individual artist or attributed to a specific gang that uses the artwork to delineate its neighbourhood within a city. Some styles are inseparable from types of music, such as hip hop, house, garage etc., while others are the product of crews developing a collective approach to letterform.

**Top:** The word vandalism painted on a wall in Shoreditch, east London – graffiti with irony.

**Middle and bottom:** Details reveal how the lettering resembles some of the slab serif outlines and three-dimensional forms of fairground signwriting (*see* pp.32–39).

**Right:** A jagged style from Sweden, Bates shows considerable refinement of complex letterforms with graduated colour fades. The highlight is derived from the lens flare associated with fairground lettering (*see* pp.32–39) and the graffiti is set on a red ground.

1

2

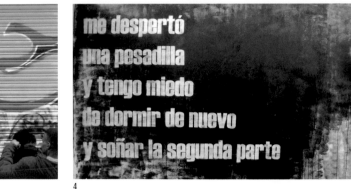

1 A relatively simple throw-up style by Nylon. The white ground is sprayed, or in some cases rolled, on to the wall and the black letters are sprayed over it.

2 Lettering, again by Nylon, with colour bands, a strong drop shadow and a fluorescent keyline surrounding the entire motif

3 A crew at work on a shopfront grille. Here the graffiti has been officially agreed.

me desperté
una pesadilla
y tengo miedo
de dormir de nuevo
y soñar la segunda parte

3

4

5

6

7

8

4 A painterly approach to street art by Einsamkeit. A black ground with hand lettering with san serif type forms and the image defined by white highlights.

5 An artist uses spray paint for a mural.

6 A complex form of wild style, seen on a street in east London. Letterforms sit amongst a tangled ribbon which threads its way between the maroon blocking-out.

7 Detail from 'Spat', a jagged style with a drop shadow.

8 From a distance this form of wild style by Siner resembles woodcut or linocut. The hard black outline and the detailing within the forms look almost scratched.

9 A subway train which still carries the legendary tag 'Stayhigh 149'. Simple black aerosol-sprayed lettering is on either side of the windows above the later addition 'Jamar'.

9

# 1.4 Tattooed lettering

The techniques used for tattooing have varied throughout history. Modern tattooists, like the ones at Wizard Tattoo featured below, use electric guns with multiple needles. New needles must be used on each client and the equipment must be regularly sterilized. Here 'fridge magnets' is tattooed on a client's back in the lettering style of such magnets.

## Lettering on skin

**1** The design for the tattoo is drawn in outline at full size on paper. A photocopy is made and a colour selected from a limited range for each letter. Most tattooists have a book of letter styles from which a client may choose, but the example shown here is not characteristic as it uses fridge magnet letterforms.

**2** The final design is copied on to the reverse of a sheet of tracing paper (here seen from the front).

**3** The paper design is positioned with the right-reading lettering facing out of the body (the lower back). Alcohol is rubbed on the front of the tracing paper, the outline of the lettering is transferred on to the skin.

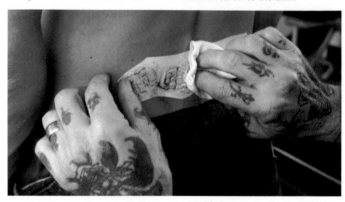

**7** A single needle is used to trace round the design in dark blue ink. It is operated electronically and penetrates the skin, injecting a small quantity of ink just below the surface.

**8** The skin is irritated by the ink and the outline of the letters becomes raised and slightly inflamed.

**9** With the client seated and bending over the back of a chair, the process of filling in the colour according to the design begins. Here the drop shadow (the shadow around the edge of a letter) of each letter is broadened with the dark blue ink used for the outline.

**4** The paper is removed leaving the traced outline of the letters on the skin.

**5** The sterilized tattooing needle is fitted into an electric pen which carries the ink.

**6** Colours can be mixed on a palette but must not be too subtle as they will fade on the skin and lose their contrast.

**10** Adding the colour is achieved more quickly by using multiple needles which cover a larger area with a single injection. The dark blue keyline serves as a guide for the colour. However, using multiple needles is a slow and painful process.

**11** As the skin is now very tender, the area of the tattoo is covered with antiseptic cream.

**12** Finally the whole area is covered with cling film to keep it sterile while the inflammation heals.

**Right:** The finished tattoo reflects the quirky nature of the three-dimensional fridge magnet letters by graduating the tone of the coloured face and blocking out one side. The irregular alignment and deliberately uneven intercharacter spacing reinforce the trompe l'oeil effect: the letters seem to be stuck on the skin as they would be on a fridge.

1

2

3

Throughout the nineteenth century and until the late 1950s, signwriting (literally making signs with words and not pictures) was the principal process used in environmental and transport lettering. Prior to this period, stone-cut and woodcut letters were the predominant forms – their use dates back to ancient Roman times.

Painted lettering on shop fascias did not develop until the sixteenth and seventeenth centuries when a rich merchant class who built shops (permanent retail spaces) rather than temporary market stalls emerged in Europe. The shops were at first identified by their trade signs, pictorial symbols devised for non-readers – a pair of shears for a tailor, a pestle and mortar for a chemist, a bull's head for a butcher and a last for a cobbler – which hung at 90 degrees to the façade. As literacy levels across Europe began to rise in the seventeenth century, painted letters started to appear on the exteriors of inns, public houses and shops. The address of a business or house was described by its proximity to other notable buildings, areas or long-standing businesses – the baker by the spire for example, or the butcher on the square – a practice that gave sign-painters much work and continued long after street numbers were adopted in the eighteenth century. When a business changed premises, its sign was physically moved to the new building but was amended to reflect its previous location. Lettering on a shop fascia that stated the proprietor's name came to be associated with a 'better class of trade' as it implied the clientele of the business could read. Signwriting was important as part of the painting and decorating trade until it became a designated trade in the 1850s.

Throughout the late nineteenth century a range of signwriting styles developed for different trades. Those for shop fascias differed from the livery used by steamship, coach and railway companies. Freight trains in the United States were adorned in a box cart style (bold condensed caps), but in Europe agricultural carts and gipsy caravans were predominantly floral. Canal (narrow) boats had their own distinctive castles and roses style (*see* pp.40–41). Advertisements differed from street signs, and circuses, menageries (touring shows of exotic animals) and fairgrounds had bold, highly decorative three- dimensional lettering. Although signwriting has declined in popularity due to the introduction of cheaper acrylics, vinyls and illuminated light boxes, many of the distinctive styles remain today. While most signwriters are capable of painting in several different ones, they may develop a specialism for a particular clientele. The descriptions and processes on the following pages show some of the styles.

**This page:**

1 Water transfer corporate crests formed a principal element in the design and livery of nineteenth-century railway companies and featured on both sides of every carriage.

2 As trams worked the same route daily, a permanent route number could be painted on them. This renovated tram from 1919 shows the route number 74 positioned below the single headlamp. The nineteenth-century, bold block lettering style of the number contrasts with the plain sans serif caps on the destination board. Signwriters hand-painted destinations on canvas fixed between two rollers, which the driver could wind on to the appropriate name.

3 Some corporations, like the owners of this tram company in Southampton, England, for example, or combined signwritten lettering and decorative borders with large, printed water-based transfers that were applied as decal and varnished over.

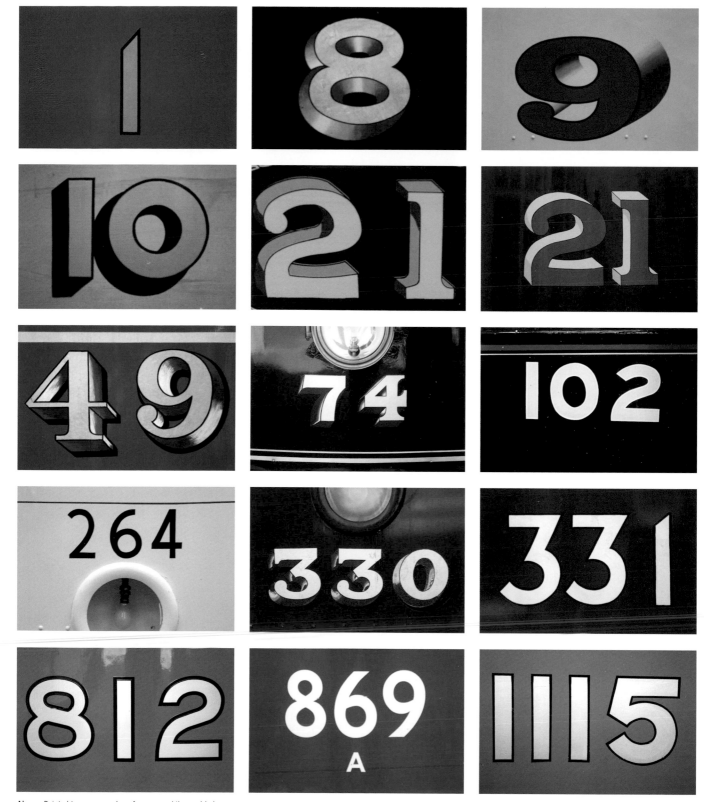

**Above:** Painted tram car numbers from around the world show a wide variety of styles. Some of the numbers clearly relate to insignia derived from painting on carriages while others have picked up on lettering styles associated with railway livery.

# 1.6 Fairground painting

**Above:** Strong, colourful lettering typical of the nineteenth-century travelling fair. The square, blue tops of the letters appear to burst out of the lower forms just above the green-leafed lozenge – sometimes referred to as an ivy. The signwriter must make careful decisions about the levels of tonal contrast between the ground and each of the elements. The front face of a letter is often lighter in tone than the back shading, which in turn must be different in tone, either lighter or darker than the ground. The shadow is generally the darkest of all the elements. Here the lining out (painting a thin line around a coloured letter or shape within a design, often to cover the edge where two shapes butt up to one another) is the lightest colour. The decorative ropework acts as a border. The three-dimensional block is to the right; this is called front shading. If the block is drawn to the left of the letterface (*see* Modern opposite ), it is referred to as back shading. The shadow is generally drawn as though the letter is illuminated by strong sunlight and falls below the character. The shadow does not usually match the depth angle and so is either 45 degrees (when the depth is 30 degrees) or 60 degrees (when the depth is 45 degrees). If the letter it is to touch the ground, it is drawn from the bottom serif; if it is to appear to hover above the ground, it is drawn from behind the face.

Nearly all travelling fairs are owned by long-established fairground families where the business has been handed down from father to son and the rides form part of the inheritance. Some rides have mechanisms, carvings, gallopers (horses on a roundabout or carousel), boards, mirrors and pay boxes that are well over a hundred years old, and have been in the same family for generations.

Painting a ride is a slow process as its every visible surface is often covered. Many fairground owners are sensitive about the designs, and the painting and lettering schemes used on their rides. Some families, keen to preserve the traditional aspects of their fair, re-create the painting scheme and a new design is not required. Others wish to retain a particular set of colours for both rides and the vehicles that transport them. Carter's Steam Fair, for example, uses predominantly maroon. This approach may allow for new designs but within a restricted palette, which serves the same purpose as a corporate brand or railway livery. Other owners have patterns and specific lettering styles which are developed by a fairground painter for their use.

At the initial consultation with a fairground painter, the owner identifies themes, decorative patterns and appropriate lettering styles for the ride by reviewing a huge photographic collection of previous work. Following the design briefing the price is haggled over and finally agreed with a handshake – few fairground owners make contracts. Fairground painters tend to develop an individual approach to the layout and designs of lettering. Some spend time measuring up the exact panel dimensions and make 1:12 scale drawings before making a pencil sketch of a complete design which is presented to the owner for amendment, final approval and agreed colouring. Some owners prefer to see the design drawn out in full size. The owner delivers the major decorative panels to the workshop, and continues to run the ride.

Carter's Steam Fair is the most complete touring steam fair in Britain. Jody Carter is keen to preserve the living tradition of the fairground and its associated skills, and is vehemently opposed to the use of vinyl. To achieve his aim, he runs residential courses where he teaches students fairground signwriting. Carter emphasizes the importance of learning how to draw Roman capitals and then lower-case letters as a prerequisite to working in the more florid styles associated with fairground painting. The height and width of the letters, and the thickness of the strokes, are drawn out between baseline and cap line with a chinagraph pencil. Most fairground letters are robust – described by Carter as 'letters with girth' – and have strong serifs and internal florid embellishments, lozenges and scrolls. The letter is fattened and a midpoint between cap line and baseline is established from which scroll forms are drawn. The signwriter considers both the proportions and style of each letter and the number of coloured elements within it.

**Left:** Blockwork is used to give lettering the appearance of depth. Here they are blocked out at 45 degrees to the left while, unusually, the shadow has been painted at 45 degrees to the right.

## Painting a winged roundel and lettering

**1** The winged roundel boards are traditionally used at the top of a waltzer pillar. The single wing to the right gives the impression that the ride is rotating. Here the lining out of the stylized feathers is carefully applied.

**2** The cap line and baseline are drawn across the roundel and wing with a chinagraph pencil. In this design they will not run parallel but will reflect the shape of the cut-out wing.

**3** Bold sans serif letters are sketched between the cap line and baseline and deep maroon gloss paint is applied with a long-haired brush. Carter rests his hand on a daub stick to avoid smudging the wet paint.

**4** The letters are painted in quickly and evenly.

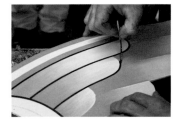

**5 and 6** (right) As the letters in this example are gradually decreasing in size, the stroke widths vary. Carter reviews the relative weights of each of the characters and slightly thickens the initial 'C'. The chinagraph outline of the letter is used as a guide for the painting rather than as an exact line.

1

2

3

4

5

**This page:**

1 Italic lettering arranged on the cant.

2 Two-tone bold italic lettering.

3 An expanded block form where the shadow emanates from the corner of the block. The lettering appears to be touching the ground.

4 Classic, exuberant fairground lettering.

5 A stylized italic with a capital 'F' that resembles a 1920s Ford car logo.

6 The back of a waltzer shows a stylized brush script. The cross bar of the 't' resembles wild-style graffiti with layered strokes.

6

8

7

9

10

11

12

This page:

**7 and 8 (detail)** The rich mixture of eclectic fairground painting styles is illustrated on the panelling of the steam-yacht organ.

**9** The painted letterface and the blue blocking on this penny arcade sideshow do not butt up to one another.

**10** The shading and highlights on this lorry number give the impression that the numeral is illuminated from the right.

**11** Lettering derived from Art Deco forms, using outline and decorative stripes. The cut-out form behind is colour-blended black at the top and red at the bottom, as on nineteenth-century, woodblock letterpress posters.

**12** Slab serifs on the word Carters combine with a condensed san serif. The gold block gives the letters depth; it falls to the right in Carter's and the shadow falls to the left; the maroon block on Paramount falls to the left and has no shadow.

## Panel painting

Peter Tate is a specialist signwriter and fairground painter, and works for both static and travelling fairs at his workshop in Derby in England. He began as an informal apprentice to a signwriter and has continued painting on his own for over 40 years. Fairground owners choose the decorative style and colour they require and deliver the ride panels to the workshop where Tate paints.

### Painting a decorative panel

**1** In cases where the agreed design must be reproduced on several panels or cars, the painter must make a copy before painting can begin. The design is traced from the original panel on to paper. The tracing paper provides a pattern which is used to ensure consistency between the panels

**2** A detail from the traced pencil pattern is drawn over with a felt-tip pen to make the image stronger. Many of the panel pieces on fairground rides are mirrored through matching left and right panels, but a pattern that does not include lettering can be reversed. The design lines are traced over with a pounce wheel: its rim of tiny spikes leaves a trail of evenly spaced holes in the paper.

**3** The pattern is taped to one of the panels. A pounce bag containing blue chalk is patted over the design lines. The chalk passes through the tiny holes in the paper on to the surface of the panel. This chalk line is then drawn in pencil. The tracing process is repeated for all the panels; the pattern front and back are alternated to produce mirror images. To ensure consistency each stage of the painting is completed on every panel before the next stage is begun.

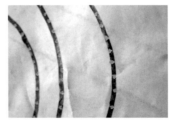

**7** Tate does not use a daub stick to support his painting hand when lining out but, prefers to trust his hand and eye to sustain a smooth and even stroke.

**8** If a second line is required, the process is repeated with a thinner brush.

**9** Opaque coach paints are used for solid colours. Where the artist wants to indicate depth, shading or shadow, flamboyant enamel paints are used. These are translucent, which means they carry a colour but allow the base colour to show through. Above is a detail from an opaque, red letter with a yellow border with a 6.4-mm (¼-in) lining out. The letter appears to throw a shadow on to the blue stripes. The shadow is painted with a flamboyant blue enamel.

**Left:** Peter Tate's workshop with panels for a waltzer top board arranged around the walls on easels. The boards are painted in sequence: a single part of the decorative design or lettering is painted in one colour and this is repeated on the next board. Painting in this way ensures that colours are identical. Painting an entire waltzer takes three to four months working a 50 to 60-hour week.

**4** Long, ox hair brushes are used to paint the design line, while broader, squirrel hair brushes are used to paint in solid areas of colour. Sufficient paint must be mixed to cover all the panels as any remixing may show up as a colour change. Here black paint is mixed with tiny amounts of thinner to make it flow easily.

**5** Lining out is highly skilled: the artist follows, by eye, the edge of the painted designs or lettering. The paint must be thick enough to load the brush but thin enough to flow easily.

**6** The breadth of the brush defines the width of the line. The paint must leave the brush evenly on both sides of the line. The very long hairs of the brush carry a lot of paint which, in the hands of a skilled artist, allow 60cm (24in) of lining out to be done with a single stroke. Seated in front of a panel, the painter works from top to bottom.

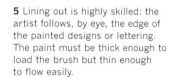

1

3

2

**1** The neon halo effect around this 'A' may at first appear to be airbrushed but in fact it is painted with a pink flamboyant enamel.

**2** A detail from a marbling effect inside lettering on a waltzer. The flamboyant blue and green enamels have been blended into one another. Black, opaque coach paint has been painted across the area and then partially ragged off (dabbed with a rag) while the paint is still wet, leaving a deep lustre.

**3** Here the flamboyant enamel is painted on in several layers so that the light appears to diffuse. Painting with flamboyant enamels is often referred to as clear over base. When the painting is complete, the panels are varnished with seven coats, giving a smooth surface and enriching the colours.

## Painting a top board

**1** The tiger image would stand to the left of a large ride name with the same image flipped to the right. Here the panel has been primed and base-coated with three layers of white. The lightest opaque coach paint was then put on, followed by the yellow and blue. Painters tend to paint from the lightest colour to the darkest when using opaque colours.

**2** The tiger's black stripes are painted in with opaque black before the yellow and orange of the body, which will be done in flamboyant enamels.

**3** The yellows and oranges of the body have been blended and model the shape of the body. The lettering has been painted in white opaque on the blue before being lined out and coloured with flamboyant enamels. A letterform is generally painted from the inside to the outside and the artist is aware of the outline of the letter rather than forming the letter by defining the ground. Lettering usually looks stronger painted on a ground rather than painted out of it – a subtle but important difference for the painter.

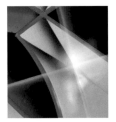

Stars are popular embellishments for fairground lettering. Here an airbrush is used to add a starburst.

A painted trapezium star; these are often drawn to surround lettering.

A simple lining-out star left with a ragged stroke end.

Like many signwriters and fairground painters Peter Tate very modestly signs his work on a single waltzer panel.

Master signwriters and fairground artists like Tate have an extraordinary ability to paint in several styles. This shows a traditional Victorian approach using a brush.

## A walzer top board

**1** The waltzer top board is made up of eight sheets put together in the workshop so that the entire surface of the sign can be worked as one. The lettering style is derived from the metal backplate of a pinball machine. It has been drawn out by hand, but as much of it is angular a straight edge is used. Solid colours are painted in with opaque paints. Here the complex blocks of the three-dimensional forms have been painted in first.

**2** This style of metallic, shiny lettering emulates the highlights and reflections of chrome. It is ideally suited to airbrush work where colours can be blended and continuous tone is easily realized. Here the base blue has been oversprayed with a black which fades very subtly from the baseline of the letters towards the vanishing point.

**3** The three-dimensional letters now appear to be flying forward from the ground. The face of the letter has a 'sunset' yellow blended to deeper red, and the edges of the letters give the impression of a chrome-finished avit (an edge cut at 45 degrees). Base colours for the swirls (ribbons that appear to wrap around parts of the design) have been put in place. The arrows and fast forward symbols have been prepared with a white ground.

**4** The completed design with swirls, neon halos and starburst highlights is darker and perhaps a little more menacing than the previous image. A lot of black tone has been sprayed into the perspective areas and even on to the top face of the central letters, heightening the contrast.

**Above:** The pink disco lettering from the car design from another waltzer shows a combination of 1970s forms and jagged underlining style derived from graffiti. Because this is fairground lettering it is blocked up as a three-dimensional form.

**Above:** The car designs are a very eclectic mix of traditional forms and ideas from many sources. The swirls and ribbons have a nineteenth-century origin but the fluidity with which they are drawn is a subconscious reference to psychedelic posters of the 1960s. The three-dimensional block caps with enlarged characters are a traditional form seen on fairground rides, traction engines, commercial vehicles and pub signs, but here they are infilled with colour schemes derived from American custom cars and have chrome edges. The twinkling starbursts reference photographic images, while the baseline of the words and the accompanying pulsing, luminous neon line, are borrowed from the graphic equalizer display on a stereo system.

# 1.7 Canal boat painting

Traditionally panels on either side of the stern cabin in a canal boat are painted. Their proportions vary: some may be as long as 3.6m (12ft) while those on recreational boats may be as short as 1.2m (4ft). The canal boat signwriter must consider the proportions of the panels in relation to the number of lines to be painted, and the relative importance of each of the words, as well as the length of the longest word.

## Painting canal boat panels

**1** A 12-mm (½-in) long, sable hair, chisel-edged brush is used for most of the painting.

**2** Moore uses a set of card strips to determine the broad stroke widths for characters. He selects one of the cards as a guide for drawing the thick strokes of the lettering, which is loosely based on the Clarendon typeface. The face of the letter is drawn inside the unit to allow for intercharacter spacing and back shading. Thin strokes are drawn in with the edge of the card, using a finger width as a guide.

**3** Paint is loaded on to the brush by rolling the hairs across the palette. If the paint is not running smoothly, it is dipped into thinner. The faces of the letters are painted with a very thick gloss paint called one coat; sometimes lettering is overpainted with a second coat. Generally the letterface is painted first in the lightest colour.

**7** Once the face of the letter is complete, the lightest blockwork is painted – here pale blue – and finally the shadow, here dark blue. While some painters blend the shadow details, working two wet paint colours into one another, Moore prefers tapering – painting little triangular brush strokes into the lightest colour. Other painters use a series of decreasing line weights from dark to light to visualize changes of tone.

**8** A small gap, perhaps 4–6mm (⅛–¼in) wide, separates the face of the letter from the block. When the face of the letter and the blocking are painted, the gap forms a line the colour of the coach painting and adds to the three-dimensional appearance of the lettering. The gap also enables the signwriter to paint in the blocking without having to wait for the letterface to dry. The two colours, being separate, cannot blend or smudge.

Unlike some signwriters, Moore uses thin, low-tack, flexible masking tape along the baseline and cap line. In his view this speeds up the painting process as he only has to line out the vertical and round strokes of each letter.

**6** Moore, describes letters as fitting into units: for him there are three unit widths: a half unit for the 'I' and punctuation; one and a half units for 'W'; and a single unit for all the other letters. As BYWATER has seven letters, one of which is 'W', it is seven and a half units long. The number of units on either side of the centre point is therefore three and three-quarters. Moore divides the space from the centre point to the end of the arc into three and three-quarter units and marks the unit width on the baseline. The unit concept includes intercharacter spacing, the letters are therefore drawn marginally inside the units. Here Moore measures off the cap height and unit division on one panel in order to transfer it to another.

**4** The traditional signwriter seeks to fill the panel and therefore makes the arc bridge the space between the vertical edges. The arc forms the curved baseline for the lettering and, as a consequence, its position on the panel is determined by the anticipated height of the lettering. The arc is drawn by measuring the overall panel length, marking the centre point, then bending a wooden strip from the centre point to the panel edge and drawing around the strip with a white chinagraph pencil.

**5** In this example the boat name BYWATER, rather than the owner's name, forms the principal lettering. A signwriter adapts the proportions of the letters to fit the space and fill the length of the arc. If the name is less than five letters, and the arc comparatively long, the letters will be expanded. A long name on a short panel will have compressed letterforms.

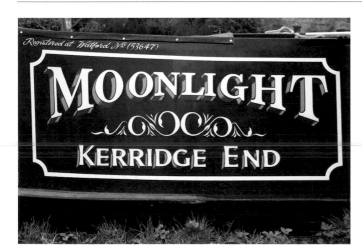

Above: Only the baseline is curved: the cap line remains straight. Stroke widths at the centre point 'N' and 'L' are thinner than those at the beginning and end of the word, while all the widths in between are incremental. To give a three-dimensional effect, blockwork is drawn in. As with most canal boat lettering, the blockwork is drawn to the left. The depth and angle of the blockwork varies from job to job but must be consistent within a single name if the illusion of solid letters is to be maintained.

Left: Flowers or decorative scrollwork are often used within lettering panels or, as here, on door interiors.

Above: A traditional bow gunnel painting colour-matched with a harlequin pattern.

# 1.8 Road lettering and markings

**Right:** Lettering and street markings are drawn out on the road surface using a temporary spray paint. Thermoplastic resin is heated in a tank before being applied to the road through a pressurized spray or series of rollers.

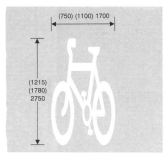

(750) (1100) 1700

(1215)
(1780)
2750

**Above:** Symbols devised to accompany words are also drawn on a matching grid so that the elliptical wheels of the bicycle painted on the road appear to be circles when viewed by a motorist approaching the sign.

Thermoplastic is used to paint markings on the surface of aircraft runways, car parks and athletic tracks. Made of a silicon aggregate and a pigment, titanium oxide (in the case of white lines) it is bound together by a thermoplastic resin. Tiny glass beads are added when reflective properties and night visibility are required. The proportions of the mix are subject to British Standards Institution (BSI) standards, which ensure a compromise between maximum visibility, durability, and how long the line stays visible on the road before being blackened or eroded by tyre and skid resistance. The same thermoplastic mixture can be coloured by adding resin-based pigments for parking restrictions and for marking out playground and factory floors.

Government transport authorities specify strict guidelines that define the colours, line weights, style and lettering sizes required on any particular section of road.

The painted lettering on a road surface differs from that used on the majority of informative road signs in that it makes use of caps as opposed to caps and lower case. In Britain three proportions of sans serif lettering are specified within the guidelines. In the first the letters are a minimum of 35cm (13¾in) and a maximum of 70cm (27½in) tall, and the baseline runs parallel to the kerb. The characters face, and are designed to be read from, the pavement by a pedestrian ('look left', 'look right'). The same proportion of lettering is used for parking restriction markings, although in this case the lettering, which again runs parallel to the kerb, is designed to be read from the road by the motorist ('School keep clear', 'doctor', 'taxi'). The second and third proportions of lettering are designed to be read from a moving vechicle and are aligned at 90 degrees to the kerb. The motorist must be able to read words at speeds of up to 112km/h (70mph) and view them from behind the wheel at an abnormally shallow angle. In order to make the characters more legible, and the words more readable, the letters are elongated. The proportional change in the lettering is determined by height. Letters up to 1.6m (5ft 3in) are drawn on a rectanguar grid made up of units 7cm (2¾in) wide and 20cm (8in) tall, while the letters with a height up to 2.8m (9ft 4in) tall are drawn up on a similar grid with units 7cm (2¾in) wide and 35cm (13¾in) tall.

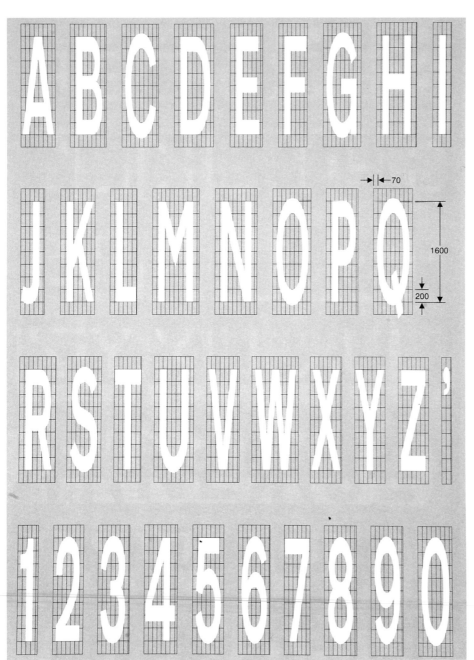

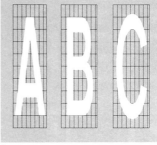

2

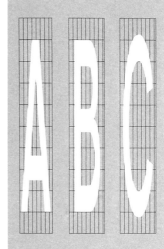

3

**This page:**

1 1.6-m (5¼-ft) high lettering from *The Traffic Signs Regulations and General Directions 1994,* p.318. Each letter is drawn on an elongated grid as the lettering is designed to be viewed from a vehicle travelling at speed. By accentuating the height of each letter in relation to the width, the letters becomemore legible.

2 Three letters from the 1.6-m (5¼-ft ) high alphabet are drawn to the same width as the taller 2.8-m (9-ft) alphabet (3), devised for reading at higher speeds. By elongating the lettering the alphabet is legible through a greater range of angles, and therefore gives the driver more time to read the message.

1

# 1.9 Painting stained glass

**Above:** The stained-glass painting process, which uses ground glass mixed with metal oxide compounds, is similar to oil painting but the artist has to anticipate how the colours will change during firing. Paint colours can be overlaid and some pieces may be fired several times with each firing changing the colour.

**Above right:** Joseph Nuttgens Fellows in his workshop surrounded by plastic bins full of coloured glass fragments which he will cut to shape before painting and lettering begin. He uses an oxide paste to paint lettering on to a piece of stained glass before firing.

Stained-glass painting is an ancient craft dating back to ninth-century Europe where it was practised by monks and artisans who were commissioned to make windows recounting biblical stories or depicting scenes from scripture.

Two major advances in glass technology – the invention of flash glass in the sixteenth century and etching in the seventeenth century – prompted the developments in the craft. Before the invention of the flash process, glass was either clear, though by today's standards it had many imperfections, or coloured. By flash-dipping a sheet of clear glass into melted coloured glass, a thin, coloured veneer was fused to the surface as it cooled. If the surface was ground away on one side, a lighter colour could be achieved. If both sides were abraded (rubbed or scraped) a white area was created. The flash-dipping process extended the colour palette available to the stained glass artist. Yellow glass could be flash-dipped in blue glass to produce a green glass which, when ground away, created tints of green. The abrasive process of wearing away the flash veneer was replaced by etching when it was discovered that concentrated hydrofluoric acid could etch away the unprotected surface of flash glass to reveal the second colour. Acid-etching transparent glass created a translucent, frosted area that enabled images and text to be read on clear glass.

Today lettering on stained glass is created through one of three methods. As shown in the following process, letters can be painted on in a metal oxide and fired. The result is referred to as black lettering as it is darker than the ground. Letters can be etched out of flash glass: clear flash glass covered in a colour can be etched so that the letters are white out of a colour or a colour letter out of a colour ground; alternatively, the flash glass can be etched so that the letters appear as colour out of transparent glass. Letters can also be etched to appear etched on (translucent letters on a clear ground) or etched out off (clear letters on a translucent ground).

Joseph Nuttgens Fellows was commissioned to make a window for Newcastle Cathedral in England on the theme of industrial heritage.

## Designing a stained-glass window

**1** The stained glass artist responds to the client's brief by researching the themes of the window. Fellows spent time in Newcastle Cathedral checking how the window was illuminated through the day. He looked at collections of old photographs in the local library and visited industrial heritage sites in and around Newcastle, a mine, a shipyard, a steelworks, railway sheds and heavy-engineering factories. Pages from his sketchbook show how imagery derived from photographs and drawings from life are combined.

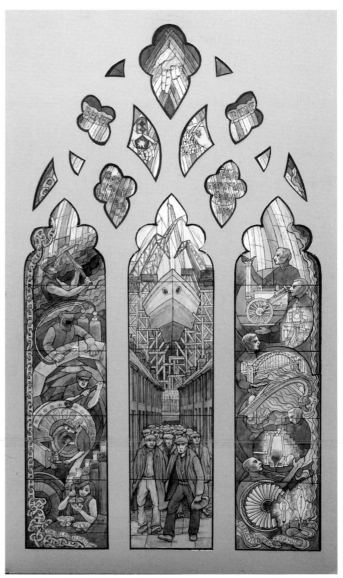

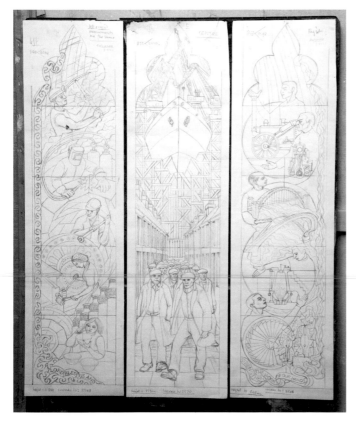

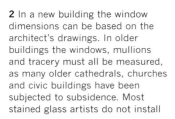

**2** In a new building the window dimensions can be based on the architect's drawings. In older buildings the windows, mullions and tracery must all be measured, as many older cathedrals, churches and civic buildings have been subjected to subsidence. Most stained glass artists do not install the windows but work with highly specialized glaziers, referred to as leadmen. Based on the leadman's measurements Fellows makes 1:12 scale design drawings. The client is consulted throughout the design process and comments are fed back.

**3** Once the scale drawing has been agreed in black and white it is traced on to watercolour paper. The colour is added in a combination of watercolour and gouache. This is done in a restrained way with the colours knocked back – painting the rich colour saturation associated with stained glass on a sunny day at one-twelfth scale creates a harsh impression of the design. The final drawing is presented to the client and design, colours and text are checked and approved before the manufacturing process begins.

# Cutting and lettering stained glass

**1** The scale drawing is enlarged on a large-format photocopier which produces an image 1m (3ft 4in) wide and up to 30m (98ft 5in) long. The photocopy is printed on tracing paper and matched to the leadman's paper patterns or measured for accuracy. Here a section of the Newcastle window is unrolled on the light box. The glass pieces for each of the shapes must be cut by hand in the correct coloured glass. The glass will be laid out on the drawing like a jigsaw.

**2** H-section lead (top) is used to join different coloured pieces of glass. Lead lines marked on the full-size photocopy are redrawn with a felt-tip pen (bottom) which is the same width as the lead – 3mm (⅛in). The full-size tracing paper design is laid flat on a light box and a piece of stained glass of the correct colour is placed over the drawing.

**3** Glass is cut with a tungsten wheel cutter and glass pliers. The glass is scored by running the tungsten cutter across the surface following the lead lines, which are clearly visible on the design drawing. The artist must ensure that the glass is scored to the inner edge of the pattern piece.

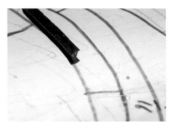

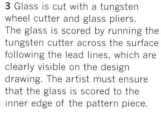

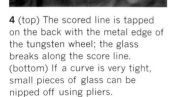

**6** Once the oxide has dried, any imperfections on the edge of the lettering is cleaned up with a scribe (a pointed instrument).

**4** (top) The scored line is tapped on the back with the metal edge of the tungsten wheel; the glass breaks along the score line. (bottom) If a curve is very tight, small pieces of glass can be nipped off using pliers.

**5** The yellow glass piece for the ribbon on which the type will be painted has been cut to shape and laid over the design. The paint is a compound of metal oxides: copper for green, cobalt for blue, manganese for purple, with lead, chromium and iron used in various combinations to produce different colours when fired. Letters painted with metal oxides are darker than the coloured glass on which they sit and and are referred to as black letters. White letters, paler than the glass on which they sit, are produced by etching flash glass. A signwriter's long-haired brush is used to paint directly onto the glass, guided by pencil letters beneath.

## Firing the stained-glass lettering

**1** (top) Once the image or lettering has been completed on each piece, it is prepared for firing. Trays filled with dry plaster of Paris are used to support the glass. A rule is pulled across the surface of the plaster to make a smooth bed on which the pieces of glass can be laid out with the lettering face up. (bottom) The tray is gently slid into the electric kiln.

**2** The kiln is designed to fire flat objects and therefore the slots that support the trays are very shallow. It takes several hours to reach the required temperature of 610–620°C (1130–1148°F). A tray with glass to be fired is placed in the top slot for three hours and heat in the other slots are turned off. When the first tray has been fired, the kiln is opened and the tray is moved to the cooling slot below. As each new tray of glass is fired the trays that have already been fired are moved down a slot until all six slots have been filled. This very slow cooling process prevents the glass cracking or exploding.

**3** The kiln is usually emptied the day after firing, once it is completely cool. The glass pieces are moved to a laying out frame which consists of a large, thick sheet of clear glass mounted in a stout, wooden frame. The design is traced on to the glass in chinagraph pencil or black felt-tip pen by laying the full-size photocopy under the glass sheet. The cut glass pieces are laid out and temporarily fixed in position with double-sided tape before they are painted, usually at an easel.

**4** A wood and glass frame for the Newcastle window is lifted into position in the studio. The glass pieces are not attached. As the artist needs the entire window to be illuminated by daylight, a conventional wooden easel is not appropriate here. A system of pulleys mounted in front of a south-facing window is used to lift the laying out frame into place so that it hangs vertically in the way the final window will be presented in the cathedral.

**5** A detail of the frame raised in position. When all the pieces of glass have been attached, including the prefired lettering (the shapes for the ribbon can be seen bottom left) the painting of the design can be undertaken.

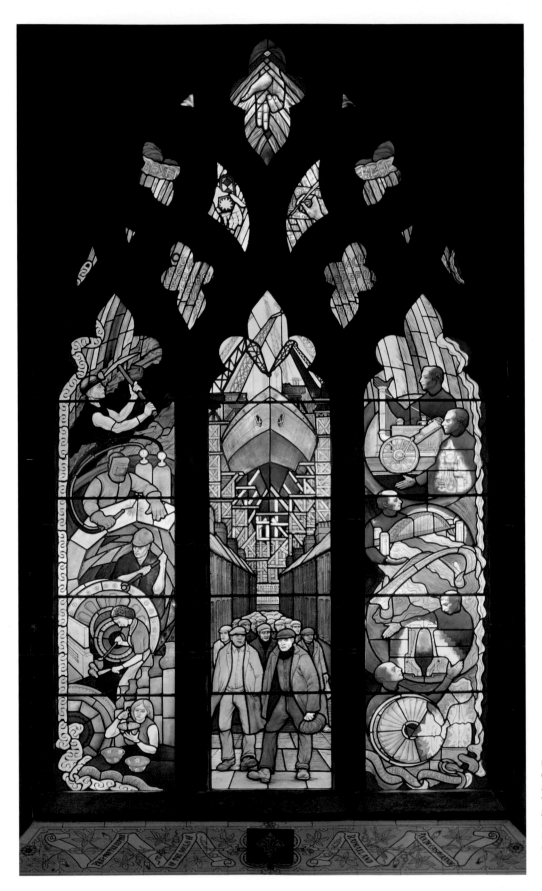

**Left:** The finished window at Newcastle Cathedral shows how the industrial imagery and colours within the design combine with the lettering. The lead physically holds the glass pieces in the design together and also serves as part of the design palette, producing a strong, opaque line that defines the major design elements. The lettering shown on the previous pages appears on the scroll in the bottom right of the window shown here.

# 1.10 Mosaic lettering

Mosaics were used for flooring and for decorating walls in ancient Greek and Roman villas and bathhouses, as well as in Mesopotamian gardens. They are made from tiny fragments of glazed tile called tesserae.

In the nineteenth and early twentieth centuries, mosaics were very popular in the halls and conservatories of grand houses and were soon adopted as a flooring and paving alternative to stone and wood in the more modest terraced houses of the aspirational middle classes. Proud hotel, restaurant and shop owners of the period commissioned mosaic doorsteps and arcade entrances which highlighted the prestigious nature of their premises. These mosaics featured decorative numerals and shop names that were often designed to match carved and painted fascias. At the end of the nineteenth century, the popularity of mosaics was spurred on by the decorative schools of Vienna and Paris, together with the Art Nouveau movement, which made extensive use of mosaic designs and lettering. In some European capitals the mosaic was elevated from floor and wall decoration to the façades of commercial buildings, restaurants, cafés and dining rooms. Mosaic techniques were ideally suited to the concrete floors and rendered brick walls of flat-roofed Art Deco buildings and swimming pools. Hollywood stars of the period developed a taste for pool bases with huge mosaic monogram or slightly racy quotes, which shimmered through the water in the Californian sunshine.

There are two principal ways of laying a mosaic: the direct method which involves the artist working on site setting the tesserae directly on to a cement ground or fascia and the indirect or reverse method which can be undertaken off site. In the indirect method the whole design is put together in a workshop before being moved to the site in sections.

**Above:** Entrance to a shop doorway showing a decorative script mosaic.

**Left:** Decorative lettering for a shop in Barcelona, Spain is arranged in an arch above the entrance.

1

2

3

**This page:**
Examples of the resilience of mosaic lettering
exposed to the environment and city grime.

1 A mosaic pilgrimage map consists of closely
packed lettering.

2 Mosaic lettering from the Parc Güell in
Barcelona, Spain, uses two colours of irregular
shaped stones to define the lettering.

3 The semi-permanent nature of mosaic
lettering is seen on this shop fascia, which
was revealed in its slightly faded glory after
a perspex light box was removed when the
premises changed hands.

4 A detail from part of the shop fascia above,
shows the white ground mosaic laid out in the
manner of brick bonds.

5 A detail of the mosaic lettering from the
Conway Hall, London shows a rich blue ground
on irregular tiles and the white and gold tiles
used for the lettering. Though the tiles are
small, the scale of architectural lettering
combined with the reading distance from the
street supports the visual impression of refined
letterforms derived from type.

6 The pavement of the Foro Italico, in Rome,
built as an entrance to what would have been
the 1936 Olympics which were subsequently
moved to Berlin. The mosaic tiles reflect
ancient Roman pavements and feature Roman
mythology and phrases.

7 The Foro Italico mosaic makes consistent
use of small, square, black and white tiles
and the visual strength of the sans serif with
a circular 'O'.

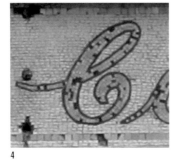

4

5

6

7

345672

# Type casting, composition and design

# 2.1 Letterpress

Letterpress printing is the cradle of type and its associated discipline typography. As such it is a technology that involves a number of interrelated processes. In this book the four principal processes of letterpress – type design, casting the type, setting or composing the type, and printing from the type – appear in different chapters. This division reflects the chronological development of diverging specialist trades over 500 years of letterpress history and illustrates letterpress's direct link to, and influence upon, other lettering processes. Chapter 1: Hand-drawn and painted lettering describes some of the ways calligraphy informs type design today (*see* pp.13–49). Chapter 2: Type casting, composition and design examines the manufacture of letterpress type, before moving on to hand-casting (*see* pp.54–55) hand composition (*see* pp.58–59) and hot metal composition and casting (*see* pp.60–63). Chapter 3: Printing describes how letterpress type is proofed and printed (*see* pp.89–130).

As casting type is the beginning of letterpress manufacture it is appropriate to define the process. Letterpress is a form of relief printing. The ink sits on the raised surface of a letterform, which is reversed on the printing block, and is transferred to paper through pressure applied by a press. Letterpress printing is literally inked letters pressed on to a page. This simplistic description of the process, however, belies its significance in the development of the modern world. The invention of movable metal type in Europe is attributed to Johannes Gutenberg (*c*.1400–82) a metalworker from Mainz in Germany, who printed his *Forty-two Bible* (so called because the column depth was 42 lines) in *c*.1455. Although movable metal type is attributed to Gutenberg, the same process had been invented in Korea as early as *c*.1377. Gutenberg's invention of modular lettering (type) spawned the discipline of typography (the arrangement of 26 modular letterforms, numerals and punctuation). Mechanical lettering in the form of fonts and typefaces has become the principal means of preserving written language. While it remains true that handwriting is learnt, and many of the processes celebrated in this book are calligraphic, the influence of typographic letterforms has spread well beyond their letterpress roots.

The process of making matrixes (a flat brass or copper blank into which a right-reading impression of a letter has been made) and movable moulds is based on that invented by Gutenberg. This remained the principal means of type produced for the next 350 years and continues as a craft today. The process begins with cutting the design of an individual letter (in reverse) on to the end of a steel bar known as a punch. The bar is worked at the same size as the required type. Working the end of a steel bar in reverse, at sizes as small as 4pt, is highly skilled and today there are few punch-cutters left. The outside of the character is shaped with files, while the counters are made with a separate positive punch, called a counter punch. The counter punch is struck into the punch, creating the impression of the counter. The shape of the letter can be reviewed periodically by making a smoke proof. Here the punch is held in a candle flame, blackened with soot and then pressed on to paper so that the letter can be read the correct way round. Skilled punch-cutters can make up to four punches a day. Once the punch has been shaped into a letterform it is hardened or tempered by repeated heating and cooling of the metal.

The hardened steel punch is hammered into a flat bar of copper, called a strike. The impression made in the copper blank (a rectangular slug of copper cut to fit within the mould) is right-reading. The punches for each character in a font have to be struck with the same force so that the impressions in the copper are of consistent depth. The copper is then justified (filed so that the edges are square to the letterform and the base of the letter is a common distance from the bottom of the blank). Finally, the distance between the edge of the impression and the blank is resolved. This determines the shoulder of the character and, therefore, the kerning (the space between the letters). Once the process of justification is complete, the copper blank is referred to as a matrix. Overleaf Nigel Roche, a typographic historian and letterpress printer, and senior librarian at the St Bride Library of Printing, London, demonstrates the making of punches and the casting of letterpress type.

**Above:** A detail of italic capital punches showing the letters in reverse and the tapering from the steel bar to the letterform.

**Above:** The print workshop of Christopher
Plantin in Antwerp, Belgium, was established
in 1555. It has retained many of the features
of its original layout, with some of the oldest
presses in the world, dating from c.1600.

## Hand-casting metal type

Cast metal type is often referred to as lead but is actually made up of an alloy of three metals. Lead alone is soft and does not produce a durable printing surface. The three elements of the alloy are 75 per cent lead, 15–19 per cent antimony and 6–10 per cent tin. These proportions have been adjusted through time to produce harder more durable type, and vary for machine casting. Some type foundries have also added tiny amounts of copper. The melting point of this alloy varies slightly depending on the proportions in which the metals are combined but at 327°C (621°F) is relatively low. Tin and antimony, a bright crystalline and very brittle metal, combine to strengthen the alloy, making it harder than lead alone. Antimony has a unique property that makes it ideal for casting: unlike other metals, it expands as it solidifies. This ensures that the molten alloy is forced into the smallest details of the type mould.

### Casting the type

**1** The type alloy is heated in an electric crucible to 327°C (621°F), at which point it becomes molten. A small ladle is used to scoop off impurities that have risen to the surface before it is dipped into the centre of the crucible and the alloy is poured into the type mould.

**2** The caster grips wooden blocks which insulate the mould while gradually pouring the molten alloy into the opening at its top. Just as the metal rises above the opening, the caster throws the type (see step 3).

### Breaking open the mould

**1** This eighteenth-century, adjustable mould has three principal elements which can be dismantled. This view shows the base of the mould with the reverse of the type matrix held in place by a wire spring. To remove the cast type the mould must be dismantled.

**2** The type matrix has been removed from the base of the mould and the silver cast type face is visible just above the tip of the wire spring . The impression on the matrix casts the type face and the mould casts the body of the type.

**3** (Above and detail below) Half of the mould is removed to reveal the silver alloy body and shank of the cast type nestling neatly in the mould.

**3** The throw involves the caster quickly lifting both mould and ladle, in a single movement, above his head. This forces the molten metal down to the bottom of the mould, ensuring that all the fine type details, such as serifs, are filled with the molten alloy and any air bubbles are forced to the surface, making the cast solid.

**4** A detail of the top of the mould shows the solidified metal, which takes only seconds to harden. By the time the the cast type is separated from the mould, it is cool enough to touch.

**4** The bright silver alloy type is picked from the mould. The shank is waste material and will be broken away from the body and returned to the crucible to be smelted and cast again. The point at which the shank is broken from the body becomes the foot of the type.

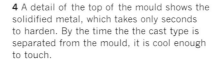

**Left:** Detail showing the four elements of the cast type. (From the left) The small, silver cone is the bevel of the typeface raised above the square section of the body; the groove on the body is the nick which aids the compositor in setting the type to the correct orientation; the long, triangular piece with a pool of solidified alloy at one end is the shank.

**Left:** Type was traditionally bought by weight and delivered to the printer wrapped in paper and bound together with string. Different languages use different letters more frequently, so foundries created font assortment tables for languages and different sorts of setting.

**Above:** Type frames are large steel or wooden cabinets that hold 20 shallow wooden trays called 'type cases'. Each case contains type of a different size and cases are usually arranged in the frame with the smallest, and therefore the lightest, type at the top. Printers generally store families of type in a single frame: 6pt, 7pt, 8pt, 9pt, 10pt, 12pt, 14pt, 18pt, 24pt, 36pt, 48pt, 60pt and 72pt are all standard sizes which are arranged in size order from the top of the frame. 'Bastard' or non-standard sizes – 7.5pt, 8.5pt, 9.5pt, 10.5pt, 11pt, 16pt, 22pt, 28pt, 42pt etc. – may be inserted. Some printers organize the frames by size and weight such as Bembo 6pt roman, italic and bold, followed by the same order for 7pt.

**Right:** The terms upper case, here, for majuscule and lower case (opposite) for minuscule, describe a pair of cases stored in the frame with upper-case letters positioned in a case above lower-case characters. The case is lifted from the frame with the case below pulled out about halfway as a support.

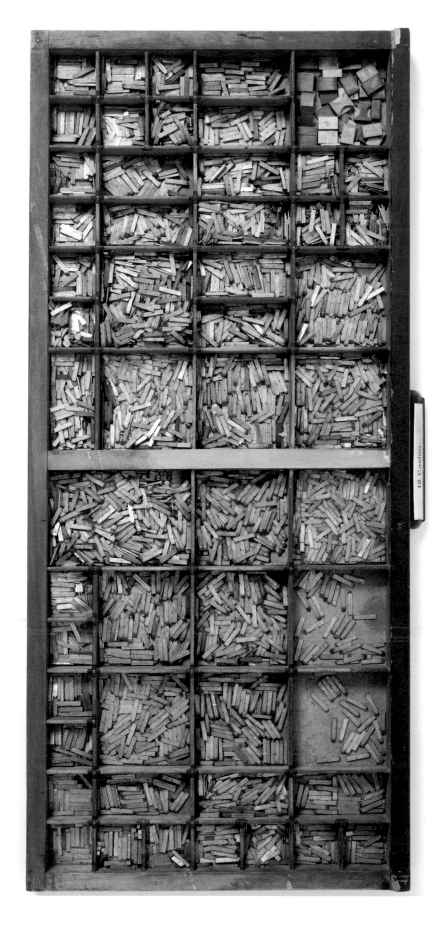

**Right:** The lower case contains all characters, numerals and punctuation for a single font in one point size. Type is stored in compartments in a consistent arrangement known as the lay of a case so that a compositor can quickly pick up individual characters. Each compartment contains one character in a single size and weight. The size of each compartment relates directly to how often a character is used within the language being set. Vowels occur more frequently than consonants and therefore have larger compartments. The most frequently used letters are arranged near the centre of the case, so that the compositor's hand travels the shortest distance when picking up or distributing the type.

# Hand composition

**1** The metal composing stick is used for setting type into lines. Sticks vary in design but usually have a plate about 5cm (2in) wide as a base, a flange on the long side which is slightly shorter than the type height, a fixed stock on the short side, and an adjustable lever or 'knee'.

**2** The distance between the stock and the adjustable knee of the stick determines the length of each line of type. This distance can be adjusted to match the width of the column required for a book or newspaper, which is referred to as setting the stick. The width of a column and, therefore the distance between stock and knee of the stick, is referred to as the measure and is traditionally specified in picas (units of 12pt). The compositor places a set of slugs to set the measure. The lever on the adjustable knee is pushed down; the slugs must be firm but not wedged.

**3** From the case type is picked up one letter at a time with thumb and index finger. The first character is placed in the stick against the adjustable knee and held in place with the thumb of the other hand before the next character is picked from the case. This process is repeated until a word is completed

and a spacing unit, usually what is known as a thin (one-sixth the size of the type body), is inserted. Spacing units are the same depth as the body of the type but do not have a raised letterface and are therefore not inked when the press roller passes over them. This leaves a white gap between words.

# Proofing

**1** Type is now moved from the stick to the imposition stone – a process referred to as dumping the stick. Today the stone is actually a milled metal bench that stands 96.5cm (38in) from the ground, a comfortable height for the compositor when standing. The surface dimensions of imposition stones reflect the type of work undertaken in the print shop and are designed for imperial paper sizes. The stick remains clamped while the slug of type is gripped between forefinger and thumb and slid on to the stone.

**2** A metal frame called a chase is placed over the type to secure it. One edge of the type is pressed close to the chase, while the remaining three sides are packed out with what is called furniture (strips of wood or metal cut to specific measures). The type must sit square in the chase and is secured with 'quoins' (expanding metal wedges or bars that enlarge with the turn of a key). The process is referred to as locking up, while the type and chase together are referred to as a form.

**3** The type secured in the chase is wrong-reading so that when it is inked up by the roller of the press the printed impression will be right-reading.

**4** Once the type is locked into the chase, it can be lifted on to the bed of the press and secured by a lever. The size of a press bed determines the size of paper used. This 1960s, electric, single-colour cylinder press is used for proofing and printing short runs. An electric motor turns the cylinder but the paper is fed and the impression made by hand-cranking. The press consists of a bed and two steel cylinders, one level with the bed and the other above it. The cylinders are connected by a series of rubber-coated rollers, which touch one another.

**5** The bodies of the letters in a typeface are of many different widths. The number of characters per line is determined by the width of the individual letters and the length of the measure to which they are set. The optimum number of characters per line in a book where sustained reading is required is often defined as 65, although lines can be shorter. When no more characters can be added to the line in the stick, small spacing units are inserted to fill out the space and secure the line. A vertical spacing unit, called a lead, after the metal from which it is made, is placed below the first line before the next character is set up against the knee on the line below.

**4** The nick – the groove on the body of the type – must face forward and be visible as the type is set. This ensures the type is sitting in the stick the correct way up. The stick turned on its side shows type with the nicks correctly aligned.

# Lettering & Process

**5** A palette knife is used to smear the top cylinder with a line of ink straight from the tin. The electric press is started and the lowest cylinder rotates, causing the smooth rollers above it to turn and transfer the ink from one roller to another. Once the ink is evenly distributed across the cylinders and all the rollers, an impression can be pulled.

**6** Once the printing is complete, the type is cleaned with a spirit-soaked rag, wiping towards the closed corner of the form. The ink is broken down by the spirit and is wiped away promptly to stop it soaking down into the form between the type bodies. A small, soft brush is sometimes used to rub away surplus ink trapped in the counters of the characters.

**7** The face (top) and reverse (bottom) of the impression are examined. The print is checked for typos – mistakes made during the composing stage – for the evenness of the ink coverage and the crispness of the impression. If the proof is approved the run can be printed on the chosen stock.

# 2.2 Hot metal composition

Hot metal composition is a process in which type is composed (arranged in a line) and cast by machine. The lead type is made in a mould similar to that used in hand-casting, but each letter in a line is cast in succession rather than being picked from a case and ordered in a composing stick (*see* pp.58–59). There are several systems of hot metal casting. The most popular forms, which remain in use for very high-quality letterpress work, are Linotype, Monotype and the Ludlow system (used exclusively for display faces). Their names reveal the differences between the systems: Linotype casters cast a line of type as a single form, while Monotype casters cast individual characters in sequence. Both systems make use of specially designed keyboards to determine the order in which the matrixes are to be positioned prior to the casting. The Linotype caster has an integral keyboard and the type is cast a line at a time, while the Monotype system divides the process between two compatible machines. Here and overleaf a compositor and caster demonstrates hot metal composition and casting at Gloucester Typesetting in England.

## Monotype composition

**1** The Monotype keyboard is different from the familiar QWERTY layout. The keyboard bank is split into two separate elements of 162 keys (324 in total). The keyboard can be set into five, six, or seven alphabet layouts. Here the two principal elements of the keyboard are divided into three, giving six variables. Rows of keys are organized from the top left as small caps, normal caps and roman, and from the top right as italic caps, italic lower case and bold caps.

**2** Keyboard banks are detachable and can be changed to set the machine up for a particular magazine or book. The buttons for individual keys can also be changed to reflect a customized matrix case.

**3** Directly beneath the keyboard are the key frames which are activated by the compositor depressing one of the keys. This triggers transverse bars to open pneumatic air valves and operates the punches which cut a hole in the program ribbon, seen here as four spikes creating the holes on the left of the paper strip.

**4** The round justification drum above the keyboard determines the space between characters. The setting can be minutely adjusted to provide consistent interword spacing along a line. Numbers on the drum show the constant to the left – this scale is divided into 71 sections. Intersecting these lines are 20 horizontal divisions. As each key is tapped, a pointer moves to show the exact width of every letter. The machine can register up to 71 divisions of a unit in a line.

**5** The em scale marker is a straight rule with sliding pointers that can be set as tabs dividing a page into many columns. This feature is particularly useful when setting tabular matter and figures.

**6** Above the justification drum a scroll of paper is stretched between two spools. This paper tape is referred to as ribbon. When the operator pushes a key, the action eventually cuts a hole in a specific position on the ribbon. The ribbon is divided into 31 channels of perforations. Each hole cut is positioned in relation to a set of coordinates that determine the character to be cast.

**Below:** A spread from the *Book of Information*, produced by the Monotype Corporation Limited (1970) featuring a diagram of a 16 x 17 character (272 character set) unit-shift matrix case arrangement. The positions of all the characters are shown in relation to their respective coordinates. The lines above a character indicate that the unit shift is incorporated and the character will be allocated the unit value of the row above.

**Below:** The following spread from the *Book of Information* shows the unique basic Monotype keyboard arrangement and finger chart learned by every compositor.

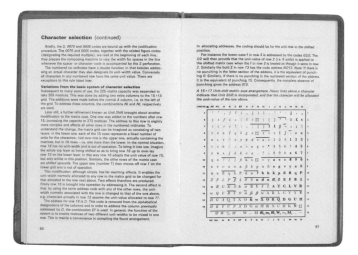

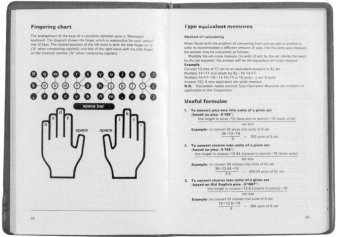

**Right:** A detail of the matrix, reproduced actual size. Monotype machines originally had 225 characters arranged in a grid of 15 x 15 units. Monotype matrices can also be 15 x 17 characters (255 characters) or 16 x 17 characters (272 characters, as here). The horizontal coordinates were identified by the letters 'A–O', while the vertical used the figures 1–15. Skilled compositors and casters learn to read the ribbon notation, translating the holes into letters and words.

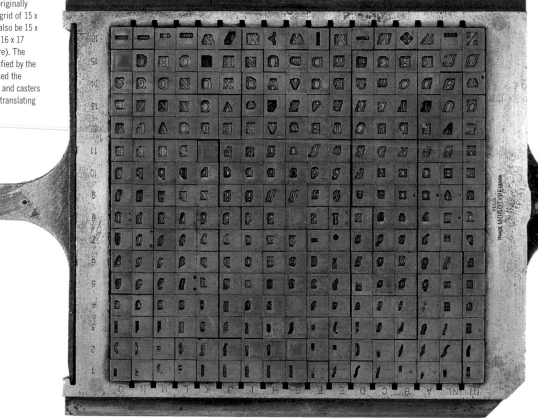

Type casting, composition and design

**1** The Monotype caster is a separate machine from the compositor. The perforated ribbon from the compositor is transfered to the caster. The position of the perforated holes on the ribbon define the individual character and the spacing and position of the type in the form. Compressed air passing through the holes in the ribbon triggers each command.

**2** The matrix case on a Monotype caster holds all the bronze moulds for a font in a single point size – here Times New Roman in a 15 x 17 character matrix. The edge of the case is marked horizontally with the coordinates A–O and vertically with numerals.

**3** The mould performs the same task as a hand-casting mould (*see* pp 54–55) and like its predecessor is movable. The bottom of the mould (here facing upwards) has a square orifice. The two fixed side walls determine the point size of a font. The movable mould blade, which narrows or widens with every character cast, is referred to as the set wise.

**7** The molten metal in the crucible is forced through a nozzle into the mould (not shown) and on into the matrix. The mould closes the set once the molten metal has entered its inner chamber. The matrix case is held upside down and receives the spurt of molten lead, which is forced into the smallest detail of the bronze right-reading letterform. As the tolerances are very fine, the mould is described as kissing the matrix. The cast type cools immediately and is pushed out from the mould.

**8** Each piece of type exits the caster on a line carrier and is 'dumped' into a stick, (*see* type to the right of the yellow pencil) and moved line-by-line on to a galley (bottom right).

**Left:** In the first 80 years of the 20th century, when hot metal casting was in its heyday, huge quantities of lead were required to sustain the typesetting of newspapers, books and periodicals. Lead alloy was supplied in cast ingots to a specification determined by either Monotype or Linotype.

**4** Here the 11pt mould orifice is closing, the position it maintains once the lead has been injected. The mould is opened and closed with every piece of type cast. The casting speed can run at up to 140 revolutions per minute producing up to 8,400 characters per hour. This is perhaps 20 times as quick as hand-casting. Throughout the casting process the mould is constantly subjected to intense heat from the molten metal and is cooled by water which hastens the solidification of the lead.

**5** The cast lead ingot is suspended above the electrically heated crucible by a counterbalanced chain. Running the machine at maximum speed to cast 6pt type will require 3.2kg (7lb) of lead per hour, while 36pt requires 19.5kg (43lb).

**6** A thermometer in the crucible measures the temperature of the lead, which melts from a solid ingot to a liquid state when heated. The crucible temperature for type above 12pt is approximately 343°C (650°F), while smaller type is normally cast at 371°C (700°F).

**9** (top) All the letters are individually cast on a Monotype machine (hence the name). When the caster is running at maximum speed, it may be producing a line every 20–30 seconds. After proofing, if a correction needs to be made to a letter, an individual character can be removed with tweezers and a new character cast and inserted. (bottom) A detail of the interword spaces in Monotype casting, they sit lower than the body of the type, enabling the compositor to remove words easily.

**Above:** The Monotype caster in operation; it is extremely robust in construction yet very delicate in movement. The Monotype Super Caster, which operates on similar principles to the caster, was developed to manufacture type above 14pt and up to 72pt, as well as leads, rules, furniture, block mounting and decorative borders. The Super Caster is even stronger as the volume of molten lead that must be forced into the mould when casting large pieces of furniture or display type, is over 100 times greater than that required for casting 6pt type.

# 2.3 Book finishing

Lettering can be applied to the cover and spine of a book in several ways. Hand-tooled lettering is used to title one-off or very short print run editions of precious books. Gouge work lettering (pronounced 'googe' work in the binding trade) uses heated, curved gouges with different arcs to form letters. It is considered a free style enabling the individual finisher to create his or her own letterforms. Brass type can be mounted in a type carrier (a form that holds a line or lines of type and which can be heated to nearly 100°C (212°F) and the title debossed with a single hand impression if a short run is required. All of these process variations can be blind debossed (where the impression is below the surface and contains no gilding or printed colour infill) or make use of gold leaf inlay.

For longer runs, an electrically heated type carrier is positioned in a pragnant machine which resembles a platen press (*see* p.116). The heated type is levered down on to the book cover and rests on an inclined metal plate. This process is suitable for blind debossing or foil blocking, which is far cheaper than gold leaf and gives the binder a wider range of metallic colours and matt, lustre, pearlized or mirror finishes to choose from. Lettering can also be created through onlay – cutting out letterforms in leather and pasting them to the surface of the cover in a similar way to appliqué. Finally, coloured leather lettering can be inlaid (embedded) into the surface of the cover. Here 'gentleman binder' John Goss of the specialist book binders Savilles, who has mastered the trades of collating, folding, stitching, rounding and backing, works on the lettering of a cover.

## Hand-tooled lettering

**1** Letter tools of a single typeface and size are stored in wooden boxes and referred to as 'alphabet sets'. Character sizes are specified in either points or didots, here 18pt York. Each box has 26 letters; some include numerals. Caps and lower case are stored separately.

**2** Each tool consists of a brass type-character attached to a shaft topped by a wooden handle. Brass and not lead is used to make the type as it can be heated without distortion during the branding process.

**3** A pair of dividers, set to match the cap height of 18pt York type, mark the leather of the spine with two pricks. This measurement is repeated at the base of the spine.

**7** The letters are spaced by eye on the guide sheet. The spacing is generally wider than that used for printed type as the leather is drawn into the impression when branded.

**8** A scrap piece of leather from the same skin as the cover is now marked out with dividers and ruled with baselines and cap lines. This is used to check the spacing from the guide sheet and the quality of the impression.

**9** The letter tools are positioned in order on a gas-fired plate and heated to a temperature of just under 100°C (212°F).

## Gouge work lettering

**Above:** Gouge work lettering makes use of curved brass tools, all of which have arcs with slightly different radii. The tools, like those in the alphabet set opposite, are heated on a gas plate and the design is test spaced on paper in the same way as for hand tooling. The major difference is that the finisher designs the letterforms through combinations of short, arc-shaped impressions.

**Left:** The title *Fairy Tales* and the scalloped, panel edge make use of gold-leaf gouge work and are combined with more conventional roman caps for the author's name.

**Below:** The spine of a book entitled *A Book of Mediterranean* Food illustrates how gouge work can be used with flair to create exuberant, informal lettering.

---

**4** The baseline and cap line are gently pressed into the leather using a ruler and a round-topped palette knife. These impression lines are temporary and can be altered if necessary.

**5** The branded lettering on a book is permanent and the spacing must therefore be checked on a spacing guide before the type impression is made. The spacing guide is created by printing the type on to the edge of a sheet of paper with water-based ink from a pad.

**6** The letter tool is inked on the pad and positioned right way up; a small nick on the shaft indicates the top. The edge of the sheet of paper is used as a cap line while the tool is guided by the thumb of the left hand and pressed with the right hand.

**10** Tiny nicks are made in the top of the baseline marking the centre of each character. The heated tool is then flash-dipped in water, positioned between baseline and cap line and held in position with the thumb. The brand dwells for seconds to make the impression even.

**Left:** This detail shows the evenness and crispness of the branded impression. The lettering can be left plain as here, or be gold-leafed. Gold leaf is positioned over the letter impression and the finisher guides the hot tool through the leaf back into the plain letter impression, fusing the leaf to the leather. Excess gold leaf is simply rubbed away.

## Foil blocking

Foil blocking is a cheaper and quicker alternative to debossed gold-leaf work. It is used for hardback books with longer print runs and makes use of brass type which is arranged in a type carrier rather than a stick (*see* pp.58–59). Brass is used because, as with hand-tooled lettering, the type must be heated to just under 100°C (212°F) before it is debossed into the book cover by a pragnant machine.

## Using heat to deboss lettering

**1** The brass type is stored in small cabinets but the lay of the case (the arrangement of the characters within their boxes) is very different to the letterpress case. Caps and lower-case letters are stored separately.

**2** A detail of the brass type shows that it is wrong-reading. Brass type is used for foil blocking as it is far harder than the lead type used for letterpress printing. Each character is subjected to far greater pressure and heat during the debossing process.

**3** Type carriers are designed to take a single line of type, and are either size specific (here designed to carry any 12pt type) or universal.

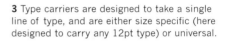

**7** The type is secured in the carrier by tightening the screws and is made square on the pragnant machine.

**8** The pragnant machine consists of an inclined plate (right) on which the book cover rests. The type carrier (centre, the carrier handle is visible top) is electrically heated to 97°C (206°F) and the impression lever (left) is pulled down by the operator to force the hot type into the cover.

**Above:** Each case contains a single font (here 18pt Edinburgh) in one size and is divided into 42 boxes, 26 characters, numerals, punctuation and brass spacing units (which are shorter than lead type).

**Above:** The universal carrier has a movable plate held in place by a leaf spring which can be adjusted by a small screw.

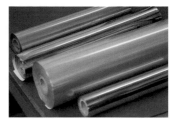

**Above:** Foil comes in roll form and in many different colours and finishes. Here mirror, matt silver and gold are shown, though coloured metallics, and gloss and satin finishes are available.

**4–6** Here gentleman finisher Derek Reid sets the type into a type carrier.

**5**

**6**

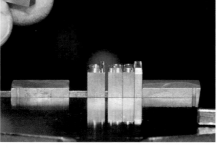

**9** The cover board is positioned on the plate and supported below by a metal fence. Once the type is at the correct temperature and the cover appropriately positioned, the first blind pull, to deboss the lettering, can be made by applying downward pressure to the handle and allowing for a short dwell to give the type time to brand the cover.

**10** The pressure on the handle is released and a sheet of metallic gold foil is immediately placed over the cover and a second pull is made. The hot type is forced into the foil and on into the debossed impression. As both pulls are in register, the foil is applied exactly to the face of the impression.

**11** The debossed foil-blocked letters on a blue leather cover.

**Right:** The finished foil-blocked lettering shows the depth of the debossing and the lustre of the foil. The combination of pragnant machine and foil make short and large runs possible: an experienced operator can produce as many as 200 covers per hour; a gentleman binder working by hand with gold leaf may produce only two or three covers an hour.

### Block line plates

When a designer wishes to use an image, logo or calligraphic lettering in either debossed, onlay or inlay form, a block or plate must be made from an artwork. Traditionally, these decorative plates were hand-engraved into brass, but the process is very expensive and has become the preserve of only the most prestigious limited edition books. A cheaper, block-making alternative is produced by machine-engraving zinc alloy; the plate is referred to as a zinco. The block is engraved in reverse, wrong-reading. A block press consists of a flat, metal platen that the book leather rests on, above which is suspended an electrically heated plate where the zinco or brass engraving is attached.

### Using heat to emboss lettering

**1** A zinco plate showing hand-drawn outline lettering for an expensive edition of the children's book *The Travels of Babar*.

**2** The zinco plate is mounted in the top of the block press and electrically heated. Leather of the required colour for the onlay or inlay lettering is placed on the metal platen.

**3** The press is pulled down. The combination of heat and pressure provided by the press cuts almost completely through the leather. For onlay work the letters are picked out using a scalpel and pasted directly to the surface of the cover. The depth of the relief depends on the thinness of the leather, which can be paired down to as little as 0.4mm (approx. ⅛in).

**Above:** In this example of inlay work, *Lullaby Land*, the spine leather was placed under the press and the plate cut directly into it. The positive letterforms were removed, leaving negative shapes in the spine. A second pressing was made using the same zinco plate to cut a piece of pale green leather, followed by a third separate pressing in a piece of yellow leather. Following the second and third pressings, the positive letters were picked out. These letterforms fitted exactly into the negative shapes and were glued down. The lettering sits flush with the surface of the spine.

**Left:** A detail from the cover of *Lullaby Land* shows a combination of inlay leaves, onlay signs and blind debossing using hand-lettering tools.

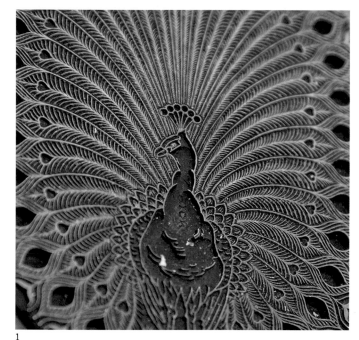

**This page:**

**1** The fine detail of a 40-year-old hand-engraved brass plate (showing a peacock) designed for a gold-leaf cover impression.

**2** Decorative border wheels for line work.

**3** All hand-bound books are pressed for at least 24 hours following finishing. Alternate books in the stack are spine forward, and each book is separated by a metal cover plate.

**4** Boxes of alphabet sets for hand-tooling, many of which are over 100 years old.

# 2.4 Punch-press stencils

Punch-press stencil lettering is used to label goods from tea chests to military equipment and is made by punching out the letterform. A strip of brass or zinc is trapped between a male and female letter die-form (a hardened steel letterform that consistss of two dies that fit together and is used to press letters out of sheet metal) and huge force is applied. The two dies interlock, punching out the stencil letter. The metal is literally sheared or torn along the edges of the die-form. The positive letterform is waste and the stencil is the flat plate with a letter-shaped hole. Stencil letterforms, such as these produced by A.T. Brown Precision Engineers, are designed without enclosed counters as these would drop out during manufacturing.

## Brass lettering created through pressure

**1** The female die (left) and male die (right). A brass or zinc strip is trapped between them. Each size of letter requires an individual die-form, and a standard caps set of 26 caps, ten numerals and six punctuation marks: in all 42 interlocking dies. A caps and lower case set uses 68 die pairs. Machine tooling for the dies is expensive so the number of sizes of stencil fonts is limited.

**2** A 50-m (164-ft) reel of brass strip is mounted below the punch. The width and thickness (gauge) of the strip varies depending on the cap height of the letter. Small letters are made from the thinnest brass, while letters with a cap height of over 7.6 cm (3 in) tend to be produced in a heavier-gauge zinc.

**3** The brass passes through a pair of metal rollers. These flatten the strip, removing the bend formed by the reel, and ensure the strip is aligned with the punch. The rollers are changed to accommodate different strip widths for different sizes.

**4** The flattened brass strip is drawn between the male and female dies. Hydraulic pressure forces the male die down on to the female die, punching out the stencil letter. The strip is pulled forward a set distance that allows for kerning and for a folded interlocking strip on either side of the letter. The operation is repeated and a strip of stencil plates for the same letter is created. This is then automatically guillotined into individual letters. The waste positive letterforms are put into a bin, to be collected, smelted down, rolled and recycled into another brass strip.

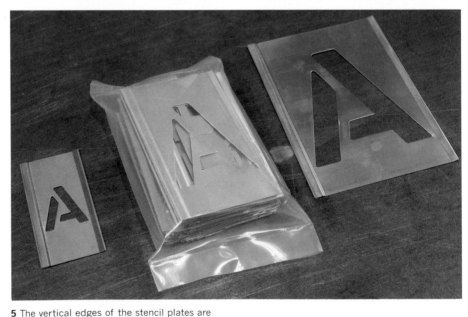

**5** The vertical edges of the stencil plates are folded over on themselves so that any two letters can interlock. A raised pleat is put into each plate so that it sits flat on the surface. This process of folding and pleating is done with a hand press and takes a matter of seconds. Letters are stored alphabetically by size before being sorted into packs.

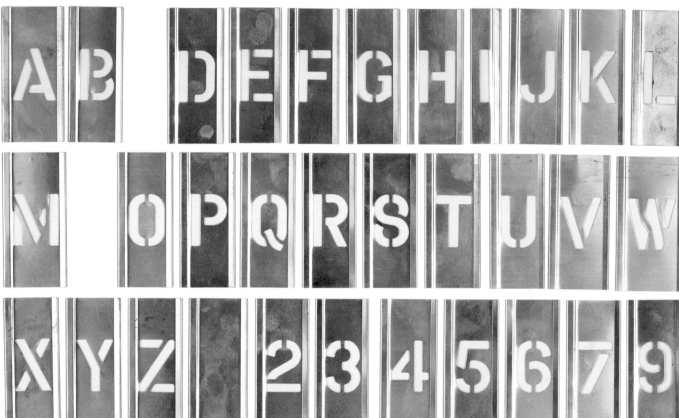

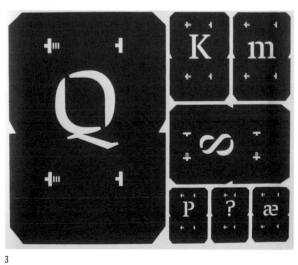

**This page:**

1 Stencil letters from a 3-cm (1½-in) alphabet. The company has been producing stencil letters for the military since before the First World War.

2 Stencil lettering on a circular template is produced for labelling the tops of beer barrels, for the military and for theatre lighting.

3 A screen-print of a stencil letterform designed by David Ottely.

4–5 Military stencils applied to the emergency exit hatch in a Royal Navy helicopter (4), and a US Army truck hood (5).

1

2

3

4

5

**Right:** The first typewriters only produced caps in a single font, but the development of the 'shift key' (seen here on an 1878 Remington model) supported both caps and lower-case on a single machine. Refinements in 'pitch' (the space between lines), the addition of 'tabs' (alignment points for margins) and a bell signalling the number of characters remaining in a line before the carriage needed to be returned, made for practical and typographic refinement.

The typewriter was first patented in 1714 by the British engineer Henry Mill (*c.*1683–1771). However, it was not until 1868 that the first practical typewriter using the now familiar QWERTY or universal keyboard was designed and manufactured in the United States. The design was developed and sold by E. Remington and Sons, famous rifle and sewing-machine manufacturers. The typewriter was in the vanguard of typographic democratization; for the first time mechanical and identical letterforms were at the fingertips of anyone who could write. From 1900 until 1980 it was the 'iron horse' of government, education, journalism, military and business correspondence. Secretarial colleges and typing pools sprang up across the world, training men and women in shorthand and typing.

The lever action, which punched a letter into an inked ribbon and on to the paper, affected the form of the letters themselves. All the characters on early mechanical typewriters were of the same height, and had to fit on a single body width as there was no facility for varying the intercharacter spacing to compensate for characters of different widths. This mechanical design constraint meant that new monowidth type had to be drawn so that the space occupied by the lower-case 'i', or punctuation marks, was of equal width to that of the upper-case 'M'. Narrow characters were expanded or drawn with extremely long serifs, while wide characters were condensed. The space bar produced a far larger gap between words than was customary with metal type.

## The QWERTY keyboard

**Right top:** The QWERTY or universal keyboard, named after the first six letters in the top alphabet row, was first patented in 1878. A typewriter's mechanical linkages in part determined the arrangement of the keys. The QWERTY keyboard was designed to separate the most commonly used letters and position them towards the outer ends of a row where they would be depressed by the weakest fingers. This slowed down the maximum typing speed, giving the returning levers time to regain their position without colliding with levers of keys that were being depressed.

**Right middle:** In 1932, Professor August Dvorak (1894–1975) proposed an alternative layout which grouped together the most frequently used letters and minimized the finger travel distance. The home row letters on the Dvorak keyboard are used 70 per cent of the time compared with only 32 per cent on QWERTY, which has been preserved as a matter of custom and practice. In an age of digital type unrestricted by mechanical linkages typing is still done on a less than efficient keyboard layout.

## IBM Golf ball typewriter

**Right:** IBM's Selectric Typewriter featured 88 characters on a revolving sphere referred to as a golf ball. It was capable of printing characters of different widths and, therefore, re-creating the proportions of metal type. The golf balls came with different fonts and sizes, and were interchangeable. They could be purchased by the general public at a stationer's – perhaps the first phase in the direct sale of typefaces to the non-specialist.

# 2.6 Braille

**Above:** The dimple-like depressions in the Braille matrix that are used to create the raised lettering are made by hand using a stylus. Each cell has six dots (shown here actual size). The matrix sets a consistent interline spacing (equivalent to leading in type) as it is important that the reader is able to consistently locate the beginning of the next line.

**Above right:** A detail of a Braille embossed card shows the crisp definition of the raised dots. Reading Braille relies on sensitive fingertips that can detect relative positions on the six-dot matrix and the blank, flat cell space between words. The matrices carry the alphabet, numerals and punctuation, though caps and lower-case letters are not used in the same manner as type. Skilled readers reach reading speeds similar to those of sighted readers looking at type.

Braille is a tactile lettering system used by blind and visually impaired people throughout the world. It consists of a matrix of six dots arranged in two columns with each letter, numeral or punctuation mark identified by an individual dot pattern raised above the reading surface. The Braille reader moves his or her fingers across the raised dots, identifying letters and words by touch. Braille takes its name from the French inventor Louis Braille (1809–52), who completed his raised lettering system in 1824.

All the principal Braille symbols are made up on a matrix of six dots arranged in two columns of three dots. The matrix is referred to as a Braille cell. The dots are numbered 1, 2 and 3 from the first column, top left, and 4, 5 and 6 from the second column, top right. Originally Braille was read from left to right but versions have been developed for representing languages with alternative reading directions. Each letter has a specific pattern – either raised dots or blank space – which the reader learns to recognize. The dots in standard size Braille are raised between 0.4mm and 0.5mm (approx. ½in).

There is no visual relationship between the dot pattern of the Braille symbols and the Latin letterforms they represent. The characters 'a' to 'j' make use of the top four dots of the Braille cell. Dot 3 (bottom of the first column) is added to each of the 'a' to 'j' symbols, which are repeated with this addition to represent the characters 'k' to 't'. The first five symbols of the system, 'a' to 'e', are repeated with the addition of dots 6 and 3 to represent 'u' to 'z'. The letter 'w' is an exception to the pattern as at the time of Braille's invention it was not in use in France. It has, therefore, had to be encoded subsequently. These basic letter symbols are used consistently in many languages that make use of the Latin script for the sighted reader. However, variations in the code have developed. English Braille, for example, encodes letters, punctuation and some word signs but uses a prefix symbol to represent capitalization and numerals. Experienced Braille users may also learn Braille shorthand.

There are four principal ways of writing Braille which are shown overleaf: using a slate and stylus, on a manual Braille typewriter (called a Perkins Brailler), on a computerized refreshable Braille display, and on a computerized Braille embosser. In some countries, embossing using Braille type pieces that resemble those used for letterpress printing is still used for major publications, but elsewhere this has largely been replaced by computerized embossing.

1

2

3

**This page:**

**1** Braille typewriters and embossing machines can be used to create relief lettering on crack-back tape which can be attached to cupboards, filing cabinets, books and food products, etc. enabling a blind person to identify their contents through touch.

**2** This simple book designed to teach both blind children and those with limited vision makes uses of large, black type and Braille embossing. The blind child must develop a refined touch, learnt alongside the phonetic sounds the dot patterns represent.

**3** A page from a Braille book embossed on both sides, to make more economical use of paper. The dot matrix on either side of the page must fall out of register so that dots on one side do not destroy those on the other.

# Writing Braille by hand: slate and stylus

**1** The slate and stylus method was first developed by Charles Barbier and Braille. The slate is made up of two elements: the matrix (top) which consists of a hinged grid of open rectangular cells, and the slate (which is held in register within the matrix). Today the slate is a plastic sheet with small dimple-like depressions in the Braille six-dot pattern. The stylus (below) has a blunt, rounded metal tip and a plastic handle.

**2** A sheet of paper or card is placed between the slate and the rectangular cells and is held in place by small pins or grips. Virtually any paper can be temporarily embossed, but very thin papers are inclined to tear and quickly lose their raised surface as the reader's fingers gently press down on the cells.

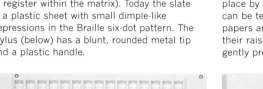

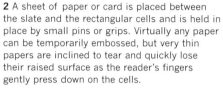

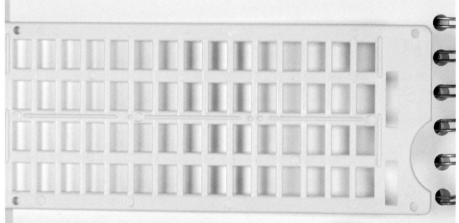

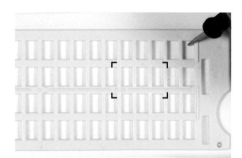

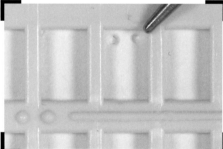

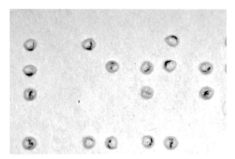

**3** The Braille symbols must be written wrong-reading from top right of the matrix. This requires the blind reader to reverse the dot patterns representing each letter. The writer positions the stylus by feeling the edge of the cell. He or she then gently feels for the appropriate dimple beneath the paper before pushing and twisting the stylus to force the paper down into the dimple and make the impression.

**4** The process is repeated for every dot within every cell until a word is spelt out and then a cell is left blank to create the interword spacing. Proficient writers are generally slightly slower at writing than sighted readers using pen and ink. When a line is complete, the writer moves to the right side of the second line.

**5** Most slates allow five or ten lines to be written before the matrix is moved down the page. The top line of the matrix is aligned by touch with the bottom line of Braille. Slate and stylus Braille, unlike some computerized embossing, is produced on only one side of the sheet.

## Writing Braille mechanically: the Perkins Brailler

The Perkins Brailler was invented in 1951 by David Abrahams and Edward Waterhouse, respectively woodwork and maths teachers, at the Perkins School for the Blind. They had responded to a task set by the principal of the school, Gabriel Farrell, to produce an inexpensive machine that allowed blind pupils to write efficiently.

### Typing Braille

**1** The Perkins Brailler has six principal keys for each of the dots within a cell, as well as a space, backspace and line space key. Like a manual typewriter, it has two side knobs to advance the paper and a carriage return to move the paper on at the end of a line.

**2** The paper is fed between two rollers and advanced to the required position by twisting the advance knob.

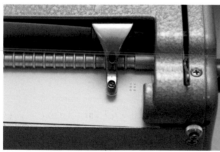

**3** The margins are set by positioning carriage return stops. The small, evenly spaced grooves represent the common character width of the Braille cells.

**4** Each character is typed by pressing the appropriate number of keys that make up the dots for each symbol. The keys are linked to the embossing carriage and a wire stylo that makes the impression on the reverse of the paper. The carriage repositions itself when the next character is punched.

**5** When the sheet is complete, it is rolled out and the next page is fed between the rollers. The Braille typist can check the text by 'touch reading'. Copies can be made by placing two sheets of paper in the machine, one behind the other in a manner similar to using carbon paper.

### Refreshable Braille display

A refreshable Braille display enables blind and visually impaired people to type on a word processor in both Braille and roman script. This means they can communicate directly with both blind and sighted readers without recourse to a sighted Braille translator. Many blind operators type texts from dictation machines. They listen to the words, type on the QWERTY keyboard, and then read back the Braille to check their text using the refreshable Braille display. They are able to print out either a roman script document for a sighted reader or a Braille copy for a blind reader using a computerized embosser (*see* opposite).

## Digital Braille setting

1 The refreshable Braille display unit is positioned below the conventional QWERTY keyboard. It is able to present two lines of Braille at a time. Each Braille cell is represented by eight small holes drilled through the plastic reading surface. When a letter is typed on the QWERTY keyboard, small nylon pins with rounded tops push up through the appropriate holes to create a raised symbol which the operator can read through his or her fingertip. The position of the cursor on screen is represented by vibrating dots in one cell.

2 Dots are raised using the piezo effect where some crystals expand when an electrical charge is applied. Each dot is connected to a crystal by a small lever. When the charge passes through the crystal, driven by the Unicode command, the tiny crystal expands, moving the lever, and the pin is lifted through the hole and raised above the reading surface.

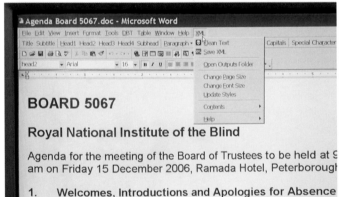

3 The text on screen as roman script. It refers to the Royal National Institute of the Blind, which in 2007 changed its name to the Royal National Institute of Blind People.

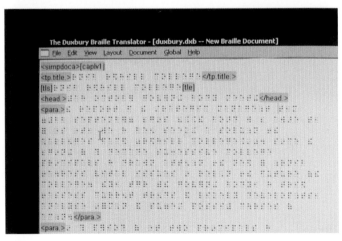

4 The same text presented on screen as Braille symbols. The software that controls the Braille display generically known as a screen reader, converts roman text into Braille characters or vice versa.

## Printing and binding Braille documents

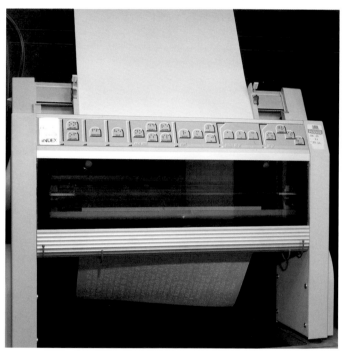

**1** Once a document has been checked through the refreshable Braille display, it can be 'printed' using a computerized embosser. In a large office the computer is linked to the embosser through a central server. Smaller embossers have been developed for personal computers, but they are significantly more expensive than equivalent ink printers used by sighted people.

**2** The embosser works on a similar principle to the Braille display. Embossing pins are lifted, wrong-reading, into the appropriate position to make each of the cell symbols, before being pushed into the back of a thick sheet of paper to produce right-reading Braille. Here the embossed sheet of Braille is exiting the printer.

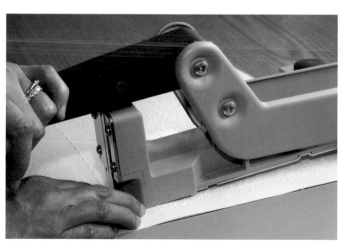

**3** The finished Braille sheet can be embossed on both sides, which saves on paper and, according to Braille readers, is no more difficult to read than a sheet that is embossed on only one side.

**4** The completed document is stapled together to make a book.

# 2.7 Transfer lettering

For many years water-based transfers were used in the ceramics industry to add pattern and lettering to crockery. A transfer was printed on to a waxed paper which, when dipped in water, could be slid on to the surface of a tile, cup or plate. Dry transfer lettering was invented by 'Dai' Davies, who with Fred McKenzie founded the Letraset Company in London in 1959. The very first sets, like the transfers designed for use on ceramics, required water to separate the lettering from the backing paper, but by 1961 the process had been refined. Dry, rub-down letters were screen-printed on to the back of a matt, polythene sheet which was protected with blue, waxed paper. To use the transfer sheet, the designer drew a blue baseline across the artwork, positioned the dotted baseline on the sheet along this line, and rubbed over the sheet with a burnishing tool. The letters had a slightly tacky back which adhered to the paper. If the letter was correctly positioned, the blue backing sheet was placed over it and rubbed down with the burnisher. If the designer made a mistake, the misplaced letter could be removed with masking tape or a scalpel. The process was slow and it was often difficult to space letters evenly. Letraset was designed for working with short texts and headlines but not for body copy.

## Rubbing down a dry transfer lettering

**1** Dry transfer lettering is screen printed, wrong-reading, onto the reverse of a semi transparent carrier sheet. This sheet is positioned over the artwork and may be taped down. A blue pencil line is often used as a baseline along which the type is arranged.

The designer transfers the selected letter from the sheet to the artwork by rubbing it down with a burnishing tool. Letraset printed letter-spacing guides on some sheets, but refined, even spacing generally relied on the designer's eye.

**2** If a mistake is made, the individual rub-down letter can be removed with masking tape or scratched off with a scalpel. When a line of type is completed and checked, it can be burnished down. The opaque backing sheet is placed over the line and the

lettering is rubbed down, fixing it on to the artwork. A clear spray varnish makes the artwork permanent.

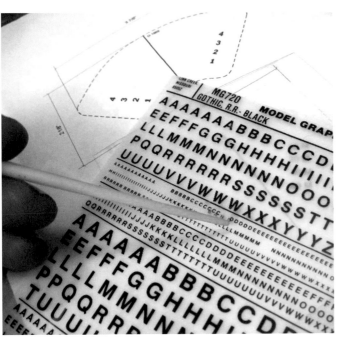

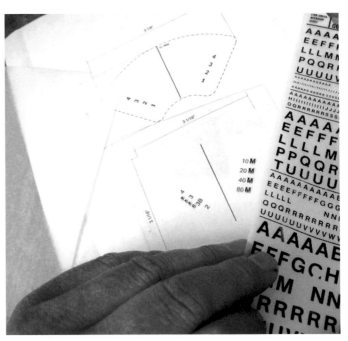

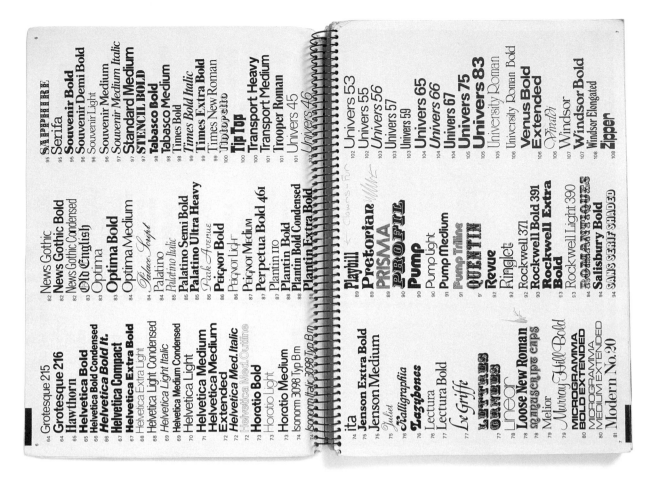

**Above:** An index page from a Letraset catalogue shows the range of faces. Many of the fonts are designed to be used for headlines. Letraset produced over 1,200 fonts in dry transfer formats, many in an extensive range of sizes; a large studio would store several thousand sheets at a time. Letraset commissioned 474 original fonts, many of which are now available digitally.

**Right:** Letraset developed larger self-adhesive lettering for internal and external signage, and enviromental and retail use. Like the rub-downs it was modular and came in sheet form. Letterforms were die-cut into the adhesive surface of crack-back sheets. This page from an early Letrasign catalogue shows (from left to right) 1. the waste vinyl being removed, 2. the individual character being lifted from the sheet with a scalpel, 3. the character positioned on a page, 4. the final arrangement, which must be burnished down, removing any air bubbles trapped between the letter and the surface.

### Letrasign sheets

Letrasign self-adhesive vinyl lettering sheets are an easy and economical way to make signs, notices and identifications. The robust letters are easy to position, and reposition, to achieve good results quickly. They are ideal for most applications including house and boat names, vehicle markings, notice boards, direction signs and for exhibitions and displays.

Letrasign lettering has a matt finish and the letters are sharp and highly legible. The permanent adhesive adheres to most surfaces and when burnished will resist abrasion.

They are designed for use indoors and outdoors and with proper application will resist most weather conditions.

Letrasign can be applied to most surfaces provided that they are smooth, clean, dry and free from grease.

1 Remove the waste vinyl from the backing paper by gently peeling away from one corner, taking care not to remove any letters.

2 Letters can now be lifted easily with the fingers or better still by using a thinbladed knife.

3 The letters can be positioned directly onto the working surface. Press the bottom of the letter lightly into contact with the surface to hold it in position until the whole word is assembled. The letters can then be repositioned if required.

4 Those letters with a flat base should sit on the line but those curved at the base must be positioned slightly lower to be visually correct.

When the entire word or notice has been assembled the letters should be firmly rubbed down to remove any air bubbles.

The lettering will now be firmly bonded.

**Number of letters per sheet**

To test visual impairment opticians assess eyesight on a similar premise – letters are read from a chart at a set distance and are presented in progressively smaller sizes. The medical term for the quality of eyesight is visual acuity. Visual acuity, derived from the latin *acuitas*, meaning sharpness, is a measure of the eye's central sharpness rather than peripheral vision.

Dutch ophthalmologist Hermann Snellen (1834–1908) devised a scientific test for eyesight in 1862 which remains the standard today. It requires the person being tested to cover one eye and read the smallest line of type they can. This process is then repeated with the other eye. A reading of 20/20 is considered normal vision. An example of impaired sight would be a reading of 20/40 meaning that the subject can read at 6.1m (20ft) the row that a person with normal sight can read at 12.2m (40ft). A person with a reading of 20/200 is considered legally blind.

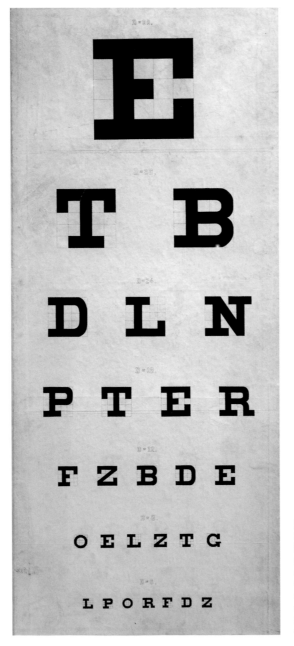

**Left:** Snellen designed a set of letters reproduced in different sizes to be read by the subject from 6.1 m (20 ft). Egyptian or slab serif letters were arranged in rows of diminishing size. To compensate for the variation in the angle of the reader's gaze he designed the letters to subtend a visual angle of five degrees and for each component part to subtend an angle of one minute (one-sixtieth of a degree).

# 2.9 Ishihara's colour-deficiency lettering

**This page:**
Letters that a normal viewer can see are less well detected by the colour-blind viewer.

**1** The protanomalous observer does not detect the red within violet and violet appears as blue.

**2** People who are colour-impaired are less sensitive to green in colours; it appears to shift towards red.

**3** Others perceive no difference between red, orange, yellow and green.

**4** In another condition brightness of red, orange and yellow is reduced to the extent that the colours are seen as black or grey.

The standard way of testing colour deficiencies was devised by Dr Shinobu Ishihara (1879–1963). Ishihara was asked by the Japanese army to develop a colour vision test for soldiers. The basis of the test is termed pseudo-isochromatic. This means that at least two different colours appear equivalent to someone who is colour-impaired when they are, in fact, distinct. A person with normal colour vision can distinguish distinct numbers or patterns which are unrecognizable to anyone with colour impairment. Ishihara drew a circular field and filled it with dots of different sizes. By colouring the dots with different hues he could create figures. The only clue to the form of these figures was the hue. The original drawings made use of Japanese characters but these were soon replaced by Arabic numerals and wiggle paths. The numerals were often drawn over one another, making it very difficult for a colour-impaired person to distinguish the figure.

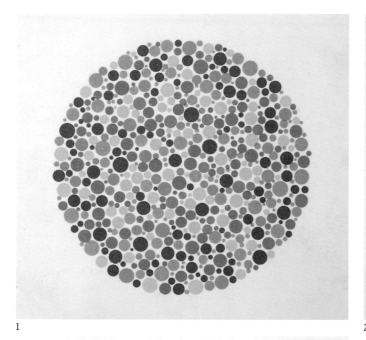

1

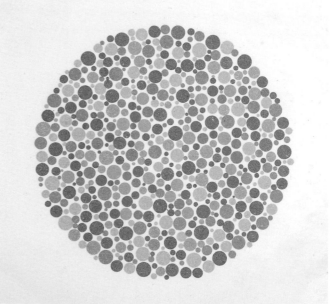

2

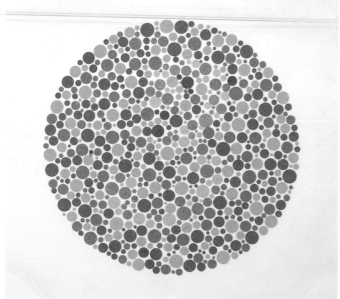

3

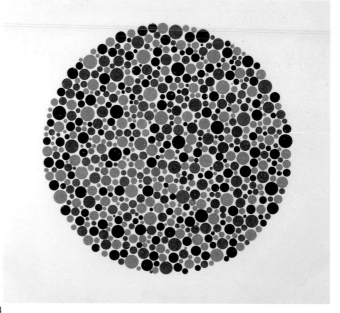

4

# 2.10 Designing type (1)

Type designer Jeremy Tankard was commissioned by Christchurch Art Gallery in New Zealand to design a font family for its identity and publicity material. Pages from his sketchbook and laser printouts show his process of reviewing, editing and redrawing elements of each letterform and reveal how a type designer searches to make compatible letterforms within a font while retaining its desired character.

**This page:**

1 Early sketches of numerals.

2 Visualizing the potential form of an 's'. By writing comments, the designer feeds back on to the page, in words, an internalized critique received through the eye.

3 Hand-drawn pencil roughs in the sketchbook are redrawn, digitally printed out and reviewed. Corrections to terminals, junctures, character width and bowls are indicated in a personal shorthand.

4 Tankard moves between sketchbook and screen, drawing and redrawing a form.

5 The rough for a special character.

6 The bold form of the character shown at two sizes allows the designer to evaluate its visual impact.

7 Text samples of the complete lower-case alphabet are stored in a file and ordered chronologically so that the designer can trace the development of an idea for a character. The predominantly mono stroke with pronounced square-cut serifs, together with the quirky use of a looped form (note the 'k'), give the font its visual character.

8 By combining pairs of letters as ligatures and kerning pairs the designer is able to work through a range of approaches to connectives and also establish the intercharacter spaces.

9 The upper- and lower-case versions of the name of the gallery showing an alternative 'ch' with a connective and how the intercharacter spacing works within the name.

10 A page from publicity material that uses alternative lower-case forms.

11 A more decorative expression of the word 'construction' using tracery to interlink upper-case forms.

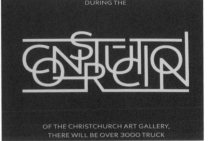

# Designing type (2)

Sheffield City Council commissioned Jeremy Tankard to design a san serif font for Sheffield Connect, a transport system in the city in the north of England.

**1**

**2**

The forms of the developing typeface† Sheffield Sans. City signage type. However as a straße style galileos forms explore a far wider [matrix] these include ‹condensed› and wide «fonts» and a variety of weights from light to heavy in total. ¶There nœl twenty four fonts the (numbers) are semi-lining so a line of text numbers will not be so overþowering‡ or it cøst the upper cáse are short to the {ascender} height "how many" and hæw much is the use of the question? and exclamation! marks. (The quick brown fox 'jumps' over the lazy dog). info@sheffieldcity.org

**3**

THE FORMS OF THE DEVELOPING TYPEFACE† SHEFFIELD SANS. CITY SIGNAGE TYPE. HOWEVER AS A STRASSE STYLE GALILEOS FORMS EXPLORE A FAR WIDER [MATRIX] THESE INCLUDE ‹CONDENSED› AND WIDE «FONTS» AND A VARIETY OF WEIGHTS FROM LIGHT TO HEAVY IN TOTAL. ¶THERE NŒL TWENTY FOUR FONTS THE (NUMBERS) ARE SEMI-LINING SO A LINE OF TEXT NUMBERS WILL NOT BE SO OVERÞOWERING‡ OR IT CØST THE UPPER CASE ARE SHORT TO THE {ASCENDER} HEIGHT "HOW MANY" AND HÆW MUCH IS THE USE OF THE QUESTION?

**4**

85

Designing type

**This page:**

**1** Early drawings reveal Tankard's inspiration: English Grotesque forms.

**2** A second sketch shows the 'i' and 'j', which borrow their dot from the London Transport font designed by Edward Johnston. The form of the 'a' is heavily influenced by the 'a' drawn by Eric Gill and Johnston.

**3** The condensed bold form set in lower and upper case.

**4** Detail from a sketchbook showing the development of ideas for monetary symbols.

**5** The lower- and upper-case alphabet sets in roman. Note how the punctuation makes use of the inclined point of the 'i'.

**6** This sample, ranged left, shows how upper- and lower-case combine. The condensed forms are well suited to close interword spacing.

**7** The laser printout showing the bold roman forms has been drawn on by hand to visualize the italic version. Careful choices must be made concerning the angle of incline.

**8** Here the bold italic forms have been digitally drawn and compared letter for letter with the upright bold roman forms.

**9** Italicized ligature or special character (top line) and some accented characters (bottom line).

**10** Two weights of the italicized lower-case dipthongs and accented characters.

**11** By setting words containing kerned pair combinations the designer can assess how the intercharacter spacing relates to letters set as single characters. The pair 'bj' have been negatively kerned so that the loop of the lower-case 'j' overlaps the interspace of the 'b'.

abcdefghijklmnopqr stuvwxyz-.,:; aaccggttuuyy ABCDEFGHIJKLMNOPQR STUVWXYZ CCGG

**5**

Sheffield Sans sample setting. This type showing is here to see how the developing font appears in small column width setting. The typeface is created for Sheffield City Council for the Connect Sheffield project. It will be produced as an OpenType font, it is a semi con densed type style based on English Grot forms.

**6**

a a b b c d d e e f f

**7**

a a b b p p q q c c d d r r s s e e f f t t u u

**8**

Æ Æ Œ Œ Ø Ø Ð Ð Þ Þ

**9**

æ æ œ œ ø ø ð ð þ þ

**10**

bj
object
subjunctive
bk
yubka

vicar
wildcat
cb
macbeth
Mcbride

**11**

**Left**: A black and white print from a woodcut is scanned at high resolution to provide a pattern from which the letterforms can be redrawn. It is interesting to note that Reynold Stone's original woodcut contained a significant omission: he apparently forgot to cut the number 5.

The majority of standard fonts used today on personal computers precede the invention of digital type in the late 1960s. Since then, designers have been converting analogue (non-digital) fonts and letterforms for digital use, using Fontographer, FontLab and FontStudio. This process is ongoing and many designers are beginning to take an interest in digitizing letterforms from a wide range of historical sources in an attempt to preserve the nature of type cut in wood, stone-cut letters, calligraphy, signwriting, and steel and wood engraving. The digitization and conversion of analogue letterforms, which were not originally drawn as type but are being translated into type, sets a difficult challenge for the type designer. The visual conventions of type – evenness of appearance, consistency of proportion, regular intercharacter spacing, considered variations in weight – may be partly at odds with the spirit and intention of those who first drew the letterforms.

The process of converting an existing analogue letterform into type has perhaps ten phases: 1. scanning; 2. grouping the letterforms; 3. evaluating vertical and horizontal proportions (cap, ascender, descender, cross bar etc. and common letter widths); 4. tracing; 5. unifying common letterform components (stroke widths, serif forms etc.); 6. justifying (establishing the shoulder widths); 7. defining kerning pairs and ligatures; 8. testing (sentence construction); 9. hinting (determining how a font is presented on screen); 10. interpolation (adjusting the weight of a face at different sizes). Although the phases have been numbered 1 to 10, each phase is not self-contained and completed before the next is undertaken. The process is iterative, the designer moves fluidly between tracing and testing, drawing and redrawing. The designer's quest is to identify and preserve the character details of the original features and balance these in relation to the unifying constraints of typographic convention.

The partnership of Michael Harvey and Andrew Benedek at Fine Fonts combines lettering experience in calligraphy, letter-cutting and carving, type design, customization and digitization of historical analogue letterforms. The following example shows Fine Fonts creating type based on a woodcut by Reynold Stone (1909–1979). Interestingly the woodcut was redrawn as the font Janet for metal type but the drawings and matrix (*see* pp. 60–61) have been lost. All that remains of the font are private press books published at the time.

## Converting hand-drawn letterforms to digital type

**1** The letterforms from the original scan are divided into upper-case and lower-case italics and numerals then copied into Illustrator software so that they can be digitally traced. The baselines, cap lines and ascender and descender lines are defined. This is something of an imposition on the spirit of the woodcut where these proportions, being hand-drawn, were not perfectly consistent between characters.

**2** The letter 'O' is scanned in the background as a guide and ellipses are drawn to match as closely as possible the outer and inner form of the character. The Bézier curves are infinitely adaptable and the outline is worked until the designer is satisfied with the line of best fit.

**3** The letter 'I' is approached as the second symmetrical letter but this creates the challenge of developing a characteristic serif for the font. One serif is carefully drawn around to establish the line of best fit with the original. This line is then copied and flipped to make the termination of the downstroke.

**4** The provisional serif from the 'I' is now copied on to other letters to see how it compares. This exercise reveals some of the fundamental differences between the wood-engraved letters and type. The serif widths are all different and some vary significantly. By checking against all the serif letters the designer begins to establish the range of variables, and is in a position to develop one or more compromise serif forms.

**5** The serif form can be flipped vertically and placed over other characters (here the 'H') and further adjustments made. Options are considered, drawn, matched, reviewed and redrawn.

**6** The range of stroke widths is established by a similar process of digital tracing, copying and placing over other woodcut characters.

**7** When several characters have been drawn in outline they are copied into Fontographer or FontLab for an initial assessment of how they begin to work together. The designer is trying to identify the spacing between letters. Here the space between straight-sided letters based on 'H' is being assessed.

**8** By trying various combinations of straight-sided and round letters (here 'n' and 'o') approximate side bearings or shoulders (the space either side of the face of a letter-form) can be established. In digital type these are invisible and are determined by the type designer who defines the optimum spacing between letters so that printed type is even.

**9** A return to the tracing process. The left side-bearing for vertical letters can be provisionally applied to 'B', 'D', 'E', 'F', 'I', 'K' and 'L', the right side-bearing to rounded letters 'O' and 'D', and the left side-bearing to 'C', 'G' and 'Q'. Here the vertical stroke is being checked and a limited set of widths is established.

**10** Digital type enables the type designer to vary the spacing between any two characters within a font individually and automatically in a way that is not possible in metal setting other than by creating special characters or ligatures. The designer assigns special commands to the kerned pairs when the two characters appear successively. These commands override the established side bearings, closing or opening the space. Here the original side bearings for a lower-case 'g' are adjusted.

**11** Hinting is the process of adjusting the presentation of a typeface on screen with the aim of improving its legibility. As the resolution of screen displays vary, a single typeface can appear differently at different resolutions. Hinting determines how the pixels are most accurately used to represent the vector outline of a font on screen.

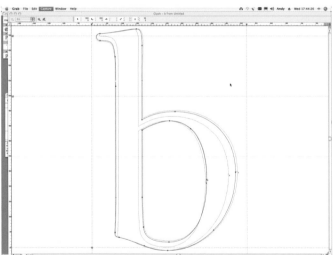

**12** There are three levels of hinting: manual, delta and fast. Manual hinting is the most detailed and involves the type designer reviewing every character, at every point size, and checking and adjusting its screen presentation. This may involve checking 300 characters at 20 sizes – up to 6,000 characters. Few fonts are hinted entirely manually due to the expense. Interpolation is the process of adjusting what a font looks like at different sizes when printed, to retain its character, visual consistency and legibility. The relative weight of 6pt type and sizes up to 72pt varies, the characters are not merely scaled up. The type outline is influenced by a mathematical formula which is expressed as a percentage. This example shows some of the variation in character widths.

**13** The designer begins to make up words using the font, constantly reviewing on screen, and uses high-quality print outputs to check the evenness of the strokes, consistent tone of the letterforms, kerning combinations and the appearance of the type in different sizes. He will begin to consider how the roman form will link to different weights and italics to create a type family.

45673

Printing

# 3.1 Woodblock printing

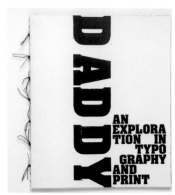

**Above and opposite:** Bjørn Ortmann, a student at Central Saint Martin's, College of Art and Design, London, adapted the classical approach to woodblock carving by using large sheets of thin plywood to design *Daddy, an Exploration in Typography and Print*, these pages from the book feature a poem by Sylvia Plath. Like Ilse Buchert Nesbitt, Ortmann worked with a reverse-reading paper guide but one from a digital output. He cut around each of the characters before stripping away the top surface of the veneer to create raised typographic letterforms. The woodblocks were printed page by page in imposition on signatures on an Albion press. Some of the text, such as KILL, bleeds off the fore-edge of the page and continues on the reverse. The lettering was based on typographic forms but, being hand-cut, the letters are not absolutely identical either in form or in the way they are printed. The distressed patina reflects the nature of the poem.

Woodblock printing is a process that dates back to second-century CE China where designs and writing were printed on to textiles and paper. The tradition of printing continued throughout the Far East for over a thousand years before there is evidence it developed in the West. By the seventh century, parts of China had introduced woodblock printed paper money. The earliest surviving printed book is the *Diamond Sutra* of *c*.868, Buddhist teachings printed from woodblocks.

The earliest surviving Western so-called block books – such as *Biblia Pauperum*, *Apocalypse* and *Ars Moriendi* – featuring woodblock illustrations and written in the roman alphabet date from *c*.1460. The technique was most widely used in Germany, France and the Netherlands but its popularity declined rapidly with the introduction of copper and steel engraving, which reproduced finer printed lines and, therefore, smaller letterforms. Although woodblock printing was superseded in terms of speed by letterpress printing, it remained popular until the second half of the nineteenth century. It was associated with fine printing and championed by William Morris (1834–96) and the Arts and Crafts Movement. Morris ensured it was taught in the emerging art schools. Other technical developments were introduced by the Post-Impressionist painter Paul Gauguin (1848–1903) who began carving plains (areas of wood cut to two depths) and inking them with separate colours to produce two-colour images, often black and brown, from a single pull.

The side grain of soft fruit woods, such as pear and apple, as well as hardwoods like poplar, lime and maple, are ideally suited to woodcutting as the long grain is fine and even. The wood must be well seasoned and free of any knots before it is mechanically planed flat to 2.3cm (⅞in) or type high (the standardized height of letterpress type).

The lettering design must be drawn in reverse on the surface of the woodblock. Because of this requirement few cutters draw letters directly on to the block. One of the finest American cutters, Ilse Buchert Nesbitt (*see* opposite) is an exception in that she can draw a wrong-reading image directly on to the block. Most calligraphers like to draw right-reading letters on to tracing or typo paper using pencil or ink. The paper is then flipped and glued to the surface of the block and provides an accurate visible outline for the carving. If the lettering is to be printed black, the majority of the surface wood surrounding the letterforms must be cut away. If the lettering is to be reversed out (the black ground is printed, and the lettering is defined by the white unprinted surface of the paper), the cutter must remove the wood inside the letterform. Woodcutting like engraving allows no space for mistakes, as any slip or misplaced mark on the surface of the block affects either the letterform or the ground, and will be reproduced in print.

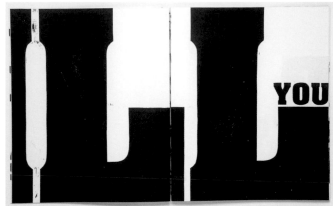
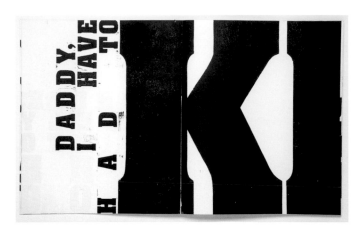

## Cutting the letters

**1** Woodblock cutters make use of a range of tools. They tend to use a burin with a V section. After writing the text, with a pen and ink on tracing paper, Ilse Buchert Nesbitt pastes it to the surface of the block wrong-reading and begins to cut away waste wood around the outline of the letters using a paring knife. Note the oilstone for sharpening the knife.

**2** Ilse cuts away from the letter outlines towards the waste wood using a double-handed grip; the left hand pushes behind the blade and the right hand resists. This approach offers both power and control at the cutting edge.

**3** The work is slow and painstaking as each letter and connective must be cut around, and the interline and word and character spaces cut away to an even depth, allowing the lettering to stand proud. Outlines of the letters are cut with a slight avit, which means the base of the letter is broader where it meets the newly cut surface of the block than at the letterface. This minimizes the edge of letters being chipped when under pressure during printing.

**4** As the work progresses, Ilse can make test proofs to review the quality of the cut and refine the letterforms. This detail shows the exquisite quality of the cutting.

# 3.2 Letterpress printing

Gutenberg's first press was based on the technology used in winemaking. It differed from all previous presses in that it combined both an up-and-down movement, applying pressure to transfer ink from the type to the paper, and a separate in-and-out motion, positioning the form and paper. This type of press, made almost entirely of wood, is referred to as a joiner's press. A solid, wooden frame supports a large, wooden screw which, when tightened, exerts pressure on a plate or platen, forcing the paper down on to the inked typeface and creating the impression.

Simple wooden presses offered the printer a good impression and were successfully used for two-colour work that required accurate registration. Letterpress printing enabled a single printer, having set a text, to reproduce multiples and thus industrialize the production of language. Printing in the sixteenth century was often referred to as mechanical writing. Although far quicker than the human hand, the new technology could produce no more than 100 sheets per day. Printing was slow as each impression involved re-inking the press by hand, moving the protective frisket (stencil), positioning a new sheet of paper and pulling and tightening the screw thread. The economic incentive to reduce the time and, therefore, the cost of each pull (while retaining or improving the crispness of the impression) became the printer's obsession. By 1600, two printers working on a single wooden press at Christopher Plantin's publishing house in Antwerp, Belgium were capable of printing 1,250 sheets per day on both sides.

Letterpress was to remain the most important method of reproducing text until photo composition was more widely adopted in the 1960s, after which magazines and illustrated books could be reproduced lithographically (*see* pp.102–05). Letterpress remained the means of producing newspapers until the mid-1980s when digital technology in the form of the Apple Macintosh computer enabled designers to create digital typesetting that could be read straight to a lithographic plate by a process known as Computer To Plate (CTP, *see* pp.104). The decline in letterpress printing was almost terminal as in the late 1980s thousands of compositors and printers lost their jobs. The rapid change in technology was particularly devastating for many long-standing family-owned letterpress printing firms who simply could not adapt. Their customer base fell away, labour costs were too high and their capital assets – the type and the presses – were deemed obsolete and plummeted in value. As a consequence, they did not have the money to reinvest in new equipment, were unable or disinclined to acquire digital typesetting skills, and could not afford to invest in lithographic presses.

So what is the future for this obsolete process? Letterpress, the iron horse of printing, has in a sense turned full circle. It has returned to its craft roots as a resurgence of interest in small-batch production among younger designers, combined with the experience of older printers and devotees of the historical letterpress, has ensured its survival as a craft in some enlightened art and design schools. There it forms a key element in the teaching of typography. It is also used in private presses that produce limited editions and in small workshops such as Phil Able's Hand & Eye Press. Able demonstrates printing on a small rotary press (opposite) and on a larger Heidelberg book press (overleaf); the type is composed by Gloucester Typesetting Services on a hot metal Monotype caster.

## Letterpress: block printing

As well as text, letterpress printing is used to print images, drawings, diagrams, illustrations and simple maps that often include letterforms. This type of printing is called blockwork. The artwork can either be hand-drawn in black ink or, as in this case, designed digitally before being output as a high-resolution black print. The block is made photographically by a specialist block maker, using an acid-etching process.

## Block printing

**1** Here a second solid colour (blue), is to be spot-printed into a lozenge already printed in black. The plate is attached to a special block, a metal matrix of holes with hardwood cores. Holes are drilled into the plate and tiny panel pins are hammered through the plate into the wooden cores.

**2** The proof is pulled and the colour matched against a Pantone swatch book. The registration is checked and minor amendments made to the position of the block on the bed, to avoid the white line and ensure that the trapping (the dark colour overlapping the light one) is clean.

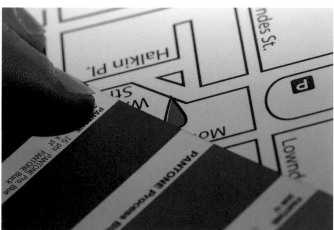

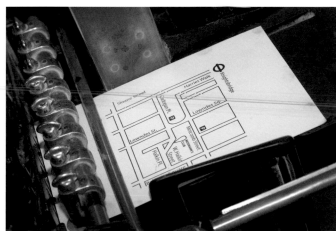

**3** The block is positioned on a small, single-colour platen press, and sheets with the previously printed black map are fed into the press by hand. The paper is lifted on to the block and the blue lozenge is printed inside the black outline.

**4** A detail of the final print shows the correct colour and clean trapping.

**Right:** A small single-colour invitation card includes a letterpress-printed block of a drawing.

English Eccentrics
invites you to
a private view
of work by
*Christopher Brown*

**1** A letterpress book is printed several pages at a time on to a large sheet of paper, which is then turned over and printed on the reverse. The sheet is folded into a signature before being stitched into a book and cut down to size using a guillotine. The process of arranging the galleys of type into book pages is called imposition. Here a large book chase is blocked out with furniture and quoins to secure the form.

**2** The type for the book – the script for *King Lear* – shown here has been set using hot metal on a Monotype compositor as opposed to cold metal or hand setting. The detail shows the large amount of spacing material used in setting plays: dialogue is set line for line.

**3** Once the form has been locked up, it is lifted from the stone and placed on the bed of the Heidelberg cylinder press. The form is gently lowered into place and positioned square with the cylinder.

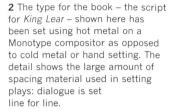

**7** The cylinder, like the proofing press is inked with a pallet knife.

**8** The large press has an automatic paper feed. A single sheet of paper is picked up from a stack by little vacuum suckers, and travels around the cylinder, over the type where the impression is made and back to rest above the original paper stack. The pages of the book generally have consistent margins, so the printer positions the printed type in the same place on every page. The baselines of the type on one side of the sheet should match those on the reverse.

**9** To ensure the baselines are consistent, the printer takes a sheet from the previous signature and makes a pull. He then holds the sheet to the light and marks any correction that must be made. The type form can be moved marginally forwards or backwards until the baselines match.

**Far left:** The Heidelberg book press is robust yet allows for very fine adjustments. In the hands of a master printer the quality of impression is crisp, even and clean.

**Left:** The locked up pages, referred to as a 'form', are secured in a book chase. This chase is made up of four rectangles, one for each page. The chase must have minimal flex as all of the type characters, lead spacing units and furniture are secured only by the pressure applied between the quoins and the chase.

**4** The quoins are loosened just a little and the type is tapped down with a small wooden block and a mallet. This ensures that all the type is level, as it can rise slightly in the form during the short lift from stone to press bed.

**5** Two screws are adjusted to make the form square on the bed.

**6** A large press shares some of the principles of the smaller proofing press but allows far finer adjustments to be made. Here the gap between the top roller and the steel cylinder is adjusted by turning little tappits to ensure both parts are parallel and that the space between the two is even.

**10** The printer now looks at the quality of the impression: evenness, consistency of inking and crispness of type. The whole type form on a cylinder press is not in contact with the paper through the entirety of the impression. The paper is progressively forced down on to the type as it is drawn around the cylinder and progressively released. Although the process is very quick there is what printers refer to as a dwell (a pause when type and paper are in contact). As the cylinder passes over the type, the release of pressure on the form may cause it to lift slightly, a characteristic referred to by printers as spring – an undesirable effect that can slur the type. Here the printer marks up uneven areas of type.

**11** Crispness of impression on a cylinder press relies on the paper being evenly forced down on to the type. The distance between cylinder and type must be consistent throughout the rotation. If the type is slightly proud, the impression will be bold; if the gap is too great, the impression will be weak. The steel cylinder is surrounded by packing (sheets of paper that cushion the impact and prevent the type being crushed). The sheets are held in place by a blanket or tympan (an oiled sheet of Manila card). The blanket can be removed and the packing behind it increased or reduced.

**12** By taking a printed sheet from a previous signature and placing it under an impression from the new form, the printer can mark with a scalpel where pressure needs to be increased or reduced – a process referred to as make ready. Holes that can be cut into the packing sheets for pages or individual lines to reduce pressure or sections can be pasted over one another to increase pressure. This adjustment process may take up to two hours before the final print run can be made. The press is run at 2,000 sheets per hour.

**Right:** When all the fine adjustments to the impression are complete, the press can be rolled and printing begins.

## Storing forms and distributing the type

**1** Once the sheet has been printed the form is removed from the press bed and returned to the stone and unlocked. The press is then cleaned.

**2** Any loose type that has lifted during the move from the press to the stone is tapped down and the form is unlocked.

**3** Individual pages are separated, tied up as a smaller form using a thin binding string and stored on a galley (a thin, three-sided metal tray on which the type is laid and tightened). Furniture blocks out the side of the galley and a sheet of card is taped over the form.

**4** The galley is slid carefully into a galley frame for storage. Only when a book is printed and bound are these forms broken up and dismantled.

**5** The process of returning hand-set type to the individual boxes within the case is called distribution. Machine-cast metal type such as Monotype, Linotype and Ludlow setting and casting is usually returned to the compositor in a galley to be smelted down. All the type must be returned to the correct box within the right case. This is checked by selecting a wide cap, such as 'H', from the galley and removing the same cap from what is thought to be the correct case and comparing them. If the case is the right one, the type is lifted from the galley, held in the left hand and returned to the correct box with the right hand. Damaged type is smelted down and cast into new type.

**Left:** Special characters and scripts used for setting non-Latin languages such as Hebrew are cast on metal body sizes which match with the Latin alphabet enabling languages to be combined.

**This page:**
The versatility of letterpress printing
is demonstrated by the range of
work that makes use of the process.

**1** A title page from *Hamlet* published by the
Folio Society, set by the Monotype metal caster
(*see* pp.60–63) and printed on the Heidelberg
press by Phil Able at Hand & Eye Press.

**2** A letterpress gift voucher printed two-colour
for St. Jude's Modern British features a
range of decorative metal fonts and a lozenge
combined with a wood-type £75.

**3** Michele Jannuzzi produced a series of
letterpress numerals for a calendar. The large
number 12 is made up of decorative border
elements and overprinted in several colours.

**4** A design by Martin Z. Schröder laid out on
the imposition stone.

**5** Schröder used similar decorative border
elements, associated with nineteenth-century
design, in the production of this
three-colour card.

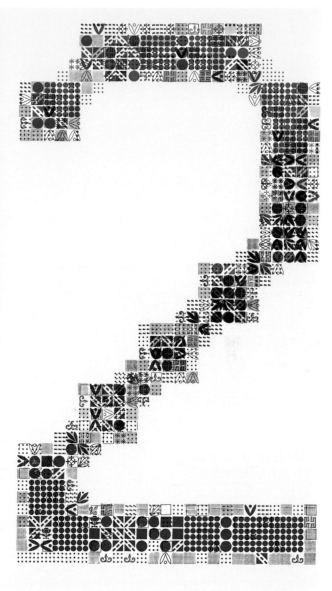

3

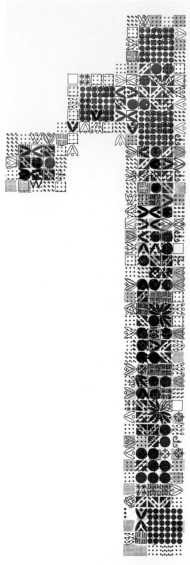

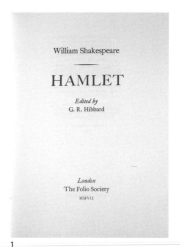

1

2

4

5

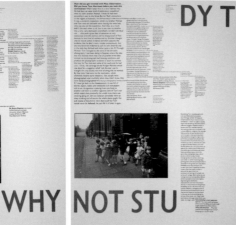

2

1 Front and back cover and a series of spreads
from *TypoGraphic no. 60*, designed by A2-
GRAPHICS/SW/HK. The large, wooden letters
printed by Stan Lane of Gloucester Typesetting
Services (*see* Hot metal casting pp.60–63)
spell out the title throughout the publication.

2 A series of pages from 'In Darkest England',
a boxed set of loose sheets primarily printed by
letterpress, designed by David Jury and
reproduced at Foxash Press. The type
visualizes memories of the same event.
Different opinions are linked in progressively
smaller type sizes and narrower columns
as they move further from the original text.

3 Frost Design produced this catalogue for the
publishing group Fourth Estate. It is printed
entirely by letterpress and makes extensive use
of woodblock and metal letterpress characters.

4 Martin Z Schröder's DANKE makes use of the
expressive qualities of letterpress printing.

5 A detail of the woodblock 'A' which shows the
ink spread across the surface responsible for
the patina of the print shown above.

3

4

ASHIRE, THE   HEAD HUN   RS OF STEP   EY?

TE   N

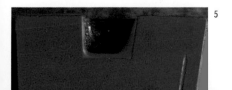

Thermography is a print process often used in combination with lithography and letterpress printing. Powder or crystals are sprinkled over wet ink, and, when placed under a heater, the lettering rises above the surface of the page. It is sometimes referred to as imitation engraving and has been widely used for printed stationery, letterheads, envelopes, business cards, invitations, Braille and, occasionally, in publishing. Some letterpress printers in the early twentieth century experimented with crystals ground from hardened tree sap, which expanded when in contact with the wet letterpress ink. Today's process, developed in the 1970s, uses thermographic powder ground from a plastic resin. The thermographic crystals produce a range of different finishes – gloss, semi-gloss and matt – and metallic powders produce a metallic sheen which is less expensive than foil blocking (*see* pp.66–67). Glitter can be added to make a kitsch, sparkling effect. Pearlescent resins separate the ink pigment to produce a soft, pastel, rainbow finish and high-viscosity powders thicken the ink, preventing infill and preserving fine lines, serifs and counters in small type. Laser-safe powders have been developed to allow thermographic type and logos on letterheads to pass through photocopiers and laser printers without the raised surface being destroyed by re-exposure of the sheet to a heat source. This form of thermography uses ultraviolet-sensitive inks which are sealed, like tin plate printing (*see* pp.117–119), with ultraviolet exposure units. All the finish variables are available with different particle sizes: extra fine particles are used for type under 14pt, fine for type between 14pt and 30pt, medium for sizes up to 48pt and coarse for all sizes above 48pt. Thermography is sometimes used to create the relief dots in Braille as an alternative to embossing. This is particularly useful when print for sighted readers has to be combined with Braille, as the thermographic dots can be printed in a clear yet raised varnish.

**This page:**
Examples of thermographic printing, the lettering is lifted above the surface of the printed card.

1 The rounded forms of the thermographic printing are visible when the printed surface is viewed from an oblique angle.

2 Large script type must be evenly sprinkled with powder so that all the thin connectives are lifted above the sheet.

3 The patina made by the reaction between the ink and the thermographic crystals is clearly illustrated when coloured letters with a large surface area are viewed from an angle.

4 and 7 A gold, metallic ink is thermographically raised above the sheet (4), but is slightly less crisp than the foil blocking debossed through a gold metallic foil (7).

5 A detail of 6pt type shows how the counter forms hold up if the finest crystals are used.

6 A detailed enlargement of 8pt type.

1

2

3

4

5

6

7

## Raising the type above the surface of the page

**1** Thermography occurs immediately after the sheet of paper has been printed, while the ink is still wet. It can be done by hand process, sprinkling the crystals over the ink, removing the excess and drying the lettering under a heater. However, at Postglow and Frankel Printers, London the process is far more sophisticated. The printing and thermography are combined into a single production process referred to as in-line thermography.

**2** Sheets from a stack of paper are fed one at a time into the press, which has a small bed that prints sheets up to A3 – and is typically used to print stationery.

**3** Sheets move through the press and the impression is made. They exit the press print-side up and are moved along a sealed conveyor belt into a chamber (not shown), where the thermographic crystals or powder are dispersed by a mechanical shaker. The crystals cover the whole sheet, both printed and non-printed areas, but stick only to the ink. The sheet continues down the conveyor belt and passes under a vacuum which sucks up all the loose crystals.

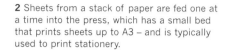

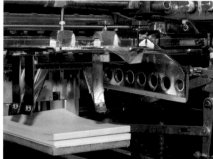

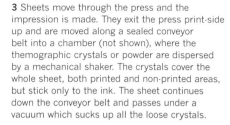

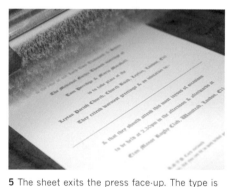

**5** The sheet exits the press face-up. The type is hard and can be stacked and knocked up (the sheets are made square and parallel) without interleaving (the insertion of blank sheets to prevent the accidental transfer of ink from the face of one sheet to the reverse of another).

**4** The sheet now passes through an electrically heated oven. Here the heating unit has been lifted above the sheet-conveyor belt to show the glowing elements. While the machine is operating this unit, like the crystals' chamber, is closed. The oven reaches temperatures of between 480°–670°C (896°–1238°F) depending on the type of powder or crystals. The resins in the crystals melt and combine with the pigments in the ink to form a congealed solid, which is slightly domed in profile. This part of the process is referred to as curing.

# 3.4 Lithography

**Right:** Two massive litho presses arranged in parallel on the print room floor. Each press features ten ink pyramids, which, when run in line, can print up to ten colours at a single pass.

**Opposite:** A poster designed by Studio Dumbar. This example shows some of the refinements made possible with lithographic overprinting.

Offset lithographic printing is the most common form of printing used to produce books today. The term lithography is derived from the Greek *lithos*, meaning stone, and *graphein*, to write: writing on stone. The process was invented by the Bavarian dramatist Aloys Senefelder (1771–1834) in 1798. Lithography transfers ink directly from the surface of the stone or plate to the surface of the paper. It is based on the simple principle that grease and water do not mix. Thin aluminium or zinc plates with a finely-grained surface are prepared: a fine film of water is applied to the entire plate, then a greasy substance is applied to the image areas of the plate and the water is retained on the non-print surface. Ink adheres to the greasy image areas, but is rejected by the wet, non-print areas. The inked image is transferred to the surface of the paper while the clean, damp areas of the plate leave no mark.

Photography was invented in the late 1830s; by 1851 experiments had culminated in a light-sensitive lithographic stone from which a photographic image could be reproduced. As photography developed, it became possible to separate a full-colour image into three process colours (cyan, magenta and yellow) and a fourth tone (black). Using these four process colours (known as CMYK), full-colour reproductions of half-tone images were possible. Lithography, which made use of colour separation, registration and multiple-roller cylinder presses, had become a sophisticated commercial print process.

By the beginning of the twentieth century, offset lithography, in which the ink is transferred, or offset, from the printing plate to a rubber-covered cylinder before being printed on paper, could lay down more colours more quickly than letterpress machines and was ideally suited to the reproduction of images. Its drawback lay in its reproduction of type. Lithography was principally a way of reproducing drawn and photographic images. Calligraphic lettering and engraving were reproduced lithographically throughout the nineteenth century, but books, being text-led, were not commonly reproduced using offset lithography until the 1960s, when the uptake of photo-typesetting enabled type to be transferred to a lithographic plate through a photographic negative.

Offset lithographic presses are either sheet-feed (one sheet at a time) or web-feed (a continuous roll of paper). Large sheet-feed presses can run at 12,000 sheets per hour but their capacity is dwarfed by web-feed presses, which are capable of 50,000 sheets per hour. To ensure high quality, books tend to be run at slower press speeds than newspapers, cheap brochures, or packaging, where high volumes of more than 100,000 per run are required.

Lithographic presses are typically either single-colour, two-colour, four-colour or six-colour, although specialist presses have been built to deliver more selected colours at a single run. Single- and two-colour presses may be used for four-colour printing, with the sheet passing through the press in registration several times.

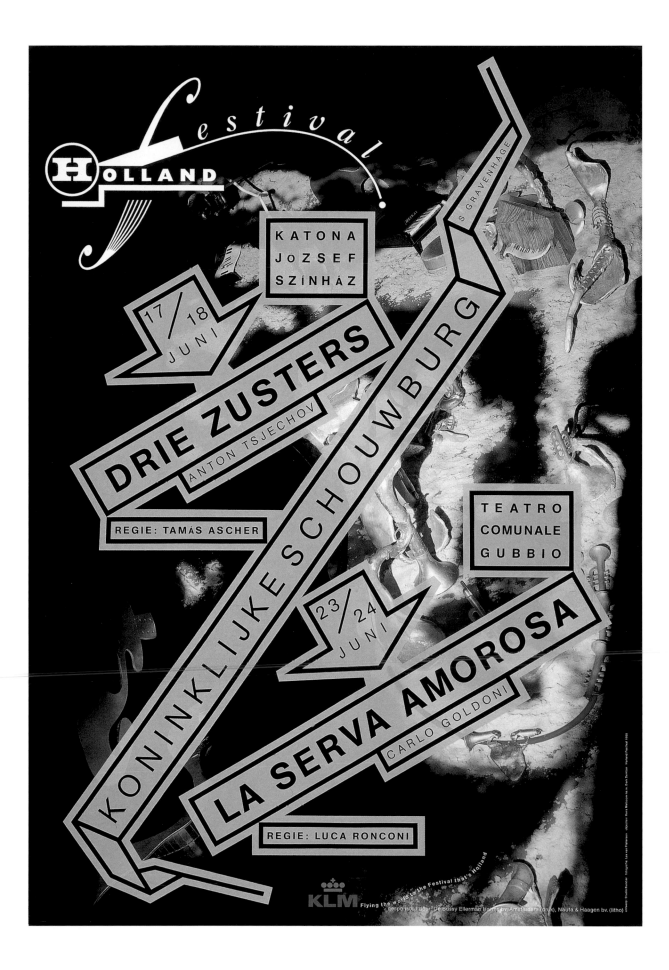

103

Lithography

**1** Today virtually all artwork for lithographic reproduction is prepared digitally on screen. Software such as Quark Xpress and InDesign enable the designer to specify all the colours within a digital artwork. Some smaller presses have retained photographic processes for making the colour separation films for each of the plates.

**2** Lithographic plates, thin sheets of aluminium, plastic – or for the cheapest short-run jobs paper – coated with a light-sensitive substance. The substance varies depending on the plate manufacturer, examples are a diazo compound or a photopolmyer. Plates must be thin and flexible as they have to be wrapped around the cylinder of the press. The texture of a lithographic plate is slightly granular, which traps moisture on its surface. Here the plate (blue sheet) is placed in a tray before being slid into Computer To Plate (CTP).

**3** The Computer To Plate (CTP) machine uses a laser to guide and write or expose the type, and half-tone imagery in the form of a dot screen, on to the plate guided by the digital postscript file. Each separation – cyan, magenta yellow and black (CMYK) – must be exposed on a separate plate. Special, additional selected colours or varnishes also require individual plates. Here the plate has been laser-written and is being removed from the CTP machine.

**4** The exposed plate is manually moved into a Kodak processing or developing unit. Some CTP machines laser-write and develop as an uninterrupted, automated process.

**5** The plate exits the processing unit. Where the laser has exposed the plate, the image and lettering are retained while the unexposed areas are washed away. The type and imagery on the plate is wrong-reading.

**6** Once all the plates have been written and processed, a short run of the job is printed on a proofing press and a proof is pulled. The proofing process provides a traditional wet proof, using ink. This enables the designer and client to view the colour on the paper stock that will be used for the final job. Plates on the proofing press are laid flat on the bed. Here they are being secured.

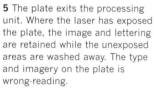

**7** Printing wet proofs requires press time and a printer to set up the press and oversee a short run. It is therefore slower and more expensive than producing dry proofs. Here the ink rollers and paper carriage have moved over the plate of the proofing press before the sheet is removed.

**8** The plate (left) and the CMYK paper proof (right) rest on the bed of the proofing press. Cheaper dry proof techniques have been developed. Some use photographic processes and other dyes. Not all require a press, yet enable the designer to check layout and registration, and give a good, though not exact, indication of colour.

1 This large incline press has eight ink pyramids – towers of rollers that move the ink down on to the lithographic plate before it is transferred on to the cylinder roller and finally on to the paper. Here three plates lean against their appropriate ink pyramids before the pressman attaches them to their plate cylinders.

2 The flexible aluminium plate is wrapped around the plate cylinder (top) and secured. The rubber blanket cylinder (below) is used to offset the image and text wrong-reading from the plate and print it on to the paper right-reading. An impression cylinder (not visible) beneath the blanket cylinder provides sufficient pressure to transfer the image evenly on to the paper.

3 Before ink is applied the lithographic plate must be moistened so that the non-image areas reject the ink. A very fine film of water is rolled over the surface of the rotating plate cylinder. It is delivered to the plate via a series of rubber rollers linked to the dampening fountain (a reservoir of water and alcohol). Here the damper fountain is checked.

4 Yellow ink from the can has been scooped into the ink reservoir with a palette knife. All lithographic presses are made up of many rollers which move the ink from the reservoir at the top of the press down the ink pyramid to the plate cylinder. The order in which the four colours are applied can be varied depending on what the designer wants the overprinting to look like. The lightest colour yellow is usually printed first followed by magenta, cyan, black and, where required, an ultraviolet (UV) seal or varnish.

5 Presses are either sheet-feed like this one, or web-feed like newspaper presses. In the latter the paper is printed as a continuous strip. Individual sheets are picked up by tiny pneumatic vacuum suckers that lift them from the hopper into the press. The paper is then moved through the press to the first ink pyramid (yellow) by a series of rollers and air beds which form a continuous conveyor belt.

6 The pressman can monitor all the ink pyramids, and the pressure between the individual blanket cylinders and plate cylinders remotely from a screen that also regulates the speed of the press.

7 Ink flows down from the reservoir through a series of rollers to the plate cylinder and adheres to the exposed surface of the image but not to the ground. Text and image are transferred to the blanket cylinder as a very thin layer. The sheet of paper passes between the blanket cylinder and the impression cylinder. Ink is transferred from the blanket cylinder to the paper. The sheet is then moved to the next ink pyramid. The sheet passes through all four colour pyramids and the UV seal.

8 Every so often sheets are removed from the run and taken to the inspection table where they are checked for registration, the alignment of the colours, dot gain (the quality of the half-tone and ink density). The ink density is measured using a densitometer, a hand-held electrical instrument. Fine adjustments to the press can be made instantaneously on the touch screen. Finally sheets are passed through an electrical drier.

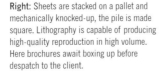

Right: Sheets are stacked on a pallet and mechanically knocked-up, the pile is made square. Lithography is capable of producing high-quality reproduction in high volume. Here brochures await boxing up before despatch to the client.

# 3.5 Screen printing

**Above:** A vandalproof external sign designed for the post office is screen-printed on the reverse of the flexible plastic before being hot-moulded into a blister.

Screen printing evolved from stencil-printing (an ancient process in which ink is forced through a mask to create an image). The Romans, Chinese and Japanese made use of stencils to make patterns on tiles, ceilings and cloth more than 1,500 years ago. The Japanese used a matrix of human hair, but this was gradually replaced by a mesh of silk threads. The stencil was laid over the mesh and coloured ink was dabbed through it to create a pattern. Stencil printing continued in this form until the early nineteenth century, when it was realized that the stencil could be attached to a fabric screen, thereby making it more durable. Silk-screen stencilling then replaced silk-stencil matrixes.

A first patent for silk-screening in 1907 specified that the process involved a mesh screen and a squeegee (a length of wood housing a rubber blade) for pulling the ink and driving it through the mesh. In screen printing some areas of the mesh are masked to prevent the ink passing through them. The image on the screen is right-reading, like the printed image. Screen printing allows flat, opaque or transparent coloured inks to be laid over one another. The amount of ink laid on the paper is far greater than with other print processes and the saturation and vibrancy of the colour give screen-printed images greater appeal. Colour separations can be made and half-tone photographic screens can be reproduced.

## Vinyl-cutting artwork for screen printing

**1** Vinyl-cut letters are used for internal and external signage (*see* pp.124–25) and to make large-scale artworks for screen-printing. The vinyl is generally cut by a cutting plotter (a knife attached to a plotting machine). The lettering design is converted in a vector-based program, usually Coral Draw for a personal computer and Illustrator or Freehand for a Mac.

**2** The plotter consists of a cylinder that holds a roll of vinyls, here Rubylith the red opaque film used for screen-print artwork – and a cutting blade mounted on an arm. The depth of cut can be adjusted so that the vinyl is cut but not its backing paper. The cutter moves quickly and precisely over the vinyl surface.

**3** When the lettering has been cut, the film must be weeded out. Either the lettering or the background must be stripped away so that the lettering can be used to prepare a screen for screen printing.

**Below:** The author tests the flexibility of the vandalproof, screen-printed sign. It makes use of polymer inks, which expand and contract, but do not crack or become detached when the plastic sheet of the blister is squashed.

**Left:** The background for a large panel is stripped away to reveal the positive letters that will form the same size artwork for the screen printing.

## Preparing the screen

**1** The screen consists of a stout, square, warp-free wooden frame with synthetic threads that are stretched absolutely flat. The space between the threads is referred to as mesh grade; the number of threads per 2.5cm (1in) in the weave is referred to as 'mesh count'. If the mesh grade is fine and the mesh count high, the detail will be retained and subtle half-tones can be reproduced. The four common mesh grades are 'S' (the smallest), 'M', 'T' and 'HD' (the thickest).

**2** The screen must be very clean and free of grease before it is exposed to the photographic image. This is achieved by washing it in a degreasing agent and checking that the mesh of the screen is completely free of ink particles.

**3** In a photographic darkroom, both sides of the screen are coated with a light-sensitive colloidal solution (not shown), a water-suspended emulsion made of polyvinyl alcohol (PVA) or polyvinyl acetate (PVAC). This is often combined with a blue or purple dye that makes the chemical change that takes place during exposure. The screen is then air-dried in a warm room.

**5** The exposed screen is lifted to the wash-out unit where it is wetted on both sides and then sprayed, from the printing side, with lukewarm water. The areas of the screen exposed to the ultraviolet light harden, while those masked by the film are washed away. The screen is then dried prior to printing.

**4** The screen is moved, under a safe light, to the photographic exposure unit. Black or coloured type is produced from a positive artwork, a process referred to as printing on (lettering is black or Rubylith red); reversed out lettering is produced from a negative artwork (the ground is dark and the lettering white). The screen is contact-exposed so the lettering artwork or film is 'ss' (same size as the final print).

The film is laid emulsion-side up on the glass, the screen is lowered print-side down on to the film, and a vacuum pump is turned on to suck the screen and film together so that they are flat on the glass bed. Ultraviolet light is turned on and the exposure made.

**1** The screen-printing press consists of a metal frame, about waist high, across which a melamine-faced wooden bed is secured. Its smooth surface is drilled with a matrix of tiny holes through which air is drawn by a vacuum pump. This fixes the paper on which the image is to be printed in position. The screen is locked above the bed in a hinged frame.

**2** The screen is lowered over the bed. The 'sheet fall' (position of the paper on the bed in relation to the screen) is marked and the frame is lifted again. Printers temporarily stick either masking tape or small, cardboard L-shaped guides to the bed, which locate the corners of the paper and ensure all sheets are positioned in the same place.

**3** The appropriate ink has to be matched to the correct surface and required visual finish. Screen printing is used to print opaque colours (by adding an extender base), fluorescents, metallics, pastels and varnishes (by adding tinters), solid or half-tones in gloss, silk or matt finishes, and even scratch-and-sniff inks. Water-based inks can be used to print on paper and card, while oil- and acrylic-based inks are generally used for non-absorbent surfaces such as metal and glass.

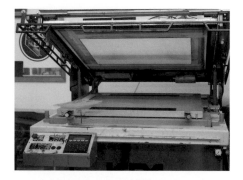

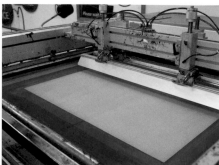

**4** Ink is poured on to the reverse of the screen at the front edge, forming a viscous pool. A squeegee at least 3.75cm (1½in) wider at either end than the lettering is used to charge or 'flood' the stencil. The frame is lifted slightly above the paper and the squeegee is used to push some of the ink away from the pool or reservoir over the stencil and towards the hinge. A thin layer of ink is absorbed into the mesh of the stencil, which is now charged.

**5** The printer places the squeegee behind the reservoir of ink at an angle of 45 degrees, before slowly and smoothly pulling it towards himself or herself at a consistent speed, retaining a firm and even pressure. The pull is continued beyond the edge of the stencil so that the ink is well clear of the stencil. Pressure applied by the squeegee to the reverse of the screen forces the ink in the stencil out through the mesh and onto the surface of the paper. A crisp print relies on a clean screen, a clearly defined stencil, well-mixed ink of the appropriate viscosity and a consistent pull.

**6** Once the pull is completed, the screen is raised a little and the squeegee is used to pull the ink away from the stencil. It is then rested against the edge of the frame where it holds back the ink reservoir. The screen is raised a little further, which automatically cuts out the vacuum and allows the printer to lift the sheet from the bed to the drying rack.

**Left:** A batch of posters is stacked in the drying rack overnight.

**Opposite:** A series of screen-printed posters promoting recycling, designed and printed by Becky Redman.

1 Black type printed over a solid yellow ground.

2 Right- and wrong-reading letters printed in two colours in register and deliberately aligned to imply recycling.

3 Repeated recycling symbols printed brown over blue and white reversed out of brown.

4 A full-bleed pink ground overprinted in black.

**Plastic can take up to 500 years to decompose.**

**RE**⊃**Y**⊂ **IN**⅁

is very important. waste has a huge
negative impact on the natural environment.

1

2

**once is not enough**

**every year the average dustbin contains enough unrealised energy**

for 500 baths, 3500 showers or
5000 hours of television

3

4

# 3.6 Vitreous enamel signs

**Above:** A German enamel metro station sign.

**Above right:** Full-size model of a London Underground platform at A. J. Wells. The illumination levels can be varied to test how signs will show up in an emergency.

Enamel is best defined by the French word from which it is derived: *esmaile* – literally glass on metal. Vitreous enamel is formed by melting glass and bonding it to a metal surface to give an exceptionally hard surface which is resistant to everyday wear and tear and requires a deliberate act of vandalism to be scratched or chipped. It has the additional properties of excellent colour saturation, luminosity, resistance to ultraviolet light, and colour retention; it is waterproof, frostproof and easily wiped clean. Throughout the late-nineteenth century these hard-wearing properties were exploited to make metal baths, tin plates, industrial lampshades and cooker hobs. The qualities of vitreous enamel also make it ideal for internal and external signage in dirty, urban environments.

Enamel signs were used in advertising from the 1910s until the late 1950s, when large-format printed billboards proved cheaper. During the 1970s and 1980s many rail networks and metro systems worldwide began to adopt cheaper vinyl signage, which adhered directly on to walls, or powder-coated platform signs. However, vinyl signs proved less durable than the older enamel versions, were subject to vandalism and, exposed to harsh exterior conditions, they faded and peeled, while the powder-coating became dull and chipped. Many European rail and metro networks have begun to review their platforms signs and enamel signs are beginning to reappear.

A. J. Wells based on the Isle of Wight, England is a long-standing enamelling firm that produces enamel-coated wood-burning stoves and baths. It has developed a signage division which is now responsible for nearly 90 per cent of Transport for London's signage. The factory manufactures signs from both sheet metal and enamel, on one site without subcontracting or outsourcing. London Underground is the oldest metro system in the world and was not designed on standard units but was developed line by line by individual companies. Many of the panels, fascia boards, platform signs and even the Underground roundels vary between stations and must therefore be custom-made.

1

2

3

**This page:**
A range of enamel car badges with cast metal lettering.

**1** The slab serif, bold expanded lettering of this cast, zinc Honda logo has been infilled with black.

**2** The much older Bugatti badge is a three-colour surface enamelled on a brass plate.

**3** The Benelli metal casting is outlined in black, infilled in old white and the keyline is polished back to the metal.

**4** The polished wings of this Hillman badge show how the very fine details of the casting can be infilled with a colour that is sitting flush to surface.

**5** The lettering of this Austin-Healey mark is infilled with a transparent enamel.

4

5

6

7

8

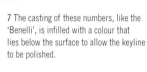

9

10

11

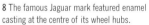

12

**6** A complex italic casting with a simple infill.

**7** The casting of these numbers, like the 'Benelli', is infilled with a colour that lies below the surface to allow the keyline to be polished.

**8** The famous Jaguar mark featured enamel casting at the centre of its wheel hubs.

**9** The five-colour infill of the Ferrari badge featuring the prancing horse.

**10** The two-colour green and yellow lotus badge; note how the yellow has been matched to the Daytona yellow of the car's paint.

**11** The simple Bentley 'B' is surrounded by a relief decorative casting of a pair of wings created through an engraving process.

**12** The metal Cobra lettering is picked out by a red enamel infill.

# Enamelling

**1** Before enamelling can begin, the metal must be thoroughly degreased. Because of the number of signs in production this process has been automated. The signs and sheets to be enamelled are loaded into racks in the degreaser which resembles a 5-m (16-ft 5-in) high dishwasher. The metal is cleaned with detergents and from this point on must be moved with gloves – even finger grease will affect the enamel bonding to the metal surface.

**2** The enamel must be made into a paint. This is done by grinding the tiny glass balls into a powder and adding water to form a thick paint. Colour is added to the mix in the form of frits (very thin, biscuit-like fragments of glass in different colours). The mixing process takes between four and six hours, and the enamel paint is stored in plastic bins.

**3** The signs must be base-coated with enamel paint. This is applied in a spray booth with an airbrush. By suspending the signs on painters' S-hooks, both sides can be sprayed prior to drying. The sign is carried to the electrically heated drying cabinet where all the water evaporates from the painted surface in an ambient temperature of 90°C (194°F). The enamel paint is now in a fragile biscuit-like form which can chip easily. The sign is carefully moved to the furnace.

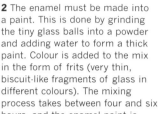

**8** The exposed screens are washed and dried before being job numbered and stored in huge racks.

**9** The lettering and lines for the London Underground track diagram shown on this screen must be printed in several colours but the artwork has been produced on a single screen as each coloured element can be masked. Only in cases where the enamel is over-printed must separate screens be made (*see* pp.106–09).

**10** The sign is positioned on the screen bed, the screen lowered over it and coloured enamel paint is poured onto the reverse.

**4** The sign is fired in the furnace for approximately eight minutes at a temperature of 800°C (1,472°F). It is here that the tiny glass particles melt across the surface, and fuse with one another and into the metal to form a cohesive sheet. The glass is no longer on top of the metal but becomes part of its surface.

**5** The base enamel is allowed to air-cool on pin racks.

**6** The screens are made either photographically on film or by a computer-controlled cutting plotter. Artwork for each job is stored until the job is complete. Here lettering cut on a plotter (*see* p.106) is weeded out by hand.

**7** The huge exposure table is designed to accommodate the largest sheet size (2 x 3m/ (9ft 10in x 6ft 8in) used on the screen-printing bed and on the London Underground panels. This ensures the lettering can, where necessary, run edge-to-edge across the panel.

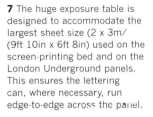
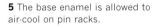

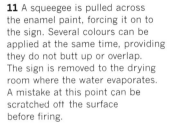

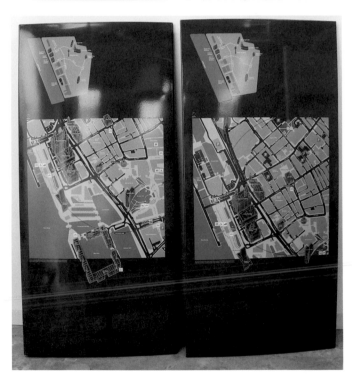

**11** A squeegee is pulled across the enamel paint, forcing it on to the sign. Several colours can be applied at the same time, providing they do not butt up or overlap. The sign is removed to the drying room where the water evaporates. A mistake at this point can be scratched off the surface before firing.

**12** The process of screen-printing, drying and firing goes on until all colours have been fired. Here a large track diagram is removed from the furnace. Repeat firing may affect colours already laid down. As there are 12 colours on the London Underground diagram, different batches of enamel are mixed which match two-colour firing with six-colour firing. The printers carefully record the order of firing on each sign.

**Above:** Front and back panels of a free-standing sign from an environmental signage system developed to guide pedestrians around the city of Liverpool.

**Right:** A detail from the map shows how the enamel process has been pushed to its limit to produce a very well-designed piece of public information. The signage system is superbly crafted, with some of the maps featuring up to 12 colours.

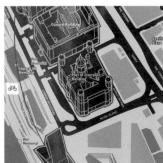

# 3.7 Rubber stamps

Rubber stamps have been used since the mid 1860s and have a wide range of applications. The term rubber stamp is often limited to small hand-held stamps associated with passports, postal franking, commercial certification and administrative approval. However, this apparently simple technology is used for a wide range of relief printing purposes which are not possible with lithography (*see* pp.102–05) and gravure printing (see p.120). The technique supports printing on to many different materials, such as plastic, polythene bags, wood (for example, fruit crates) and food products (such as eggs).

Today companies like Polydiam have developed and refined many different methods of rubber stamp manufacture, suited to the production of small-scale document stamps or large-format printing purposes. Making stamps from vulcanized rubber is the oldest process and continues to be popular, particularly when a large batch of the same stamp has to be reproduced. Naresh Kapadia of Polydiam has produced over 30,000 official stamps at a time, for electoral ratification at polling stations. The company builds many different sizes of machine but they all work on the same principles. Vulcanized stamps are hot-press moulded into a form.

## Vulcanized rubber stamps

**1** A wrong-reading relief plate is made from an artwork; the lettering stands proud of the surface. The plate can be made of etched magnesium or zinc (*see* 168–69), laser-etched metal (*see* p.155), it can be engraved (*see* p.157) or, as here, it can be made from a plastic polymer. The plate is then placed face-up in a small tray.

**2** The tray is lifted into the top of the cabinet and covered by a flat sheet of matrix board. The electric heater at the top of the unit is turned on and softens the matrix board.

**3** The handle is pulled down and an impression is made through a combination of heat and pressure.

**4** The matrix board has a right-reading impression debossed below the board surface. The plate (bottom) and the matrix board (top) are separated.

**5** The matrix board cools quickly and is placed face-up on the tray with a sheet of rubber over the surface.

**6** The tray is returned to the unit where heat and pressure are again applied. Heat makes the rubber sheet pliable, while the downward pressure forces the rubber into the letter cavities in the matrix board.

**7** Left to right: polymer plate, matrix board and a vulcanized rubber sheet ready to be cut down and glued to a stamp block and handle.

# Photo polymer stamps

**1** Photo polymer stamps are made from a light-sensitive plastic polymer. The stainless-steel production cabinet is self-contained, each of the four production phases being isolated in a drawer. A photographic negative of the artwork is placed on the glass sheet that forms the bottom of a drawer in the exposure unit. The polymer, which can be used for making stamps, or moulds, or plates for traditional rubber stamps, is in liquid form and sealed in a plastic bag. The polymer bag is laid flat on the negative.

**2** A glass lid is closed over the bag and a vacuum pump is turned on. This sucks air out from between the two glass sheets and flattens the liquid polymer (trapped in its bag) into a flat sheet of even thickness.

**3** The drawer on the exposure unit is now closed and the liquid polymer sheet is exposed to two ultraviolet light sources to harden it. The top light falling directly on the polymer hardens it to form what will become the backing sheet, while the bottom light passes through the type and image areas of the photographic negative. The water-soluble polymer only hardens in areas where it is exposed to ultraviolet light.

**4** The exposure unit is opened and the now stiff polymer sheet is removed. The plastic bag is cut away. The sheet is placed in the washing tray at the top of the unit and cleaned with water. The soft, unexposed polymer is washed away leaving the hard, wrong-reading type standing in relief above the surface.

**5** The final curing process, 'post exposure', must take place in an environment where oxygen is not present as a gas. The sheet is placed face-up in the bottom drawer of the cabinet and covered in water. It must be completely immersed before being exposed again to ultraviolet light for a further ten minutes. The curing process makes the sheet very durable.

**6** The clear polymer sheet is detacked using a powder, then laid out on a crack-back adhesive.

**7** The stamp design is glued to the stamp block.

**Right:** The finished stamp and printed image.

# 3.8 Hot foil blocking

Hot foil blocking is used in stationery, card packaging, cigarette boxes, on moulded PVC packaging and for labelling on leather products – stamping the maker's name on the sole or inside lining of a shoe. It can even be used on wood, for example, on presentation boxes for wine. As the foil is metallic, a true reflective or mirror finish, which cannot be matched by ink, can be achieved. Hot foil printing is ideally suited to type where the letterforms may be small but are printed at 100 per cent; it is not well suited to half-tone reproduction. Automated hot foiling machines, capable of printing an entire book cover with a relatively large block, are used to produce raised metallic type on best-selling paperback books and can run up to 8,000 prints per hour. Smaller hand-operated machines used for stationery can run at up to 200 prints per hour. The foils come in a wide range of metallic finishes, colours, patterns and holograms (*see* p.64) but are not produced in Pantone colours. Postglow and Frankel Printers specialize in hot foil blocking for stationery.

## Applying hot foil

**1** A platen press with a heated plate is used for hot foil printing.

**2** The metallic foil is made from several layers: a carrier film, a release layer, a varnish, a pigment layer and, finally, an adhesive layer. All the layers except the carrier film (the white sheet) and the release layer, are transferred to a sheet of paper. The foil can be produced as a roll or, as in this case, sheet form and in a range of metallic finishes.

**3** The block or die was traditionally hand-engraved (*see* pp.158–59) in copper or brass but today is made of magnesium or zinc – often referred to as a Zinco. It is produced by a die-maker from a black and white artwork. For debossed lettering, the die will be wrong-reading and printed from the front. For embossed lettering it will be printed from the reverse of the sheet and the die will be right-reading. The best embossed lettering is produced with male and female dies.

**4** For debossed work the die is secured against the heated plate, the paper is slipped into the grippers and the foil is placed adhesive side to the sheet in front of the paper. The plate is electrically heated to 97°C (206°F) and then the press is closed. The platen presses down on the sheet for a slightly longer dwell time (the duration of the impression) than most presses and bonds the foil into the debossed lettering.

**5** This finished stationery sheet combines surface-printed green lettering with foil-blocked script.

# 3.9 Tin plate printing

There are two principal forms of tin or aluminium can: one is the folded can made from preprinted sheets fabricated into a three-dimensional form with either crimped or welded seams, and the other is the aluminium, drawn and wall-ironed (referred to as DWI) can. The DWI process was invented in the United States in 1966, and the cans are printed after manufacture in their cylindrical form. The sizing, printing, lacquering and hot-oven drying process is identical to the one for sheet manufacture. Peter Luff Tin Printing and Box Decoration is a family firm that uses the same processes for printing on both tin and aluminium sheets.

1

2

3

4

5

6

7

**This page:**

1 Tin plate printing traditionally makes use of special rather than CMYK process colours. Here a 76 x 102-cm (30 x 40-in) sheet, from which glue tins will be made, is printed three up in four colours: white, yellow, green and red.

2–4 Decorated tin plate tea tins.

5 A decorative biscuit tin, printed as a flat sheet bent around a form and either pinch

folded or automatically soldered, makes use of CMYK, and special plate blue (not a tint), mid-blue, black and is overprinted in gold and then debossed.

6 The lettering design for a whisky cap lies flat on the plate; note that the baseline of the signature is curved.

7 Once the whisky cap is pressed into shape, the signature appears to run around the cap.

## Printing on tin

**1** Both tin and aluminium plate are produced in many different gauges, but boxes and cans are manufactured from 0.22mm to 0.8mm (approx. ½in to approx. ½in) sheets. Far thicker sheets can be printed but are difficult to fabricate. Here precut tin and aluminium sheets await the sizing process.

**2** The areas of the sheet to be printed must be presized, but those which form the joints in fabrication must remain raw metal to enable 'clean', folded lock joints or welded seams. Rubber rollers with a groove aligned with the box joint are made for each size of tin.

**3** To allow the ink to adhere to the surface the metal sheet must be sized with either acrylic or a polymer. The size must be printed evenly across the surface.

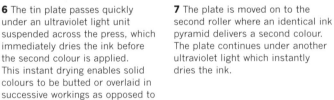

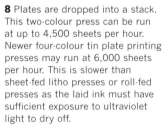

**6** The tin plate passes quickly under an ultraviolet light unit suspended across the press, which immediately dries the ink before the second colour is applied. This instant drying enables solid colours to be butted or overlaid in successive workings as opposed to organizing a printing order based on areas that do not touch.

**7** The plate is moved on to the second roller where an identical ink pyramid delivers a second colour. The plate continues under another ultraviolet light which instantly dries the ink.

**8** Plates are dropped into a stack. This two-colour press can be run at up to 4,500 sheets per hour. Newer four-colour tin plate printing presses may run at 6,000 sheets per hour. This is slower than sheet-fed litho presses or roll-fed presses as the laid ink must have sufficient exposure to ultraviolet light to dry off.

**9** The press is periodically stopped and the registration and ink lay, and the crispness of the dot screen for half-tones, are checked periodically under a daylight bulb.

**Left:** Tin plate printing is an environmentally friendly process as both the tins and the offcuts shown here can be recycled.

**4** Once the sheets have been sized, they are stacked face-up and drawn off the stack onto the press by pneumatic suction pads.

**5** The lettering artwork for tin plate printing is prepared in exactly the same way as for lithography or gravure. Tin plate printing can be in either CMYK or selected special colours. Each colour is printed by a rubber roller located at the bottom of the press and supplied with ink from a reservoir suspended on a gantry above the press bed. Ink is moved to the blanket cylinder via a chain of rubber rollers referred to as an ink pyramid. The rollers revolve against one another ensuring an even distribution of ink. Inks for tin plate printing must be solvent-based in order to adhere to the size.

**10** The plate passes through the press and the ink is printed on to the sized tin sheet.

**11** When all the colours have passed through the press and been laid they must be sealed with a varnish or lacquer. Like the size, this can have an acrylic or polymer base. The sheets are picked up off the stack.

**12** The varnish must only be laid over the printed surface of the tin, leaving the seam allowance raw for the seam weld. An identical rubber roller to the one used in the sizing process (with matching grooves) is used to lay the varnish.

**13** The sheets are lifted on a racking conveyor belt into a gas oven and heated at a temperature of 170°C (338°F). Each sheet passes through the oven for 15 minutes.

**Left:** Printed sheets are guillotined down to size so that the tins can be folded and pinched into shape.

**Right:** A heavy-gauge metal drum with very crisply printed white lettering over a red ground.

# 3.10 Gravure printing

**This page**
Gravure printing is predominantly used in the security printing industry to reproduce stamps and, in some countries, banknotes.

**Right:** The incline, roll-fed press resembles a large, modern lithographic unit. The reel of paper (bottom left) is pulled through a succession of ink pyramids. Here six pyramids with different coloured inks are aligned. The seventh pyramid carries an ultraviolet varnish seal. The slightly taller cabinet at the far end of the press is a UV drying unit. Stamps can be printed on crack-back or glue strip (traditional lick-the-back) in a single pass.

**Below:** The revolving gravure plate (bottom) clearly shows the identical laser-engraved rows of stamps. With each revolution of the roller the engraved surface is reinked. The paper is pressed on to the cylindrical engraving plate from behind by the impression cylinder and the ink is drawn out of the half-tone indentations in the plate and onto the surface of the paper. It is then UV-sealed and dried in a single operation. The stamps are perforated after drying.

Intaglio print processes including etching, engraving and gravure hold the ink in grooves below the surface of the plate. The gravure process is also known as rotogravure, which refers to the cylinders around which the plate is wrapped in a fashion similar to the system used in the offset lithographic press. Gravure has twin qualities of continuous tone and consistency of ink lay throughout a run, which make it suitable for extremely high-quality printing, such as art photography, banknotes, postage stamps, coupons and security printing, and for cheaper mass-volume products such as catalogues, glossy magazines, wrapping and wallpaper.

The artwork for gravure printing, like that for the offset lithographic process, is likely to be digital and is made in exactly the same way for either print process. The CMYK colours are separated to produce four plates. The separations are converted into plates by a digital signal that controls a diamond-tipped engraver, which cuts into a copper plate. This process can also be realized using laser-engraving, again driven from a digital colour separation. Making a gravure plate is significantly more expensive than making an offset lithographic plate, and is specified by publishers for books with very long print runs of several million copies or because of the very soft tones or exceptionally fine lines that can be printed using the process. The high cost has led to a decline in the number of printers working with the process. Attempts have been made to close the financial gap between the two processes by making photo-polymer gravure plates that use stainless steel and are as cheap as lithographic plates to produce.

The image is printed by drawing out the ink that sits below the surface of the plate. Half-tone images are broken down into a series of tiny dots. The larger or deeper the dot, the greater the volume of ink carried in that area of the plate. Large, deep dots give good ink coverage with almost no visible screen, while tiny dots create very subtle tones – a feature treasured by designers.

# 3.11 Banknotes and security printing

**Right:** Front (right) and back (far right) of a 200-franc Swiss banknote. The complexity and sophistication of the design devised to prevent forgery also contributes to the unique, beautiful visual language associated with banknotes. The face and the seated figure reading a paper (top of note) have endless subtle variations in line and colour. The tone that defines the image is created by combinations of multiple colour overlays rather than a single black plate.

Security printing is a generic term used for all forms of printing in which the sheet of paper represents value, for example, banknotes, postage stamps, tokens, cheque books and lottery tickets. The history of banknotes has seen official printers attempting to stay one step ahead of the forger. Most banknotes today are printed with combinations of photographic and hand-engraved plates using both lithography and gravure printing processes. Some countries use letterpress to mark the individual banknotes with a specific number, while many make use of 12-colour printing, foil strips within the paper, complex watermarks, embossing, tinted varnish and holographic printed elements. Most modern notes have at least 24 security 'elements' designed to prevent forgery.

# 3.12 Dye-sublimation

**Above:** Dye-sublimation printing produces vibrant colours and is ideal for printing stretch fabrics and banners and flags, as well as for sports clothing and garment labelling. Here advertising slogans and brand names emblazon the shirts and colours of professional cycling teams.

Dye-sublimation, a term often shortened to dye-sub printing, supports full-colour CMYK printing on a wide range of substrates – polyester fabrics, synthetic canvases, sportswear, carpet tiles, rugs, ceramics and many materials that have been precoated with a 60 per cent polyester compound. First developed in the late 1950s, dye-sublimation has grown in popularity since the mid-1990s – due to the increased sophistication and speeds of large-format inkjet printers – as a means of reproducing lettering, photography and artwork. An inkjet printer is used to print dye and not ink on to paper or a plate from where heat and pressure transfer it to the surface of the fabric. Sublimation is a scientific term used to describe the process in which a substance changes its state from a solid to a gas without becoming a liquid. The dye on the paper sheet is subjected to intense heat and becomes a gas, while retaining the pigment colours. The gas is trapped, cools quickly and reverts to a solid dye again. It solidifies into rather than on to the surface of the polyester, which itself has been softened by heat. The pigment particles penetrate the fabric, cool and form a bond in the surface of the polyester. This fusion of fabric and pigment make the lettering or image very durable – the fabric can be folded, crumpled, washed and even pressed without fading or peeling. The colours are vibrant and true to the printed original. Unfortunately dye-sublimation cannot be used with natural fabrics like wool, cotton or linen as it relies on ones that soften with intense heat, enabling the dye to penetrate. Nor can dye-sublimation be effectively used on dark fabrics as the dye does not sit on the surface but penetrates it.

The dye-sublimation process is used in two ways: CMYK combined transfer in which all the CMYK colours are bonded simultaneously in a single heating and pressing; and CMYK plate or special (selected colour) transfer in which each dye colour is heated and printed separately. For the latter, the plates must be accurately registered on the fabric. An additional lamination finish, which protects the fabric against subsequent high temperatures, ultraviolet light and to some extent scuffing, can be printed to seal the fabric. Opposite, Dhafer Moosa at Stylo Graphics shows how a digital image is prepared for dye-sublimation printing.

## Dye-sublimation printing

**1** The image is printed wrong-reading on an inkjet printer. However, instead of ink the cartridges contain dye suspended in a liquid carrier. The CMYK colours are used. On some printers greys are created with a separate cartridge rather than from the CMYK mix. The image on the paper looks very similar to a conventional inkjet image.

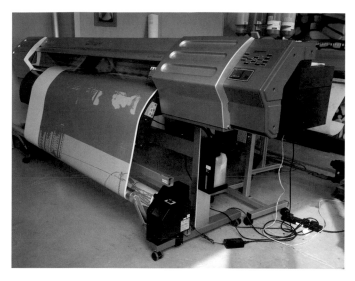

**2** The flat bed shown here, is 3 x 1.5m (9ft 10in x 4ft 11in). Resolutions up to 600dpi can be printed. As the text on the fabric will expand when hot and contract marginally when cooled the sizing must accommodate a 1–3 per cent change. The digital image must be flipped so that the text is wrong-reading.

**3** The paper is laid text- or image-up on a polyester fabric. A second strip of fabric is laid over the paper image. The heat is then set to 200°C (392°F). When the electrically heated metal platen reaches the correct temperature it can be lowered on to the bed.

**4–6** The pressure must be adjusted according to the type and thickness of the polyester. Large pneumatic rams force the hot platen down onto the fabric which is allowed to 'cook' for a minute. The platen is moved progressively down the length of the bed.

**5**

**6**

Left: Detail of a dye-sublimation print for Stella Artois lager reproduced on a heavily textured waterproofed fabric.

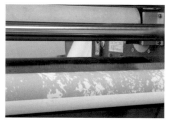

**7** The platen is lifted and the backing fabric is removed to reveal the vibrant, right-reading print. The paper is left with a very pale image and the carrier as most of the dye has been transferred and fused to the polyester.

**8** A roll printer rather than a platen dye-sublimation printer is used to print a roll of fabric 1.8m (5ft 11in) wide and over 30m (98ft 5in) long. A heated roller initiates the sublimation.

# 3.13 Vinyl lettering

Printing

**Right:** The moulded shell of this Renault F1 racing car is adorned with the printed and knife-cut vinyl lettering of its sponsors.

Vinyl is the shortened name for a plastic polymer, polyvinyl chloride (PVC), but may also be called ethenyl. It is produced in self-adhesive sheet or roll form and is a relatively cheap and extremely versatile medium for lettering. Self-adhesive letters can be cut from a huge range of colours and effects – metallics and pastels, clear and opaque, holographic patterns, high-visibility fluorescent and reflective – and in finishes such as non-reflective matt, silk or high gloss. Some vinyls can be printed single- or double-sided with CMYK or inkjet, lithography or overprinted with screen printing. Vinyl lettering can be cut wrong-reading or right-reading and comes in a wide range of weights for interior and exterior use. Vinyl is also waterproof and can be resistant to ultraviolet light. It adheres to nearly all surfaces that have a smooth, clean face. The low cost, and speed of production and application, together with the versatility of vinyl, has led to its wide-scale adoption, from signage and branding to exhibition design and packaging. It has been available to graphic production houses since the early 1980s and has completely changed the way many environmental lettering jobs are undertaken.

For the graphic designer, vinyl-cutting offers exactness of detailing: lettering can be positioned line-for-line, kerned at the required scale on screen and reproduced identically. For a retail chain the ability to reproduce identical large-format graphics for its stores reinforces corporate identity and gives visual form to the values associated with the brand. Vinyl lettering can be removed from the face of many materials without damaging the surface and new graphics can be applied directly on site without dismantling architectural elements. This facility makes vinyl an ideal medium for seasonal or short-term promotional messages and it is used throughout high-street retail stores. However, the qualities that make vinyl quick to remove also make it vulnerable to vandalism as it can be easily peeled from a surface, though the problem can sometimes be resolved by putting the vinyl lettering on the reverse of glass so that the exposed edge of the type cannot be damaged.

Many exterior-grade vinyls are today guaranteed for ten years against exposure to rain, frost and ultraviolet light. Printed vinyls are generally expected to last for seven years if exposed to ultraviolet light. Despite the large-scale adoption of vinyl by large sectors of the design industry, many graphic designers, typographers, architectural historians, architects, lettering artists, craftspeople, signwriters and, increasingly the public have begun to question the all-pervading intrusiveness of flat, plastic graphic corporate lettering in the architectural environment.

**2** This multipurpose machine is referred to as a graphic 'router' as it offers large-format CAM drafting, able to hold pens of different widths. A vinyl cutter (a jaw) can be fitted with a blade and a foamex router (a bit) can be fitted in a rotating chuck. The routing facility is not designed for metal but allows the operator to oversee the cutting of complex shapes in foamex or soft plastic sheets up to 4mm (approx. ³⁄₁₆in) thick. These are often used in retail display and exhibition graphics. The machine bed is 2.5m (8ft 3in) wide and 5m (16ft 5in) long, but lettering that occupies double this length can be cut in a single operation as the bed consists of a rotating blanket. Enough vinyl for the side of an articulated lorry or a container can be cut in single operation. For smaller vans and trucks vinyl graphics for front, back, both sides and even the roof can be cut from a single sheet.

**1** Digital design files are checked in a central digital studio, and assigned job numbers relating to the machines on which they are to be reproduced. Files may have to be converted into personal computer platform programs such as Coral Draw, which support some drafting and cutting machines. The lettering must be turned into outline to create a guide path for the cutter.

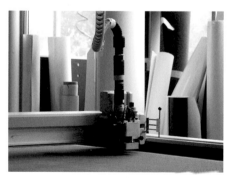

**3** A rolling flat bed is straddled by a movable bridge, along which runs the facility carriage, holding the chuck, bit, pen and cutter blade. Some vinyl lettering requires very complex decorative elements or tiny counters to be cut out from a direct-to-media (*see* pp.128–30) or inkjet print (*see* pp.126–28). A tiny camera on the carriage is directed at the vinyl laid on the bed. The vinyl surface can be preprinted with special location marks which the camera recognizes, and the cutting blade is relocated accordingly. This intelligent, self-correcting facility compensates for any stretching or contraction of the sheet.

**4** The machine operator calls up the appropriate file from the central server and creates a cutting path that links the outline of the successive letters or makes a path around a printed shape. The path includes lift and drop commands that automatically apply the blade in the correct location. The operator can limit the speed at which the blade is run depending on the thickness of the vinyl.

**Right:** A detail of the Renault's nose cone shows the printed advertising insignia. The car is painted yellow and blue. All the other colours are added as coloured vinyl, for example 'PVAX' on the right of the image; or they are printed on white vinyl, as in the case of the elf logo.

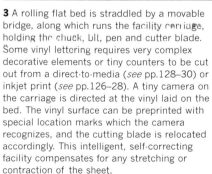

# 3.14 Inkjet printing

Inkjet printers were invented around 1976 but only really took off in the early 1980s with the increasing use of the personal computer. The manufacturer Canon claims to have been the first to develop the technology with its bubble-jet printer. As with so many technological advances, the invention was accidental. It is said that a clumsy researcher touched an ink-filled syringe with a soldering iron and the instant rise in temperature caused the ink to shoot out of the needle.

Photographic printers producing high-quality hand prints remain but the inkjet printer has become the staple for the presentation of large-format paper dummies used by design companies, advertisers and architects. Exhibition designers use inkjet prints for one-off displays as they can be surface-mounted on panels. Production houses, such as Stylo Graphics who specialize in large-format printing, use inkjet technology in dye-sublimation printing (see pp.122–23) and direct-to-media printing (see pp.129–30). Inkjet printers can be used with solvent-based inks to print on to vinyl (see pp.124–25), used for banners and the plastic tarpaulins on open-sided lorries.

Inkjet printing does not make use of plates, the ink is squirted from tiny nozzles slightly above the paper or substrate. A print head is mounted on a carriage which runs laterally across a track over the paper. The carriage is driven to and fro by small electric motors. On today's printers ink is delivered in both forward and return movements, thus reducing the print time. The roll of paper is advanced between each pass so that a new strip of ink is printed. Modern printers print groups of pixels four, six, eight, or even 12 deep with each pass. Large-format printers use 300dpi, 600dpi or enhanced resolution 1,440dpi by 720dpi. A large-format inkjet printer reproducing a landscape A1 sheet arranged across the roll puts down at least 224,688 dots per pass in approximately three seconds when printing eight pixels deep at 600dpi.

There are two slightly different technologies among the major manufacturers. Canon and Hewlett-Packard use thermotechnology, while Epson has developed a Piezo crystal system which is fired by variations in electrical current. Both systems produce ink in what is referred to as drop on demand (DOD) where small drops of ink are squirted on to the paper 5,000 times per second.

Thermotechnology has three key stages: heating, bubble bursting and vacuum refilling. A micro resistor, in contact with the ink in a tiny firing chamber above the nozzle, is electrically heated. The ink expands to create a bubble until the pressure of expansion causes it to burst and squirt the ink out onto the paper. The resistor cools rapidly, and the bubble contracts, creating a vacuum, which in turn draws fresh ink into the firing chamber from the cartridge reservoir. Print heads have up to 600 nozzles, each the diameter of a human hair (approximately 70 microns). Each DOD nozzle emits ten pico litres (a millionth of a litre) per squirt, producing a dot between 50 and 60 microns in diameter. The human eye is only capable of seeing a 30-micron dot in isolation and so reads the dots as a solid colour. Colours are mixed by combining cyan, magenta and yellow dots into different groups. Black has a slightly bigger pigment molecule and a larger dot used to create tone.

Piezo crystal technology is a non-thermal process, which does not continually heat and cool the ink in the firing cavity. Piezo was an Italian chemist who realized that certain crystals expand when an electrical current is passed through them. The degree of expansion can be varied by minute adjustments to the strength of the current, creating smaller ink dots and, therefore, higher resolution (up to 720dpi) than that currently produced by thermal technology. The Piezo crystal technology can make use of solvent inks that are drawn into the paper and dry in clean, round dots, creating a very crisp image.

# Large-format inkjet printing

**1** Inkjet printers must be regularly cleaned and checked for colour consistency. This is particularly important where finished prints are produced over a number of days and will be exhibited in close proximity to one another. To ensure colour consistency many repro houses, like Stylo Graphics, run out standard digital tint charts daily and check them by eye against those created at the beginning of a client's run.

**2** Large-format inkjet printers use outsize cartridges. As well as the CMYK colours some printers have additional grey tone cartridges which produce cleaner mid-tones. Other printers can be set up for black-and-white solids, or black-and-white continuous tone, where four cartridge slots use a black and three variations of grey tone in combination to improve the continuous tone in a black-and-white photographic print.

**3** A large-format inkjet printer outputs a sheet featuring a portrait of Shakespeare and calligraphic lettering for an exhibition panel. The roll feeder enables this Hewlett-Packard printer to output a continuous paper strip of text or image up to 30m (98ft 5in) in length and 1.40m (4ft 6in) wide at a resolution of 600dpi.

**4** A detail of the output, here on gloss paper, shows the depth and solidity of a black printed as part of a CMYK set. The image is printed within three minutes.

**5** A panel from the same exhibition features white type reversed out of a solid black. Here it is important that both blacks are identical in quality.

**Right:** A large-format inkjet-printed advert printed on polyvinyl mesh is stretched across the facade of a building; floodlighting makes it appear to glow above a dark city street. Inkjet printing of this type enables advertising agencies to make use of temporary sites that offers unusual formats. The advertisements have to be customized in terms of scale and crop, and are printed as one-offs.

## PVC banner printing

**1** Inkjet printers using solvent-based inks are used to produce large-format PVC banners. There are many grades of PVC with different thicknesses suitable for external use. The printer has an additional, electrically heated element positioned immediately in front of the printed roll.

**2** As the printed lettering descends it is immediately dried. The solvent must evaporate from the front of the PVC which, being waterproof, is non-porous and will not absorb any of the ink.

**3** A detail of the CMYK registration stripe shows the texture of the PVC banner. The printer is capable of edge-to-edge printing but this would mean that the registration and colour bands are run on the short edge. Running them down the roll ensures the operator can continually check the print quality on a long banner, although they must be cut away before the banners is displayed.

# 3.15 Direct-to-media printing

Direct-to-media printing, sometimes referred to as DTM printing, is a remarkable form of short-run specialist printing which has, over the last ten years, revolutionized the reproduction of large-format typography, photography and illustration. It supports CMYK, white solids, tints, continuous half-tone and varnishes. Direct-to-media printing can be used on a wide range of materials from paper, canvas, plastics, perspex, PVC, Formica, vinyl, wood and metal to ceramic tiles and even glass. It is referred to as direct printing because it uses inkjet technology to spray the image on to the substrates rather than a plate which transfers the lettering. However, unlike a conventional inkjet printer, the space between the bed and the jet can be varied to accommodate materials up to 4cm (1½in) thick. Special, ultraviolet-sensitive solvent inks are required which, when exposed to ultraviolet light, harden on the surface of the material. The process is ideally suited to the production of large-scale posters, hoardings, and architectural and exhibition panels. Since the adoption of digital printing technologies in the late 1980s there has been an amalgamation of many formerly separate graphic reproduction professions. Large graphic service companies have combined typesetting, digital outputs in laser- and inkjet-printing, artwork, scanning, large-format photocopying, photographic reproduction, platemaking, proofing, rub-downs and screen printing.

**Above:** A large-format direct-to-media printer represents the latest technology in print production; it enables full-colour lettering and images to be reproduced on virtually any material.

**1** The RHO 800 Direct printer resembles an enormous desktop inkjet printer but is approximately 7m (23ft) long.

**2** In a large production house the management and processing of individual jobs must be highly organized to ensure the most efficient use of machine time and turnaround. Each job has a numbered paper docket that relates to the artwork stored on the central server. The operator calls up the artwork from the server and identifies the substrate from the docket.

**3** The machine is set up for printing by controlling the position of the artwork on the substrate and defining the depth of the material. This direct printer is able to print materials up to 4cm (1½in) deep. Once the material depth has been specified, the machine automatically lifts the ink delivery nozzle a further 1.5mm (approx. ¹⁄₁₆in).

**4** The ink cartridges for the machine are CMYK plus grey, white and a varnish. It is not possible at present to print varnish with a colour tint, or metallic or fluorescent inks as these would not react appropriately to ultraviolet light. The inks are solvent-based and are pumped to the nozzle head.

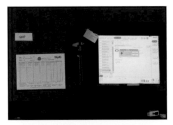

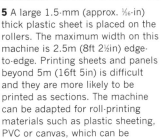

**5** A large 1.5-mm (approx. ¹⁄₁₆-in) thick plastic sheet is placed on the rollers. The maximum width on this machine is 2.5m (8ft 2½in) edge-to-edge. Printing sheets and panels beyond 5m (16ft 5in) is difficult and they are more likely to be printed as sections. The machine can be adapted for roll-printing materials such as plastic sheeting, PVC or canvas, which can be any length.

**6** As the sheet is fed into the printer the carriage head is lowered to the appropriate position, 1.5mm (approx. ¹⁄₁₆in) above the print surface.

**7** The casing of a smaller direct-to-media printer lifted up to show how the inkjet carriage shifts to and fro over the work, printing in both directions.

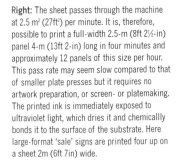

**Right:** The sheet passes through the machine at 2.5 m² (27ft²) per minute. It is, therefore, possible to print a full-width 2.5-m (8ft 2½-in) panel 4-m (13ft 2-in) long in four minutes and approximately 12 panels of this size per hour. This pass rate may seem slow compared to that of smaller plate presses but it requires no artwork preparation, or screen- or platemaking. The printed ink is immediately exposed to ultraviolet light, which dries it and chemicallly bonds it to the surface of the substrate. Here large-format 'sale' signs are printed four up on a sheet 2m (6ft 7in) wide.

5674

# Cut, engraved and etched three-dimensional lettering

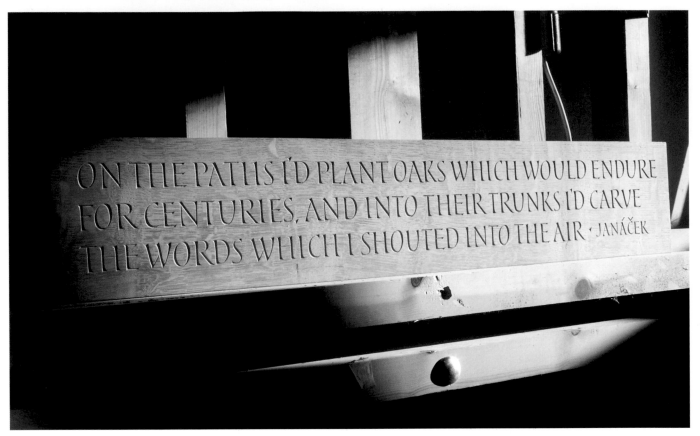

ON THE PATHS I'D PLANT OAKS WHICH WOULD ENDURE FOR CENTURIES, AND INTO THEIR TRUNKS I'D CARVE THE WORDS WHICH I SHOUTED INTO THE AIR · JANÁČEK

**Above:** An easel in Caroline Webb's studio supports an oak beam into which she has cut a text which references the wood. Oak is a hardwood, which makes it resistant to the paring knife. This lettering took over a week to cut.

Wood-carving has been a craft skill since prehistory, when stones, flints and bone tools were used to incise images into a surface or carve three-dimensional shapes from a log. The earliest surviving wood carvings of a script are ancient Egyptian hieroglyphics, some of which date to *c.*3000 BCE.

Letter-cutting in wood has always shared many principles with letter-cutting in stone (*see* pp.136–39), yet today many cutters tend to specialize in one or the other material. There are technical and commercial reasons why letter-cutting has developed in this way. Wood tended to be used for the exterior structures of small domestic and rural buildings, and the interiors and furniture of vast stone buildings. This division of the stone and wood carving trades accounts for the long-standing separation of letter-cutting along material lines. The division was further reinforced by the medieval guild and company system, under which nearly all carvers were trained.

Wood proved to be a far more appropriate material for letter-cutting broken script forms (blackletter) than stone, as the thick and thin strokes of the majuscule, and the tightly spaced minuscule of Textura (*see* p.15), could be clearly defined. Inscriptions, which were not subject to scuffing, were painted and gilded, emphasizing their forms. The lettering was made with either a deep V-cut, or carved in relief, the face of the letter standing proud of the ground, in the manner of a woodblock print (*see* pp.90–91).

Caroline Webb, originally educated as a graphic designer, began to take an interest in calligraphy and carving at the University of Reading, where she was taught to cut letters by Michael Harvey (*see* pp.86–88). Webb, who has worked in both stone and wood, now principally works in wood, which is softer and retains the finest of lines within a letterform. Her commissions include work on memorial plaques, architectural panelling, screens, interior and exterior furniture, and gallery pieces.

**This page:**

**1** A text carved into a bough of a yew tree. With a number of other artists Webb was commissioned to celebrate the yew. Each artist was given part of the tree to work with. The bough has been cut longitudinally, and the face sanded on both sides.

**2** A detail of the letter cutting reveals the fine quality of line and the variation in the depth of cut possible in wood as compared with stone.

1

2

**3** An inscription only 2.5cm (1in) in length from the piece of quarter-sewn oak shown opposite illustrates how the letterforms retain the calligraphic strokes through which they were first drawn. The carved serifs follow the movement of the calligraphic hand, beginning to touch the surface at the left of the apex, creating a single-sided serif falling to the left, drawing diagonally down the broad stroke with the full width of the pen and being lifted off to the right of the termination on the baseline, making a single-sided serif to the right.

**4** Details of a children's letter-cut alphabet infilled with a light ochre paint, which lifts the contrast between the letterforms and the wood.

**5** Relief wood-carving was a long tradition in China. Here the words happiness and long life have been carved on a sign c.1850. Like the smaller woodblock printing undertaken by Ilse Bucherl Nesbitt (see p.90) the process is very time consuming as all the wood surrounding the letterform must be cut away.

3

4

5

Cut, engraved and etched three-dimensional lettering

**1** Letter cutters who work in wood have a large collection of carving tools. Chisels with a straight cutting edge come in different widths. Gouges are chisels with a rounded blade used for cutting away large sections of wood. The radius of the arc on a gouge varies; deeper gouges can remove more wood with a single cut. Curved gouges (below right) are used for paring (cutting away or shaving) wood in a circle.

**2** Wood cutting tools must be extremely sharp to create a clean cut. Here a small gouge is sharpened by the back of the blade being rubbed on an oilstone.

**3** The letter is drawn by eye in soft pencil outline between a cap line and baseline, in the same way it would be on stone. Running the words along a plank, with the grain, ensures that the broad, deep, vertical V-cuts are cut across the grain.

**4** Here Webb uses a square-edged chisel to mark the centre of the V-cut which is estimated to be halfway between the outer and inner edges of the letter, and is not drawn. The chisel is tapped into the wood using a small, round mallet. Two nicks are cut into the wood at the base of the letter at approximately 45 degrees.

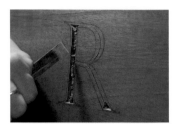

**8** Nearly all the wood has been removed from the V-cut and the edge of the cut is now very close to the pencil outline.

**10** A straight edge is used to check that the serifs extend equally from the downstroke.

**9** The piece is now laid on a flat bench and, using a chip knife, Webb pares away the final edge of the letter up to the pencil outline.

**Right:** Webb draws a design out line by line before tracing the lettering on to tracing paper. This enables her to clean up the design and centre the lines' lettering.

George
1920~2001
&
Rosemary
1921~2000

**6** Here Webb has inverted the piece on an easel to work down the broad stroke of the 'R'. Some carvers work on the refinement of a letter with fine, square chisels, but here she works with a chip or paring knife. The knife has a very short blade with a slight angle. It is worked slowly towards the carver across the grain. The blade is pushed by the handle held in the right hand and resisted by a finger of the left hand.

**5** The bulk of the wood has been chopped out using the broad chisel to make the rough V-cut. The cut finishes inside the pencil strokes.

**7** The chip knife is turned over and worked away from the carver with both hands. The left hand pushes the base of the handle and blade and is resisted by the right hand holding the handle. This two-handed cutting brings power and control to the cutting edge, and prevents the knife slipping and cutting away essential wood or creating unsightly gouges. The knife is held firmly at a consistent angle and small shavings of wood curl away from the blade.

**11** Layout paper is placed over the letter and a rubbing is made using a graphite stick. Viewing the letter in this flat, reversed-out graphic form reveals any tiny imperfections. On finishing a piece, some cutters take a full-size graphite or wax rubbing of the design as a record, and store both the original pencil design and the rubbing together. This allows a cutter to review his or her work over a lifetime and serves as a resource for future clients.

**12** The final 7.5-cm (3-in) letter has taken about an hour to draw and cut. The crispness and precision achieved with the knife is breathtaking. Where the upper bowl joins the centre bar a very fine point has been created that has a length and refinement impossible in stone. The serifs in this letter are square-ended rather than tapering to a point.

**Above:** Monoline Viking runes inscribed or scratched into a stone are far removed from the earlier, highly sophisticated Roman square capitals which appear on Trajan's Column in Rome and form the basis of what most letter cutters are taught.

**Above right:** In this carving of the word 'stone' by Andrew Whittle the surface is not merely incised, the lettering takes on a sculptural, three-dimensional form.

In cutting stone the proportions, height to width, and line widths of the letters are determined by the letter cutter, although most cutters tend to develop an individual set of proportions for roman caps. Drawing the letters requires extraordinary skill and the techniques used vary greatly between cutters. After conducting an extensive survey of historical roman forms, the lettering expert Edward Cattich concluded that the letters were first painted on the stone with a brush. Cattich, an experienced calligrapher himself, speculated on how each roman cap was broken into its constituent strokes.

While all letter cutters recognize the innate relationship between calligraphy and their own practices, few use a brush to paint the letters on to stone. Some stone cutters use a soft, chisel-pointed pencil which enables them to draw both sides of the letter with a single stroke, while others bind two pencils together, which creates two keylines with a single movement. In letter draughtsmanship all the design issues are interlinked. The size of the letters affects the number of words per line. The arrangement – which on a traditional headstone is usually centred – affects the word breaks, and hierarchy is determined by the size, position and style of the letters. Roman caps can be considered as three groups: round (C, D, G, O, Q), symmetrical (A, H, I, M, N, T, U, V, W, X and Y) and asymmetrical (B, E, F, J, K, L, P, R, S, Z). The round letters are generally wider than the other two groups with the exception of 'M' and 'W'; the asymmetrical letters are approximately half to three-fifths of the round letters. The symmetrical letters are drawn approximately five-eighths to three-quarters of the round letters. Roman letters can be drawn with vertical stress, making the 'O' symmetrical for example, or with a diagonal line of stress.

Watching the drawing of letters by an experienced letter cutter, it becomes clear that he or she is relying as much on kinetic memory (when muscles remember a repeated sequence) as eye. The width of each letter is individual but both the widths and the intercharacter spaces seem to be considered in combination. The guiding principle in drawing the letters is the search for consistency of letter pattern, evenness of line weight and spacing, uniformity of stress and logical word breaks. Lower-case and italic letters share all these considerations but the ascender and descender lengths and inclination must also be accommodated.

**This page:**

**1** Two rough-hewn, Elterwater green slate pillars with a river surface stand in a pebbled landscape. The lettering, a quote from William Blake, was designed and cut by the Cardozo Kindersley Workshop, Cambridge, England.

**2** A memorial plaque cut in dark, Welsh slate in memory of the great letter cutter David Kindersley, by the Cardozo Kindersley Workshop. The incised caps have been infilled with red paint, as lettering was on Roman buildings. The graceful lettering with embellished flourishes is infilled with gold. The variation in the form of the italic 's' shows the freedom with which a letter cutter works, considering that the lettering sits within a space.

**3** Letter cutter and calligrapher John Neilson makes use of relief forms in this piece 'Ceaseless Message', from Rilke's *Duino Elegies*, translated by Stephen Mitchell. Relief lettering involves cutting away far greater quantities of stone than incised forms, so the softer limestone of this piece is ideal. The lettering is cut in caps without interword spacing, and so stands proud of the surface as a form rather than as individual words.

1

2

3

## Hand-cutting letters

**1** Cold chisels (solid metal chisels designed to cut stone rather than wood) are made in many sizes. The cutting edge is now frequently tipped with tungsten carbide (a hard, grey metal compound). The large chisel (left) with several points is referred to as a claw. The tip of a chisel may be flat (centre), rounded (second from right) or form a point (right) used for pointing a stippled effect on the surface of the stone.

**2** The larger, nylon-headed round mallet (left) is used for heavy work with a wide chisel, where a large quantity of stone needs to be removed quickly. The small, round metal mallet (centre) is used for carving details together with a small chisel. The block mallet (right) is generally reserved for very heavy work with a broad chisel and for splitting stone.

**3** A white chinagraph pencil is used for drawing on dark stones such as Welsh slate, while a black graphite pencil is used on pale stone such as limestone or marble. The pencil is sharpened on emery paper to create a very long, fine point.

**4** Some letter cutters work out the full size design on paper before redrawing it on the stone. Others, like Fergus Wessels, design directly on to the stone and redraw until they are happy with the layout and form of the letters. For cap letters, a parallel cap line and baseline are drawn across the stone with a ruler. The cap height usually estimated rather than measured.

**9** Depending on the type of stone used, hacking back can be a delicate procedure. Softer stone with consistent gradual size, such as slate or limestone, is more easily worked than hard stone like marble or granite which have an irregular, crystalline structure. The cutter works to the keyline, striving for a clean edge between the V-cut and the flat surface of the stone.

**10** The serif on this capital 'B' is very fine and relatively long. The letter is visually weighted towards its base; the lower bowl is wider. The lower counter (the hollow, negative space within a letterform) is rounded where it meets the vertical stroke at the base of the lower bowl but the top of the upper counter is cut square. There is a gentle curve at the top and bottom of the letter, connecting the serif to the bowl. The angle of the central horizontal V-cut is consistent with the rest of the letter, but as the stroke is narrower than the vertical it is far shallower.

**5** Once all the letters have been drawn and the client has approved and checked the design and lettering on the stone, the fine chisel is sharpened and the cutting can begin.

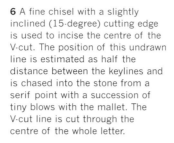

**6** A fine chisel with a slightly inclined (15-degree) cutting edge is used to incise the centre of the V-cut. The position of this undrawn line is estimated as half the distance between the keylines and is chased into the stone from a serif point with a succession of tiny blows with the mallet. The V-cut line is cut through the centre of the whole letter.

**7** The cutter works from just inside the keylines towards the V-cut centre line, chopping away stone. The position of the V-cut must remain the same but it gradually deepens as it is worked alternately from both the inner and the outer edge of the letter. The chisel is held at a consistent angle in relation to the stone as this ensures an even depth.

**8** Once the central V-cut is fully established, the cutter concentrates on refining the edge of the letter. The angle of the V is retained and tiny taps are used to hack back the cut to the drawn edge of the letter. The chisel angle determines the depth of cut; many stone cutters recognize each other's work by the depth of the letters.

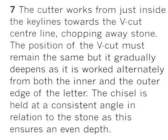

1

2

3

**1** Some cutters consider the addition of any colour or gilt to an inscribed letter to be gauche or kitsch. Others of a less purist nature seek to use selected colour, enjoying its contrast with the stone. Where the surface of the stone is smooth, flood painting can be used. Paint is daubed or poured into the letter and allowed to dry. The surface is then cleaned with fine emery paper.

**2** On dark stones such as slate the carved letter is initially far lighter in colour than the stone but if the stone is used externally the contrast begins to fade and the text loses its clarity through exposure to wind and rain. To compensate for the loss of legibility, some letter cutters infill the V-cut with a pale grey paint matched to the colour of the cut slate. Here the flood-painted letters are cleaned with wet and then dry paper.

**3** Gold leaf is brushed on to the incised surfaces of the letter, which has been coated with a paste. Gold comes in different colours – white and deep gold – and with different degrees of lustre (quality of shine).

# 4.3 Letter-cutting stone by machine

Machine letter-cutting in stone using a pantograph machine was a process invented by the Imperial War Graves Commission just after the First World War in order to make the cutting of headstones more efficient. The commission had a special font designed by the stone carver and letter cutter MacDonald Gill (1884–1947, brother of the better known Eric Gill). The pantograph process is still used today and is demonstrated here by masons at Elfes Monumental Masons in the east end of London.

## Cutting letters in stone using a pantograph

**1** The stone-cutting machine consists of a flat wooden table on which the headstone rests. Runners on either side of the table enable the machine's cutter to move above the surface of the stone. The mason draws a baseline, cap line and centre line in pencil on the stone for each element of the inscription. These lines, and the spaces between them, define the vertical spacing of the text. The horizontal arrangement of traditional headstones is centred, and therefore symmetrical on either side of the centre point.

**2** Engraved right-reading letter patterns, similar to those used on an engraving pantograph, are stored in a case like metal type. Each case holds 26 letters, punctuation and numerals in a single type style and size, in either caps or lower case.

**6** The letter patterns are placed on the pattern ruler that straddles the table. This has two flanges between which the letter patterns sit. The ruler has two scales: the top is marked off in inches from left to right while the bottom edge is a centring rule, marked left and right from the centre point. A single line of text is spelt out on the rule. Once the interword spacing is fixed the pattern is centred by ensuring the distances left and right of the centre line are equal. The patterns are locked in place with quoins (wedges).

**7** The cutting point can be moved up or down to accommodate different depths of headstone. The depth of cut is controlled by the amount of pressure the operator applies to the two handles used to guide the stylus.

**Right:** One of the first pantograph letter-cutting machines developed by the Imperial War Graves Commission in 1919. Unable to hand-cut nearly a million headstones for the soldiers lost in World War I the Commission developed machine cutting by adapting the principles of machine engraving (*see* pp.142–43).

**3** Five-cm (2-in), 3-cm (1¼ in) and 2-cm (¾-in) caps engraved on a metal 'slug' of the same height. The smallest size is 2-cm (¾-in) caps, the largest 7.6-cm (3-in). Up to 3.8cm (1½in) cap heights rise by 0.3cm (⅛in) and then rise in 0.6-cm (¼-in) increments. Minimum kerning between letters is determined by the width of the shoulder on the slug (here the distance between the serif and the edge of the metal). Spacing units proportional to the cap height are based on an em square.

**4** A line showing how much of the headstone will be under the ground is marked on the stone. Where the mark is made depends on the height and weight of the stone and how it will be set in the ground. Here two holes on the base have been predrilled to encase metal pins which will rise vertically from a stone beam. This type of setting requires only one-quarter of the stone to be below the surface.

**5** The stone's position on the table must be square to the cutter, centred, and with the base facing the operator before the clamps (on either side of the table) are moved into position and secured. As with type, this process is sometimes referred to as locking up. The gap between the pencil lines, where the inscription will fall, is painted with a brown, water-soluble dye on light-coloured stone and a white dye on dark stone, to make the outline of the lettering clearly visible to the operator during the cutting process.

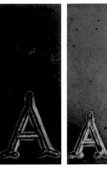

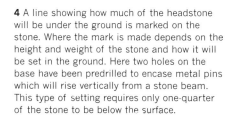

**8** The letters on this machine, unlike those generally produced by pantograph systems, are cut 1:1 – the inscribed letter is the same cap height as the pattern. The operator carefully traces the stylus around the pattern; each movement is translated directly to the diamond cutting tip. The close proximity of the pattern to the white, cut inscription, illuminated by a work light and clearly defined against the brown dye, allows the operator to monitor the quality of the cut. A suction tube sited next to the cutting head removes stone dust.

**Left:** An example of the final machine V-cut showing centred lines evenly spaced using caps. The pencil centre line, baseline and cap line marks, together with the brown dye, can now be washed off. The letterforms are far more robust than those produced by hand-carving. The inscription is typographic in form, as individual characters are identical.

**Above:** Letters cut by machine into Portland stone. The stone of sacrifice designed by Edwin Lutyens (1869–1944) for the Imperial War Graves Commission (today the Commonwealth War Graves Commission) is placed in every Commonwealth cemetery, where over 1,000 men are buried. The lettering was designed by MacDonald Gill.

The quality of computerized cutting differs significantly from letter-cutting using a pantograph machine (*see* pp.140–41), by sandblasting (*see* pp.145–47) and by hand (*see* pp.136–39). A pantograph machine has no facility to vary the depth of V-cut within a single letterform; similarly sandblasting produces only profile-cut letters with no progressive variation in depth. By contrast, letter-cutting by hand can make a progressive cut with shallow serifs deepening into the strong V of the strokes and bowls. It is this progressive cut that can now be reproduced by computer-controlled cutting. The serif can be deepened towards the stroke of the letter and the node at which the returning curve of a bowl meets a stroke. For example, a cap R has two depths, a deep, vertical V is intersected by a shallow, horizontal V. The precision of the cutting is breathtaking. As every line and edge is flawless, complex patterns, crest designs and lettering can be repeatedly incised into the surface at a scale and exactness which could not be consistently equalled, stone after stone, by a letter cutter. Some older masons and letter cutters, though impressed by the precision of computerized cutting, have criticized the cut for this very exactness, arguing that it is not in keeping with the organic, natural patina of stone. No two headstones cut by hand are identical either in the surface patina, colour or texture of the stone, or in the letterform proportion or cutting incision marks. By contrast the computerized cutter produces identical crests and lettering on every stone. The respective qualities of hand, pantograph, sandblasting and computerized letter-cutting must be carefully weighed in relation to the nature of the project, the aims of the client, the spirit of the text to be cut, the type of stone used, lighting conditions, the environment in which the stone is to appear and, of course, the budget.

In recent years, the Commonwealth War Graves Commission has invested in very high-quality computerized letter-cutting equipment, at its workshops on the Somme in France. The machines, built in Italy, are highly specialized. The only similar machine in Britain is operated by Andrew Grassby, who also works with the Ministry of Defence, cutting headstones for service personnel who have lost their lives in conflicts since 1945. In this process the design work is undertaken on screen before the digital file is transferred to the cutter. Once set running the cutter will incise a headstone in less than one hour.

## Computer-controlled machine V-cut letters

**1** The lettering is arranged on screen within a scale drawing of the headstone. Unlike pantograph letter-cutting, the size and spacing can be adjusted infinitely, and cap heights are not limited to set sizes. The text in this example is centred.

**2** Unlike sandblasting, where any font or calligraphic style can be blasted into the stone, delineated by an outline, here the centre of the V-cut defines the cutting line. The centre cutting line is crucial as it literally creates the strokes, bowls and serifs. The lettering is arranged on screen. Headstones generally feature centred lettering. Letter size, and interword, character and line spacing can be adjusted.

**3** Fonts for computerized letter-cutting must be designed with a three-dimensional element. For the letter to be effectively cut, the depth of cut must be varied between specific points on the cutting path. The font must be programmed with depth profiles for each of the elements. The stroke depth is the same for all, but serif and bowl depth vary.

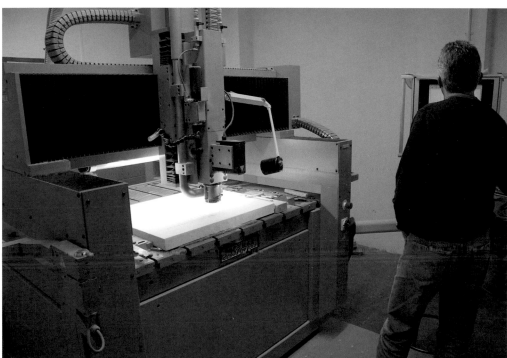

**4** Once the layout of the lettering is complete it is sent directly to the cutting machine situated in a separate workshop. The machine has a large, flat bed on which the stone lies, above which is an arm holding a tungsten carbide cutter.

**5** A detail of the tungsten carbide cutter tip. Cutters come in a range of shapes, and the machine can incise a 90-degree profile like that created by sandblasting, and produce V-cuts of different depths: 30 degrees for a shallow cut, 45 degrees for a medium cut, or, as in this example, 60 degrees for a deep cut.

**6** To compensate for the stone's minor inconsistencies in thickness a precutting program is run to form a digital, topographic profile of the surface of each stone. The cutting head has a laser (the beam is not visible) which, as it passes over the surface, continually measures the distance between the stone and the cutting tip.

**7** The depth data is automatically added to, or subtracted from, the coordinates controlling the cutting depth of each letter. The operator can stop the machine and examine the cut or allow it to run the full path monitoring it remotely. The cutting time varies depending on the complexity of the design, the number and size of the characters and the hardness of the stone – hard granite and marbles are cut more slowly than Portland stone.

**8** Each letter is cut in a single pass, and the stone dust and tiny fragments are sucked up by a powerful vacuum pump, leaving the surface clean and the letters precise. In designs with very complex imagery, or crests that require several depths of cut, the machine can be programmed to make multiple passes – cutting away stone at a single coordinate each time. As depth profiles can be developed in two planes the machine is capable of highly complex carving.

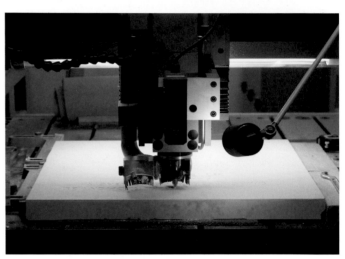

**9** The completed lettering is very crisp, the cut surface consistent and the spacing even – like type the letterforms are identical. This is an intriguing contrast to more idiosyncratic hand-cut letters (*see* pp.136–39) and lettering by signwriters (*see* pp.30–39) where on occasion the form of the letters is adapted to unify the whole design.

1
**This page:**
1 The screen design of a regimental crest.

2 The same design shows that very accurate relief lettering can be cut with a 90-degree profile, vertical sides or, like letters produced for casting patterns (*see* pp.54–55), an inclination of 10 degrees. The last is preferable if a head stone is to stand outside vertically; it ensures surface water runs away from the face rather than collecting in reservoirs between strokes and potentially causing erosion by chemicals and frost.

3 A detail of the machine-cut lettering shows the mechanical accuracy of the line work and the inclination.

# 4.4 Sandblasting

Sandblasting is a process with many different applications. It is used for cleaning metal, brick and concrete, as an opaque finish on Perspex and glass, and as a way of producing profile-cut letters in both stone and glass. It is an abrasive procedure in which compressed air is used to fire particles of grit through a tiny nozzle. The grit erodes the surface and, with the aid of a stencil resist, cuts the letters. The letters are not V-cut but have a 90-degree profile and can be either incised or stand in relief. Sandblasting is often used on granite because the rock is very hard. It is the cheapest means of producing lettering on stone and the cutting time for a memorial may be as little as 30 minutes. On glass, sandblasting can be used for small-scale, domestic and decorative ware but the process also has larger architectural applications. Today it is frequently used in preference to hand-engraved lettering as it is quicker and produces a cleaner finish. Andrew Grassby and Lesley Pyke demonstrate sandblasting in stone and glass respectively.

## Sandblasting lettering in stone

**1** The text for a headstone is laid out digitally on screen according to the wishes of the relatives. Virtually any font can be sandblasted into stone. Andrew Grassby Stone- masons worked with the stone cutter and lettering artist, Michael Harvey, to produce a font called Grassby/Harvey which is frequently used by the firm for sandblasting and stone-cutting.

**2** The cutting path controls the order in which the letters are cut into the rubber resist and determines where the knife blade on the plotter is lifted. The plotter, like those used for vinyl-cutting (see pp.124–25), consists of a rotating drum, around which the adhesive-backed, 1-mm (1/32-in) rubber resist turns, and horizontal tracks along which the carriage holding the knife runs.

**3** A detail of the plotter's cutting head. The lettering is cut through the surface of the rubber on the front of the pale grey backing paper and is right-reading. The cutting time is dependent on the length of the text, but the mask for an average headstone is cut within 15 minutes.

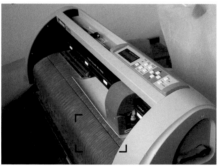
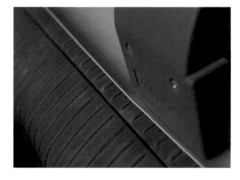

**4** The backing paper is stripped away from the rubber sheet which is then laid down firmly on the front face of a prepared headstone to prevent sand scouring the surface during the blasting. Unwanted parts of the resist are removed. Incised letters must be lifted carefully with a scalpel to expose the stone beneath. The counters must be left in place. If the lettering is to be relief, the surrounding ground and counters must be removed.

**5** The sandblasting cabinet consists of an enclosed metal box with a lid and windows. The stone is lifted into the cabinet, which is sealed. Two large rubber gloves allow the operator to hold the sandblasting gun which is attached to a large compressor that supplies compressed air. The pressure is set according to the hardness of the stone. The grade of grit used, combined with the pressure, determines the depth of the cut.

**6** The operator works across the surface of the stone in even sweeps so that all the exposed areas are cut to the same depth. If multiple depths are required, shallow sections can be masked out independently before deeper areas are repeat sandblasted. In about 30 minutes the lettering is 3mm (1/8in) deep. Once the lettering is of the required depth the rubber resist can be peeled away, and the stone wiped clean and polished.

# Sandblasting lettering in glass

**1** The artwork for sandblasting can be either hand-drawn or digital and the letterforms can be calligraphic or type. Here a piece of typesetting is run out on to film as a black positive. (It is not the artwork used in the final piece but the process is identical).

**2** A mask is made as for screen printing (see pp.106–09) using ultraviolet-light-sensitive film. The film protects areas of clear glass from grains of sand that abrade the surface. It has three layers: a backing sheet and an adhesive sheet sandwich a UV-light-sensitive centre. The positive film is placed on the exposure unit with the resist film over the top.

**3** The tiny exposure unit is turned on for 30 seconds, exposing the area surrounding the lettering to ultraviolet light. The backing sheet is peeled away and the light-sensitive area is exposed to a chemical developer, in a bucket. The areas exposed to the ultraviolet light are developed but the unexposed lettering is not.

**4** Warm water is sprayed on to the sheet and the unexposed lettering is gently washed away, leaving a clean stencil.

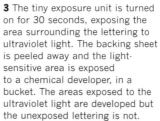

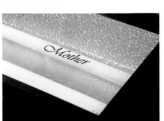

**8** The masking-off process is completed by wrapping the remaining exposed glass in parcel tape.

**9** The glass is placed inside the sandblasting unit, which contains two rubber gloves and an air gun. The lid is closed and, using the gloves, Pyke picks up the glass with one hand and the air gun with the other. The compressor is set to a comparatively low 25psi as the glass is quite soft lead crystal. The finest sand particles are fired at the glass and pass over each letter for 20 seconds.

**10** The distance between the glass and the air gun must be kept constant, as must the abrasion time for each letter. Pyke achieves consistency by counting. The used sand and glass particles fall to the bottom of the unit where they can be recycled.

**Left:** Pyke uses sandblasting in combination with acid-etching and hand-engraving to produce imagery and lettering on the surface of glassware.

**5** Using a levelling stick and a felt-tip pen, the glass engraver, Lesley Pyke establishes a baseline on the glass for the type.

**6** The film resist is positioned on the glass and the backing sheet is peeled away leaving the adhesive side to the glass.

**7** A small squeegee (a wooden-handled nylon pad) is pulled across the surface to ensure that no air bubbles are trapped between the glass and film and that all the letter outlines are glued tightly to the glass. Any lack of adhesion will allow the sand to damage the masked surface. The backing film is gently peeled away to reveal the stencil on the glass.

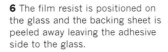

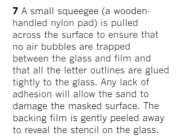

**11** The parcel tape is peeled off the glass and the residue film is washed away in warm water. The depth of the lettering depends on the softness of the glass, the coarseness of the sand, the air pressure (which can be run up to 50psi for very deep carving) and the abrasion time. Here the depth is 0.2mm (approx. ½in).

**12** The finished glass is wiped dry and the sandblasted lettering appears as an opaque finish.

**Right:** A detail of the lettering shows how crisp the outline is when it is defined by the light travelling through the glass.

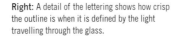

# 4.5 Machine-routed letters

Routing uses a spinning blade called a routing bit to cut shapes into the surface of a sheet of material, or to cut directly through a material to produce letter profiles. It can be used to cut lettering from wood, metal, acrylic, plastic and nylon. Letterforms can be hand-routed by a skilled operator guiding a router around the outline of a letter, but today they are more likely to be produced by machine. Routing is used to produce large-sheet letterforms for signage and architectural and retail spaces. Routed letters can be surface-mounted as a sheet or built into a three-dimensional form to stand proud of a wall or floor. Digital keyline drawings defining the shape of each letter are positioned on a scale drawing of the sheet material. The keyline forms a cutting guide for the router; letters are positioned individually rather than as words to make the most economical use of material. The router is positioned over the work at a point called the origin point, and from here begins to cut the sheet. The computer controls the cutting speed and the path between the letters, lifting the router above the cutting surface before gently lowering the bit to cut a new letter. Once the router has been set on its path, the process is fully automated.

## CNC-routed letters

**3** The largest sheet that can be cut on this bed is 3 x 2m (9ft 9in x 6ft 6in) but here a slightly narrower 1.5-m (4ft 11-in) sheet has been routed. The 'W' is 1.25m (4ft 1in) wide.

**2** With the safety curtain drawn aside, the operator can stop the routing and examine the work. Computer-Aided Manufacture (CAM) enables a single operator to oversee several router beds running simultaneously. Here there are three: one cutting stainless steel (foreground), two cutting Perspex. A vacuum pump holds the sheets firmly on the router bed.

**1** The operator is positioned just above the routing beds, behind a protective safety curtain that shields him or her from the metal swarf (chips or filings) thrown up by the router bit.

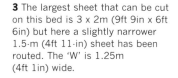

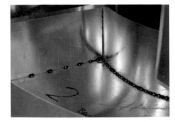

**4** A detail of a very clean 4-mm (approx. ³⁄₁₆-in) wide cut made in the 2.5-mm (approx. ⅛-in) deep stainless steel. Note the point of the 'W' (bottom left). Although the router cuts in a circular fashion (note the rounded outer corner), a perfect point has been achieved on the inner edge.

**5** Large, routed letters can be fabricated into three-dimensional forms for wall mounting. Here the reverse of the letter shows how a strip giving its depth is attached with a welded seam and a support has been spot-welded.

**6** The front face and seams of the welded letter are cleaned off with a sanding disc.

**7** A boss (a hexagonal nut with an internal screw thread) is welded to the reverse of the letter to enable wall mounting.

1

2

**This page:**

1 A stack of stainless steel letters with a cap height of 80cm (31½in) awaits painting.

2 A large, stainless steel 'R'. Note how the base of the letter is refined with a very smooth arc.

3 A huge 1.2-m (4-ft) tall, 20-cm (8-in) deep stainless steel 'T' awaits collection. It can only be moved by fork-lift truck.

4 Letters sprayed with a grey undercoat.

5 The front face of a large display letter with its final top coat.

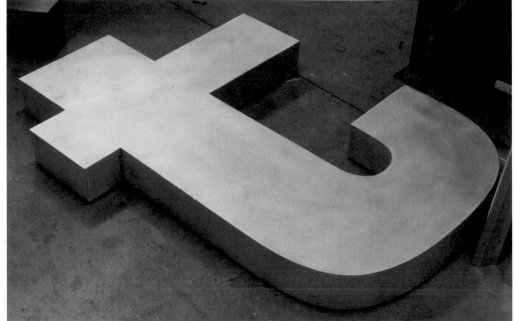

3

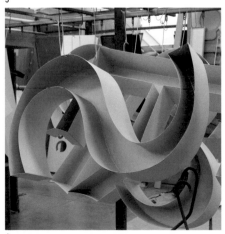

4

5

# 4.6 Water-cut letters

Water forced under very high pressure through a tiny aperture is an effective cutting agent. It is used for cutting stone, concrete and virtually any metal. Water cutting has particular engineering advantages over laser cutting and milling. As the process does not generate heat, the cut metal edge remains true and does not suffer from heat distortion or become brittle. Water cutting is capable of cutting through 8cm (3¼ in) of mild steel with a single pass. It does have some limitations – it only produces 90-degree profiles and is relatively slow. Small machines can cut fine letters with a cap height of 8mm (approx. ⅜in). Most water cutting is used for manufacturing large-scale engineering and architectural components.

## Letters cut by attrition

**1** Although water cutting is a dirty process often associated with heavy engineering, it is driven by computers. Here a series of letters 168cm (5½ft) tall and 8cm (3¼in) deep, designed to stand outside a shopping centre, have been banked together on a scale drawing of the mild-steel sheet from which they are to be cut. The keylines form the cutting path.

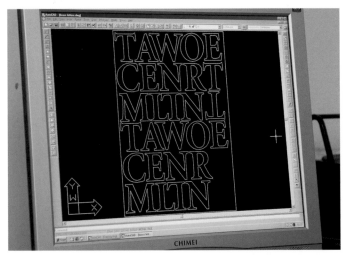

**2** The operator links the keylines together, forming a route (blue) between those elements that require cutting (orange) and areas the jet will pass over. The origin point shows where the water jet will start its journey (bottom left corner).

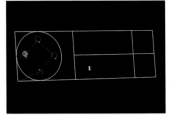

**3** Water cutting uses a combination of the mineral garnet and pressurized water. The percentage of garnet (the cutting agent) to water varies for different materials, as does the speed at which the water jets travel over the surface of the material. A digital control panel allows the operator to adjust the pressure, the proportion of cutting agent to water and the speed and number of passes. Some materials are best cut in a series of shallow passes, while others require a single, deep cut.

**6** The small hole at the tip of the water jet determines the width of the cut. Different size tips are used for cutting different materials. Although the tips are extremely hard, they last for little more than three or four weeks as the garnet enlarges the hole and the tip becomes blunt.

**7** The garnet and pressurized water combine in a chamber just above the jet to minimize machine erosion.

**8** Two jets working in parallel cut a series of strips into a stainless steel sheet. The sheet is supported by a metal grating that stands above a waste tank filled with water to a depth of 100cm (39½in).

**Right:**

**1** Water cutting leaves mild striation on the surface of the metal but has the advantage over laser cutting of not discolouring the edge or making the metal brittle.

**2** The negative letterforms cut in 12mm (approx. ½in) stainless steel…

**3** … and the positive form.

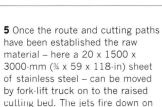
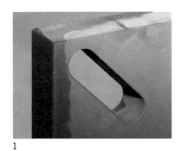

1

2

3

**4** (top) Tiny grains of garnet are sucked from their storage hopper into to a series of pipes and moved towards the water jets. (middle) A very sophisticated compressor builds up the water pressure through a series of cylinders to 281kg per cm² (4000lb per in²).

**5** Once the route and cutting paths have been established the raw material – here a 20 x 1500 x 3000-mm (¾ x 59 x 118-in) sheet of stainless steel – can be moved by fork-lift truck on to the raised cutting bed. The jets fire down on to the surface of the metal. The standing water in the waste tank below dissipates the power of the jet and fills with metal fragments and waste garnet.

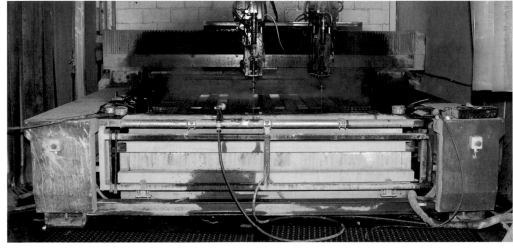

**10** Water from the waste tank is filtered and the clay-like sediment at the bottom is pumped out. This industrial waste is taken off site to be filtered and dried. The metal fragments are magnetically removed before being recycled.

**9** A detail of a cutting jet showing how the pressurized water is deflected as the cut is made from right to left. The water vaporizes into steam as it hits the metal; the noise is deafening.

**Above:** A negative shape is left in the waste steel sheet showing how the origin point for beginning the cut has been positioned away from the edge of the letterform (bottom left) so as to produce a very fine edge.

# 4.7 Hot-wire cutting

**Right:** Sam Oswick built his own long-arm hot-wire cutter to make this 3-m (10-ft) polystyrene typographic tower using the typeface he designed, called Buttress which has supporting legs for the lower-case letters.

**Above:** A detail shows the Buttress legs and connectives, and the modular structure of the tower, which was built in short sections.

Polystyrene was accidentally discovered in 1839 by Eduard Simon, a Berlin chemist, who distilled the resin of a sweetgum tree into an oily substance. After several days the resin had thickened and expanded into a jelly, which Simon named styrol oxide. It was not until 1959 that the Koppers Company in Pittsburgh, Pennsylvania, developed expanded polystyrene (EPS) foam.

Polystyrene foams are relatively cheap to produce and are as strong as unalloyed aluminium but far lighter. Their properties of low weight and high volume provide good buoyancy, sound and impact absorption, and excellent temperature absorption. Sheet and block polystyrene is produced in a range of densities and sizes. Standard sheets may be up to 3m (10ft) square and 500mm (19¾in) thick, while blocks are characteristically 2.5m (8ft 2in) long by 1.5m (5ft) square. Polystyrene can be cut cold using a sharp knife, which slices through the beads, or sawn by hand or machine with a very fine tooth blade. Lettering with complex three-dimensional curves can be reproduced in polystyrene by injecting pellets into an enclosed mould (*see* p.175), or by CAM milling. Polystyrene can be profile-cut using CAM routing (like the beads used for metal routing, *see* pp.148–49) or by hot wire. Hot-wire cutting involves electrically heating a steel wire to a temperature which instantly melts the polystyrene. The depth of the cut is limited by the length of the wire, while the length of the machine's elbow determines the maximum sheet width. Since the late 1960s large-scale letters cut with 90-degree profiles using a hot wire have been very popular with designers working on museum presentations, exhibitions, advertising, theatre props, trade shows, retail displays, shop windows and carnival floats.

The Graphics Workshop, featured in the following process, is a small, specialist company that offers a range of lettering production processes for exhibitions and retail displays.

## Cutting letters from polystyrene

**1** The hot-wire cutter consists of a long arm and a piece of wire under tension through which an electrical current is passed. The current heats the wire and cuts the polystyrene by melting it. Polystyrene letters can be cut unfaced or faced with a colour. The unfaced polystyrene has a slightly pitted white surface, but faced lettering can be smooth and produced in a pantone colour.

**2** (top) A keyline of the letter is enlarged to the correct size and printed out on a piece of paper. This guide is spray-mounted to the selected colour sheet which has a vinyl, water-resistant finish. The letter is cut along the keyline (bottom) through both layers with a scalpel.

**3** The reverse of the letter is sprayed with permanent adhesive and attached to the front face of a polystyrene sheet. Polystyrene sheets can be as thin as 4mm (approx. ³/₁₆in) or as thick as 150mm (6in).

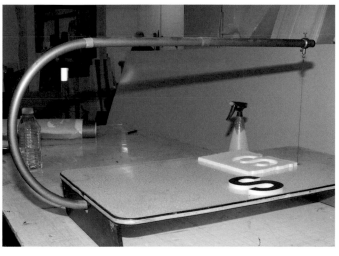

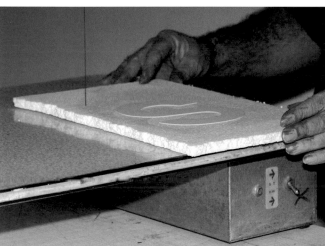

**4** The machine is switched on and the wire quickly becomes hot. A cut is made from the edge of the sheet up to the letter. The slightly raised surface of the letter forms an excellent guide. The operator slides the sheet round the hot-wire-cutter to the edge of the letter.

**5** The completed letter has a very smooth cut finish, as the hot wire melts the surface.

**6** Turpentine is dabbed on to the front face of the paper guide loosening it from the letter. The paper guide is peeled off to reveal the coloured vinyl.

**7** The remnants of the glue are removed and the clean vinyl letter is revealed. Letters can be faced with matt, silk or gloss vinyls. They can be glued or attached to a surface using crack-back paper (double-sided adhesive paper).

# 4.8 Laser cutting and etching

The word laser is an acronym for 'light amplification by stimulated emission of radiation', a term coined by Gordon Gould, a student working on his doctorate at Columbia University in the United States in 1957. A laser is a beam of light produced by passing electrical energy into a reflective cavity containing what physicists call a gain medium (any material which increases the amplification, or power, of the light by stimulated emissions). The most simple explanation is a series of mirrors positioned around the gain medium which reflect light back and forth. With each pass through the medium the light is amplified, thus increasing its power. The repetition of this process of amplification continues until eventually the light escapes the cavity through a semi-transparent mirror and is emitted as an intense, collimated beam (the edges of the beam are parallel). The gain medium can take any state – gas, liquid, solid or plasma. The first laser used a ruby as the gain medium and is therefore referred to as a solid-state laser. Chemical lasers are powered by a chemical reaction, dye lasers use an organic liquid dye as the gain medium, while phototonic lasers use photons. Each of these types of laser has a different technical specification. Some are designed to produce very high, continuous power at a specific amplitude, and some to produce consistent, low power; others pulse, and have a variable power range or beam width.

The narrow, powerful beam of the laser is perfectly suited to recreating the line of an engineer's digital drawing produced in a computer-aided design (CAD) program. As a consequence, heavy and light engineering firms were quick to adopt CAD and Computer-Aided Manufacture (CAM) systems in combination with laser-cutting technology for cutting fabricated parts.

Today, lasers are used for profile-cutting. Engineers realized that by speeding the pass time and not allowing the laser to cut completely through a surface, relief letters and patterns could also be laser etched (cut down in relief below the surface). The fashion industry picked up on the use of lasers for mass-producing pattern pieces in bulk and for removing pile from velvet to reproduce devoré patterns and lettering. In the last 15 years graphic designers, typographers, publishers and sign manufacturers have begun to use laser profile cutting and etching for the reproduction of many forms of lettering, environmental signs, printed ephemera, birthday cards, pop-up books and stationery. The process at Central Saint Martins College of Art and Design, London, shown here, is used in almost equal measure by graphic, industrial and fashion designers.

**1** The laser is positioned and guided by a keyline drawing created from a typeface or the outline of a drawn form on a computer screen. The keyline forms a path along which the laser is guided as it traverses the cutting table. The operator assigns the order and direction in which is to travel, and can identify points at which the laser is to be turned off, automatically repositioned, and turned on again to begin a new cutting path.

**2** The chosen material is positioned on the cutting bed. The origin point is set by 'x' and 'y' coordinates, through a keypad. This determines the origin point from which the laser will begin its first cutting path.

**3** The cutting program is run and the laser automatically positions itself at the origin point (seen here as a red dot) and begins its first cutting path. The material used here is unfinished 6-mm (¼-in) birch plywood. More powerful lasers are able to cut thicker and denser material.

**4** Guided by the keyline, the laser cuts curves, straight edges and square corners with ease. There is no physical contact between the wood and the laser tip which moves 4mm (approx. ³/₁₆in) above it. Heat from the cutting process may distort or weaken some materials along the cutting edge. Laser beams vary in width, only the most expensive machines allow the operator to change beam width. Allowance for the cutting width of the beam must be made when making the scale drawing of the keyline.

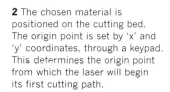

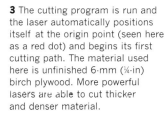

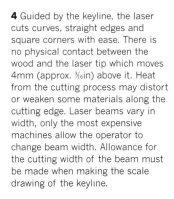

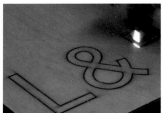

**6** Once the cutting is complete, the positive letters are lifted from the sheet. The cutting process can produce stencils, negative letterforms and positive shapes equally easily. Script letterforms with many connectives are well suited to laser cutting.

**7** A detail of the counter form, which has been removed to reveal the sophisticated curves produced through laser cutting.

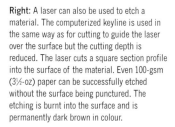

**5** Only the edge of the wood is burnt through. The front face appears to be burnt at the corners but this is merely black dust particles which can easily be wiped away.

**Right:** A laser can also be used to etch a material. The computerized keyline is used in the same way as for cutting to guide the laser over the surface but the cutting depth is reduced. The laser cuts a square section profile into the surface of the material. Even 100-gsm (3½-oz) paper can be successfully etched without the surface being punctured. The etching is burnt into the surface and is permanently dark brown in colour.

# 4.9 Pop-up and paper lettering

1

2

Lettering is often created on paper with drawing and calligraphy or reproduced in print; however, many artists and designers have used paper to create relief and three-dimensional letterforms through a range of techniques.

1 Celia Kilner, who works as a calligrapher and stone carver, produced this blind embossed lettering piece *Deep Peace*, using hand-made paper pulp pressed into a mould.

2 Illustrator Alida Sayer printed the same text on to the sheets in a stack of paper, then progressively cut away sections of each sheet. The sheets are hung slightly apart, from two long pegs, and combine to create distorted three-dimensional lettering. The quote is adapted from a line in Kurt Vonnegut's novel *Slaughterhouse-Five*.

Artists and designers have used paper to make lettering impressions or pop-up forms in a variety of different ways. Pop-up letters use sheets of folded paper which are either die-cut or laser-cut (*see* pp.154–55) to create letterforms that stand in a 90-degree fold or rise from a sheet of paper opened through 180 degrees. Pop-up cards and books, which make use of three-dimensional lettering, became popular in the middle of the nineteenth century. New techniques, coupled with the use of pop-ups in fiction and non-fiction texts, have ensured their continuing popularity.

Pop-ups are generally undertaken by graphic designers who specialize in this form of paper engineering, working with sheets of paper, scalpel, bone folders, tape and glue. They measure, draw, fold and remould sheets until the letter rises smoothly from the opening page. The designer of a pop-up makes many developmental prototypes using different techniques and paper stocks before producing a presentation dummy and drawing a production net - a flat outline on which folds, cuts and glue points are marked. Today these are drawn digitally in software programs such as Freehand and Illustrator.

Paper pulp can be moulded into letters or formed into egg boxes and similar packaging, but lettering artists have also developed ways of moulding relief letters (*see* p.174) in paper pulp, allowing it to dry and retain the impression.

# 4.10 Machine engraving

The first mechanical engraving machine was invented c.1798 by Nicholas-Jacques Conté. One of Napoleon's savants, intellectuals and academics he was given the task of studying Egyptian culture and natural history during the French invasion of Egypt. He had an aptitude for mechanical devices, and realising the enormity of the task of printing images of the expedition's findings using hand engraving (*see* pp.158–59) he set about making a mechanical engraving machine. His device featured a large table onto which the copper plate was locked down. The surface of the plate was straddled by a bridging arm which allowed the burin – the cutting blade – to move both horizontally and vertically, cutting lines in the copper to a consistent depth and width. By adjusting the cutting depth of the burin, the line width, and depth of engraving, and therefore the grey tone in the final print, could be varied. Between 1810 and 1820 a number of manufacturing companies in France and England added pantograph arms; a pantograph consisted of four arms linked in a 'v' and an inverted 'v' shape. Each arm can pivot and crucially the pivot points or linkages, such as the position of the stylus used for tracing the shape, and the cutting burin, can be moved. This allows a drawing or pattern to be copied same size; or, by shifting the relative position of the pivots, it can be enlarged or reduced from an original pattern. Here engraver Keith Raes uses a mechanical engraving machine to both engrave and profile-cut stencils from a pattern into brass sheets.

## Machine-engraved lettering

1 The engraving machine consists of two tables connected by a pantograph (a pair of interlocking arms). A 'pattern' (a series of engraved right-reading letters or numerals placed in the appropriate order to spell out a word or figure, and guide the cutting point) is locked to the upper table. The 'job' (the piece to be engraved) is locked to the lower table.

2 Engraved brass letter patterns in a range of fonts are used as guides for the pantograph. Individual right-reading letters are arranged like type to form words on the top table of the pantograph.

3 Blanks are used for inter-word spacing. The pantograph handle on the top table is used to trace around the inside of the letterform pattern and these movements are translated exactly to the cutting point on the lower table, but reduced at a scale of 1:10. This reduction minimizes minor irregularities or wobbles in the final cut.

4 On the lower table the cutting point revolves and is guided over the surface of the job producing a letter one-tenth the size of the pattern.

5 A detail of the engraving tip shows how the reduced letterform cut crisply into the surface of the brass sheet. The pantograph can be adjusted by resetting the length of the arms in relation to the pattern to create letters from a single guide at different sizes such as 1:20, 1:5, 1:4. Letters larger than the guide exaggerate inaccuracies.

# 4.11 Hand engraving

**This page:**

1 Master engraver Keith Raes at work on a goblet.

2 The engraver's tool, a small gouge with a quadrangular section, is called a burin or graver. It is made in a variety of widths; the wider the blade, the deeper the cut. The back of a steel burin is rubbed against an oilstone to sharpen it, then stroked with polishing paper to create a mirror finish.

3 The quality of edge can be checked by gently running the burin across the thumb nail. If the edge picks, it is sufficiently sharp to begin engraving.

4 Engravers work extraordinarily close to the object they are engraving and use a jeweller's enlarging eyeglass, which makes the image three or five times bigger.

1

2

3

4

Engraved letters are made by incising lines into a metal plate with a burin or graver, a small chisel-like tool with a quadrangular section. The process was originally developed to decorate precious metal objects. Throughout medieval Europe, goldsmiths and silversmiths were commissioned by the church, monarch, aristocracts and rich landowners to create ceremonial vessels, to decorate jewellery and later to produce seals and signet rings that made use of highly elaborate initials and heraldic crests. In the seventeenth and eighteenth centuries engravers began to work on decorative clocks and, later, watches. Their work was functional as well as decorative; they incised the names, numerals, increments and scale on new brass scientific instruments such as measures, rulers, thermometers, compasses and sextants. Many metals can be engraved – iron, pewter, zinc and copper – but they must be softer than the tip of the graver; the harder the metal, the greater the effort required by the engraver.

Today, although the number of skilled hand engravers has declined, the two aspects of the craft – silversmithing (decorating objects) and plate engraving (designing for print) – have survived. Apprentices are very rare and the master craftsmen of the Engravers' Guild tend to be an ageing group. There is a sense in which the process has turned full circle and returned to its craft roots so it is now cherished by artist printmakers, private presses, silversmiths and jewellers.

**1** In this example two small, silver goblets are being engraved with the same text. The engraved lettering for the second goblet must match that of the first. By rubbing Plasticine on to the engraved letters the surface of the silver is made slightly sticky.

**2** A strip of thick paper is wrapped round the first goblet, and a burnishing tool is rubbed over the lettering to transfer an impression of the letters to the paper.

**3** The centre of the lettering is marked with a silver dot, and the strip of paper is turned round so that the lettering is wrong-reading. The paper is then wrapped around the second goblet. The nick is aligned with the mark and the paper impression is matched to the height of the first goblet.

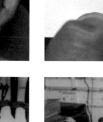

**4** By gently burnishing the back of the paper impression grease from the Plasticine, which has stuck to the paper, is passed to the second goblet producing a faint lustre and a legible letterform. To draw letters on to a silver piece, jeweller's powder in a small bag is patted on to the surface and a soft chinagraph pencil used.

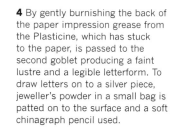

**5** Careful measurements are required to ensure the lettering is positioned in exactly the same position on the second goblet as on the first. Here the cap height of the grease impression is checked with a pair of dividers.

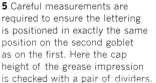

**6** The engraver uses a pile of jeweller's cushions filled with soft silver sand. These support the work and lift it above the bench and nearer to the engraver's eye.

**7** A silver duster is placed over the cushions and the goblet is rested on top of it. The engraver works close up to the goblet with a magnifying eyeglass. The engraver cuts the broad, vertical stroke of the letter using three parallel lines.

**8** With each cut the graver is dug into the metal surface, the hand turned down and then pushed forward. Waste metal is curled away from the surface and a sharp-edged V-cut is created.

**Above:** Curved lines require greater control as both the piece and the graver are gradually turned in opposition to each other. Each cut removes metal which cannot be replaced so this is no place for mistakes. The curved cuts are run into the broad strokes. As with many hand-carving skills, the engraver seems to be cutting the letterform almost as much from kinetic memory as by eye. The deeper the cut, the greater the effort required as the metal offers significant resistance. Serifs are added last and are cut from their point towards the broad vertical stroke of the letter; they define the baseline and visually unify the lettering.

**Above:** The finished lettering is polished to remove tiny burrs (rough edges) at either end of the line. The engraver seeks to keep the depth of cut consistent, the proportions of the letters regular, and the letter spacing even. The engraver takes care to place the lettering sympathetically on the piece.

**Above:** A hand-engraved, copper printing plate of an entire monogram alphabet. Raes cut this sample, using highly decorative letterforms, over two months to demonstrate the quality of hand engraving.

**Opposite:**

**Top:** In the early thirteenth century, in what are now southern Germany and Switzerland, engraving was adapted so that an image could be printed on to parchment or paper directly from a copper plate. The principle of the adaption was to make the engraved image in reverse. An image or letter was drawn on to a copper plate reverse-reading and then engraved by incising lines into the surface. This engraved copper plate shows the quality of the lettering that a skilled engraver could produce.

**Bottom:** The engraving plate was polished and rolled with ink. Excess ink lying on the surface of the plate was cleaned away with a rag, leaving a residue of ink in the engraved lines below the surface of the plate. The inked plate was then placed face-up on a simple press, a sheet of paper was laid over it and pressure was applied. The moist ink was drawn out of the engraved grooves on the plate on to the paper, creating this right-reading image.

# 4.12 Glass-engraving

**Above:** The glass engraver Lesley Pyke works at a bench with an electrical engraving tool. She wears a protective mask and glasses as small glass dust is dangerous.

Engraving images and lettering on a glass using an abrasive stone stylus is a hand technique that stretches back to ancient Roman times. Hand styli are still made but most engravers now work with an electric stylus in which a tiny abrasive stone, a burr, revolves in a small chuck (the jaws of a drill, which are tightened on the burr). This tool enables the engraver to work faster but the process is still referred to as hand engraving even though the tool revolves across the surface rather than being rubbed. There are three basic engraving depths: surface engraving, up to 10 per cent of the glass depth, intaglio or deep engraving up to 40 per cent of the glass depth (beyond this the structural integrity of the glass is threatened and is likely to break); and relief or cameo engraving where the letter is made to stand proud of the surface by engraving back the ground.

**Right:**

1 A hand-engraved plate with text.

2 Detail of the plate's edge.

3 An engraved crest which combines sandblasting for the lettering and hand engraving for the image.

1

2

3

**1** The engraver may draw lettering directly on to the surface of a glass using a fine felt-tip pen or chinagraph pencil, or set type and use a paper pattern as a guide. A laser printout in the correct size is taped inside the glass. Here Pyke uses a simple wooden frame to clamp the glass in place.

**2** The quality of the engraving is improved by wet cutting as opposed to dry abrasion. A gravity drip, a small tube that runs from a plastic bottle to a tap providing a constant drip on to the area of the engraving, is set up over the work.

**3** (top) The tiny burrs come in many different shapes, sizes and degrees of hardness and are stored in a wooden block. Burrs for cutting have tiny diamond particles that scratch the glass, while stone burrs smooth the glass. Black stone burrs take glass back to clear and rubber burrs are used to polish the glass. (bottom) A burr is set in the chuck of the electrically operated stylus.

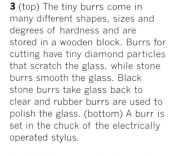

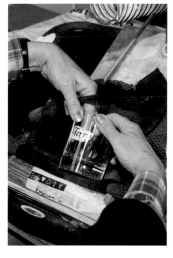

**4** Some engravers work from the centre of a letterform but Pyke prefers to trace the outline using the finest 1.2-mm (approx. 1/16-in) point burr. The electric stylus is held in one hand and the speed is controlled with a foot pedal.

**5** The outline complete, Pyke begins to work into the letterforms deepening the abrasion with a 2.35-mm (approx. 1/8-in) burr. These letters are being profile-engraved like the sandblasted ones (*see* pp.145–47) but hand engraving can be used to produce a progressive cut (one that starts shallow but gradually deepens).

**6** It takes nearly half an hour to complete the basic lettering, which can have further decoration of different depths applied.

**Left:** An enlarged detail of the engraving reveals the circular pattern within the letterform cut by the rotating burr.

# 4.13 Acid-etching glass

The process of using acid to surface-etch lettering and imagery on glass is widely used in all areas of the glass trade. A stained-glass artist will etch individual flash glass pieces as part of a large window. Acid paste is used as an alternative to hand engraving or sandblasting for small decorative pieces, while flood etching is used to create opaque imagery and large-scale lettering on architecture. Many of the acid-etching effects created on glass used for architecture have been re-created using vinyl films (*see* pp.124–25), sandblasting (*see* pp.145–47) and screen printing (*see* pp.106–09). The effects of cheaper architectural vinyls may be indistinguishable from those created by etching, depending on the viewing distance, the nature of the mounting (face or reverse) and the lighting conditions. In recent years architects and interior and exhibition designers have begun to use vinyl and acid-etched glass in combination within a single scheme – the etched glass on exterior façades and the matching vinyl on interior panes – to achieve a visually unified and quality finish.

Acid etching has some unique qualities that cannot be reproduced by vinyls – principally edge lighting. Etching leaves a recess in the face of the glass, which has a return edge that can be illuminated as light passes both through the face and along the length of the glass. If the outside edge of a sheet of glass sits directly on a light source, such as a fluorescent tube, the light will pass through the glass until it reaches the etched return which it illuminates. The illuminated return line is visible from the front and reverse face. All four sides of a sheet of glass can be edge-lit with lighting that can be varied with different colour filters. Super-clear glass, with few impurities, such as Optiwhite, allows light to travel up to 4m (13ft 1in) or 5m (16ft 5in) and through butted sheets to sucessfully illuminate an etched line. Designers and artists have been able to exploit acid-etching and lighting combinations for imagery and lettering that can appear to float ethereally within the sheet.

Acid etching is used to create several different effects, depending on the type of glass and acid combination. The length of exposure to, and the strength of, the acid determine the depth of the etch, while the type and strength of the acid determine the coarseness of the finish. Strong acid produces a rougher finish than diluted acid. Transparent lettering in clear, lead glass and some low-silicate glass is produced using hydrofluoric acid followed by a cleaning process. In other glass types it is produced with combinations of strong hydrofluoric and sulphuric acid. Translucent lettering is produced using diluted hydrofluoric acid, which leaves a slightly roughened, matt surface. Acid-etched lettering with a more delicate satin finish is made by adding potassium fluoride to a mineral acid. A pearl finish is made by first coarse-etching glass using a strong bifluoride (partially diluted) mixture followed by a much diluted version of the same bifluoride, which produces two subtle layers that refract light slightly differently. A white finish is produced with an ammonium bi-fluoride mixture.

Acid-etched letters can be painted directly on to glass with a brush, usually positive translucent on clear. Colour can also be added to acid-etched lettering in glass through painting. An oil-based ink is used, mixed with ammonium bifluoride as an additional bonding agent. Similar surface effects to those produced through acid etching, vinyls and sandblasting can be achieved through screen printing, where the colours can be Pantone-specified and slightly smaller type can be reproduced (down to 12pt with reasonably robust strokes and serifs). Acid etching can be used in combination with flash glass to produce coloured, transparent lettering out of coloured or clear glass, or clear lettering out of coloured glass. In the last 30 years glass technology has advanced significantly and glass is now used in combination with clear resins with the transparent qualities of glass. It can be cold-poured and chemically cured; therefore not requiring a furnace. Resin can carry opaque colour and translucent or transparent stains which can be poured into cavities on the front or reverse face created by acid-etching.

## Etching lettering on glass

**1** (left) A scale drawing of a design for a glass panel to be acid-etched shows the scale relative to a figure. This artwork for the acid resist is transferred on to a screen using ultraviolet light. The resist consists of a clear or white, acid-resistant oil-based ink that is screen-printed on to the surface of the glass.

**2** The etching room has metal trays for simple double-sided frosting and acid benches (shown here) for flood etching. A sheet of glass with a clear resist rests on strips of old carpet awaiting the building of a small putty wall which will retain the acid pool. Note the very powerful extraction fan and the distressing of the concrete floor caused by the acid.

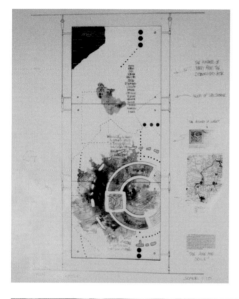

**3** When flood etching, the acid only has contact with one side of the glass. Parts of the sheet can be isolated to create different etching depths. A sticky oil-based putty is used to create a wall to contain the acid. The white, masked area around the edge and small circles will remain clear. The diluted hydrofluoric acid will be poured on to the glass and allowed to etch for 30 minutes. The etching process produces noxious fumes, which must be sucked away by a powerful air purification system.

Acid etching can be combined with gilding (where gold leaf or gold paint is applied thinly to a surface) to produce gild-etched shapes and letterforms. Throughout the nineteenth century and until the 1930s, when it fell into decline, gild etching was used on decorative mirrors, windows and shop fascias. Etched and gilded letterforms were usually produced wrong-reading on the reverse of the sheet so that the external side exposed to the elements was smooth glass. With the renewed interest in the preservation and restoration of older buildings, the skills of glass-gilding have been revived. Brewery and hotel chains, who have based their brand image on traditional values associated with craftsmanship, are using quality decorative finishes when restoring windows and mirrors. The application of gold leaf to acid-etched lettering, as well as copper and platinum gilding, is also popular for signage in the reception areas, boardrooms and offices of prestigious companies. Nero Glass have developed a range of samples using different etching techniques (*see* below).

## Gallery of acid-etched glass

Exit sign with 8-mm (approx. ¼-in) profile etched on the reverse and infilled with paint

Satin-etching on mirror glass, sandblasted and resin infilled.

Painted front face.

Tinted resin front face

Acid-etched and white gilded.

The reverse of the '507' shows how the gilding sits on the surface of the letterform.

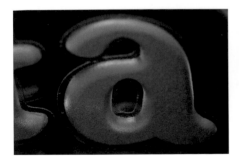

Rounded forms produced by deep sandblasting are partially acid-etched to achieve a satin finish.

Detail from an acid-etched panel. The basic panel is splatter etched (acid is dropped unevenly on the surface). The blue and black sections have been resin-infilled and the outline of the letters are gilded. The opaque inside of the word Chelsea is smooth acid-etched (evenly exposed for a consistent time).

Acid-etched glass with a numeral painted on the reverse and gilding on the left.

This is newness: every little tawdry
Obstacle glass-wrapped and peculiar,
Glinting and clinking in a saint's falsetto. Only you
Don't know what to make of the sudden slippiness,
The blind, white, awful, inaccessible slant.
There's no getting up it by the words you know.
No getting up by elephant or wheel or shoe.
We have only come to look. You are too new
To want the world in a glass hat.

New Year on Dartmoor          Sylvia Plath

**Above:** A 2-m$^2$ (21-ft$^2$) acid-etched glass installation produced by Nero glass and designed by Stuart Bourne, works within a landscape. The poem by Sylvia Plath is set in Gill Sans and is clear; the acid has been applied to the opaque back of the sheet.

# 4.14 Photographic etching

Photographic etching is a compound of two processes: photography and acid etching. It was originally developed in the 1970s for the manufacture of small, metal components for printed circuit boards, but has been adopted by a far wider manufacturing base, including architecture, exhibition design, interiors, graphic design and modelmaking. The accuracy of etching is ideally suited to reproducing letterforms. The process can be used in three main ways: surface etching; stencil or hole etching; and profile etching. Surface etching leaves the letters recessed below the surface of the metal. Stencil etching allows the acid to bite completely through the plate, creating a letter-shaped hole. Profile etching is the reverse of stencil etching: the metal surrounding the letter is etched away leaving the positive shape of the letter.

## Etching letters into metal

**1** The process must take place in a dust-free atmosphere as any tiny particles of dust falling on the plate will be reproduced through the etching. Here metal sheets up to a maximum of 75cm (29½in) square are coated with a light-sensitive photographic resist, which is black or transparent depending on the type of metal.

**2** The artwork is transferred to the surface of the plate. If the plate is to be surface etched it is exposed on one side only; for stencil or profile etching both sides are exposed. In either case a photographic negative masks the areas to be etched, which are exposed to ultraviolet light in the exposure unit.

**3** The exposed metal plate is moved into the darkroom (illuminated by a safe light) and placed on a conveyor belt from where it is passed into an automatic developing machine. The resist is developed in the exposed areas of the plate and washed away in the masked areas.

**7** Here a pile of exposed plates is interleaved with paper to prevent the surface of the resist being scratched. Any scratch or blemish would be etched into the surface of the metal.

**8** The metal sheets are laid on flat carriers which travel through the etching machine on a conveyor belt. The operator feeds them through in batches.

**9** The acid is only able to eat into the areas on the plate not protected by the resist. With each pass through the machine a depth of 0.2mm (approx. ½in) is etched. The metal sheets are returned via conveyor belt to the beginning of the process, where they are checked by the operator and passed through the process again until the required depth is reached.

The artwork can be digital or paper based and is supplied by the designer. The designer specifies the type and gauge of the metal. Virtually any metal can be etched but those used most frequently are brass, copper, stainless steel, nickel silver and mild steel. Surface etching can be used on sheets of almost any thickness but is characteristically used on sheets between 0.3mm (approx. ½in) and 6mm (¼in) as it is limited by a simple rule of thumb – the width of the hole should not be significantly less than the thickness of the plate. Therefore, if small type with very fine serifs is to be stencil etched it is the width of the serifs that will determine the maximum thickness of the metal plate.

**4** The developing machine automatically completes the plate preparation by fixing and drying the metal sheet and rolling it out into a daylight area.

**5** Like so much of this process, the etching is automated and very high-tech. Both the type of acid, and the strength at which it is used, depend on the metal and the depth of etch required. The metal sheets pass through the etching machine on a conveyor belt. The viewing windows at the front allow the operator to observe the etching as it occurs, but most of the process is monitored automatically.

**6** The metal is not dipped into baths as with traditional etching but sprayed with pressurized acid. The strength of the acid and the exposure time determine the depth of the etch. Stencil or profile etching involves dissolving large amounts of metal, so sheets are sprayed and etched from both sides. The registration of the resist must therefore be exact. The reverse of the machine shows the complex system of pipes which feed the acid to the jets within.

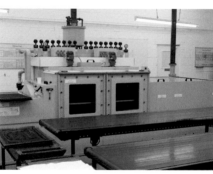

**10** When the operator is satisfied that the etch is the required depth, the sheet is passed to the cleaning area. If it has been stencil- or profile-etched the components or letters are complete. The resist is washed off in a series of baths, and finally cleaned in a stream of water before being placed in an electric dryer.

**11** A thin, etched sheet of brass is cut by hand with scissors before being bagged up for delivery to a client.

**12** Colour can be added to the surface of the metal sheet either through screen printing or by filling in an etched recess. The infill colours use a stove-enamelling process. Colour is wiped into the recess in liquid form and the surface is wiped clean. The metal sheet is then placed in an oven and heated to 120°C (248°F), to harden the colour in the recess.

Cut, engraved and etched three-dimensional lettering

1

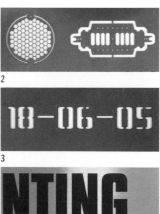

2

3

4

**This page:**
1 A record sleeve produced by Warp Records using photographically etched stainless steel.

2 The fine detail possible with photographic profile etching. Lines of 0.15mm (approx. ¹⁄₁₆₀in) can be etched into metal providing the steel is not thicker than the rule is wide.

3 Detail of photographically etched stencil forms.

4 An example of photo 'engraving'. The acid does not eat through the entire plate; here the lettering has been infilled with a coloured resin.

675

# Moulded and cast three-dimensional lettering

Moulded and cast three-dimensional lettering

**Above:** Rendered lettering was very popular in the nineteenth century. It gave the appearance of stone carving yet cost significantly less, and was frequently used on both cultural and commercial buildings. Here the lettering above the door of the Cultural League building in Bucharest, Hungary has a grey and silver paint infill.

**Right:** During the nineteenth century decorative paint schemes were used with rendering. Here both the ground (green) and letterforms (yellow) have been painted after rendering.

Rendered lettering can be incised or built in relief and is made by plastering around a profile-cut, wooden letterform. The process is relatively quick compared with stone cutting and is ideally suited to brick-built buildings. Rendered lettering varies not only in style but also in the manner of its production. Some nineteenth-century, rendered signs are made up of individual characters (no two 'Es' are identical) implying that the letterforms were hand-drawn separately. Other signs make use of identical characters which were drawn, traced, copied and finally cut out as wooden profiles. The depth of the wooden letter determined the relief height of the rendered letter.

A brick wall would be surface rendered and allowed to dry. Incised letters used positive right-reading wooden letterforms arranged along a baseline on the newly dried cement. Once the letters were correctly spaced and positioned, they were nailed to the wall. More cement was mixed and the surface built up using a trowel. The cement render was raised to the height of the wooden letterforms, smoothed, then allowed to dry and harden for several days before the wood profiles were prised away, leaving a clean debossed (below the surface) letter. The process of building relief lettering was the same but the wooden letterform was a right-reading negative, effectively a wooden stencil (*see* stencil lettering, pp.70–71). Counters were made as separate profiles. The smooth, rendered surface of the lettering was either painted a single colour, relying on the play of light and shadow to define the letterforms (*see* opposite), or infilled with a complementary colour.

Today rendered lettering has seen a small revival with the growth in popularity of traditional pubs where nineteenth-century lettering has been reinstated to the original design on many gables. The principles of rendered lettering have been adopted in many more recent building projects which use concrete cast lettering cured on site around wooden forms.

**Opposite:** The gable end of an east London locksmith shows how large, rendered lettering can be produced. This lettering was probably completed within a week, whereas carving on this scale would probably have taken several months.

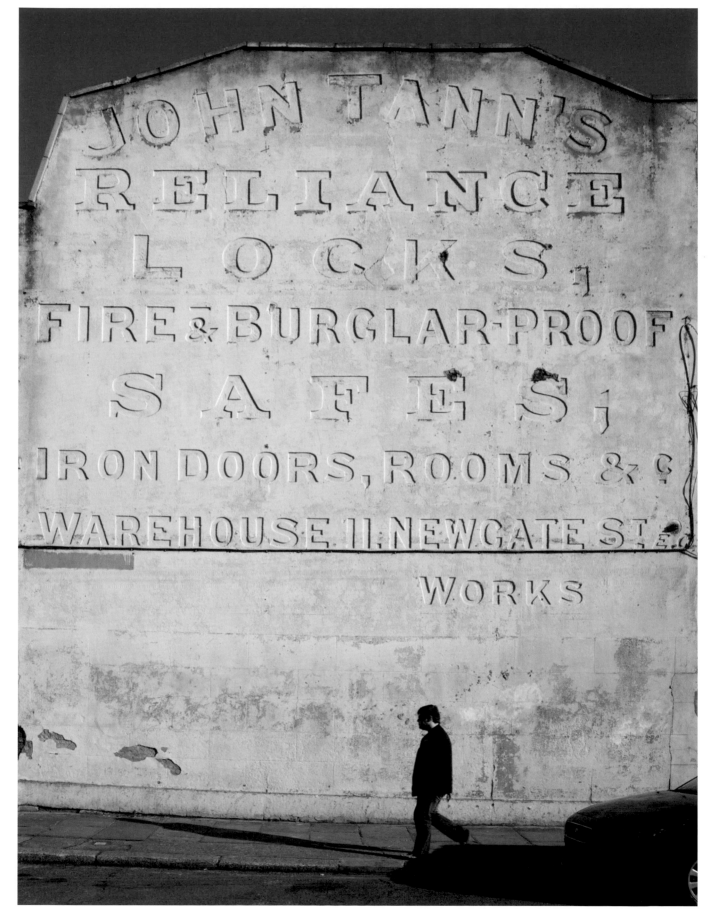

1

4

5

6

2

3

7

**Above left:**

Lettering can be moulded into paper while it is in a liquid or pulp state.

**1** The base of a strawberry punnet shows lettering which is debossed but is actually formed by spraying recycled paper pulp over a male, wrong-reading mould. The box is then dried and the paper fixed.

**2** Watermarks in moulded or hand-made papers such as Saunders Waterford produced at St Cuthberts Mill, Somerset.

**3** The watermark is visible when held to the light as the paper over the letterform is thinner than the rest of the sheet.

**Above right:**

Relief and debossed lettering are produced by trapping a dampened sheet of paper under pressure between a male and female mould. The paper sheet has been pressed down over a right-reading, male letterform. The letters appear raised on the surface. The lettering in (**4**) has a flat profile while (**5**) has a rounded letterface and (**6**) an inverted V-profile, determined by the mould.

**7** Here the lettering is debossed. The paper was laid over a right-reading, female mould and the male mould was pressed down on it.

Paper pulp, long associated with egg boxes, is increasingly being used as an environmentally friendly alternative to polystyrene packaging (see opposite). Paper is both sustainable – trees can be grown sufficiently quickly to match demand – and potentially 100 per cent recyclable. Pulp packaging can be made entirely of recycled paper. Three-dimensional packaging forms, which may include lettering, logos and symbols, are created around the outside of a gauze mould. The cost of tooling to make the mould depends on the complexity of the form required. The pulp is made by dropping bundles of waste paper into a huge cylinder of water which is then mixed with a mechanical paddle. The paper quickly becomes saturated and begins to break down into individual fibres which are stirred into a soup or slurry (a liquid paper pulp). The grey or brown slurry can be cleaned by adding bleach to remove the colour of the printing ink but this is very environmentally unfriendly as it leaves large quantities of polluted water. The pulp is pumped to a tank into which the gauze form is dipped, in a similar way to paper making. The wet pulp is sucked into the sides of the gauze form, making the individual paper fibres bond together. The paper form is then dried by electric heaters until solid. The lettering can be moulded debossed (below the surface) or embossed (raised above the surface). The outside of the form generally has a rough texture while the inside, which is closest to the gauze mesh, is smooth. A smooth surface, however, can be produced on both sides by using a double mould.

Watermarks are made by placing a letterform, made from wire thread, over the mesh of a paper deckle (a device in paper making for limiting the size of the sheet). The deckle is lowered into a vat of liquid pulp. The water drains through the mesh leaving the paper fibres on its surface.

# 5.3 Polystyrene moulding

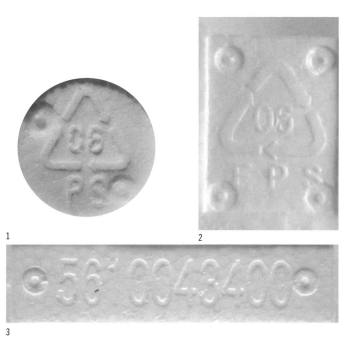

1

2

3

4

**Above and right:**

**1** Polystyrene packaging is generally marked with recycling marks and batch numbers.

**2 and 3** Numerals and lettering moulded into polystyrene packaging forms.

**4** Large blocks of expanded polystyrene can be cut into forms and sprayed with a special acrylic pigment.

Polystyrene is widely used as a relatively cheap packaging material due to its many useful properties: it is light, waterproof, impact-resistant (minimizing breakage through cushioning), has excellent insulation properties, is highly buoyant and can be easily moulded and cut with a hot wire. Lettering can be made in four ways using expanded polystyrene (EPS): moulded into three-dimensional letters; surface moulded; and profile cut or sculpted using an electrically heated hot-wire cutter. Polystyrene moulding is a three-phase process. EPS beads are tiny spheres that can be expanded to up to 40 times their original size through a controlled chemical reaction. Careful timing of this expansion determines the size of the bead: small beads produce dense, heavier polystyrene, larger beads offer a more forgiving cushion. Once expanded to the required size, beads are stored for up to 48 hours in canvas silos where they gradually absorb air. The expanded beads are poured into a metal mould in a letter or packaging form. In the mould they are subjected to an intense steam heat followed by pressure which softens the spheres so that they fuse together to form a single, dense form. The polystyrene form is then removed from its mould and allowed to cool. By introducing particles of carbon, a black polystyrene can be made. Both moulded and profile-cut polystyrene letters are not durable enough for prolonged exterior use. They also have poor load-bearing qualities and so tend to be used as a relatively cheap form of temporary interior lettering for exhibitions and retail displays.

# 5.4 Vacuum-forming and thermoforming

The terms vacuum–forming and thermoforming are frequently used interchangeably, as the processes are very similar. Both are used to pull plastic sheet materials over a mould. Vacuum-forming relies on a reduction of atmospheric pressure caused by a pump sucking air from a chamber, while thermoforming uses a combination of a vacuum and a heating element to soften the plastic first. Vacuum-forming was first used to manufacture light bulbs around the beginning of the twentieth century but, today, it is used for a vast range of products – such as liners for vehicle doors, baths, toys, shop signs and blister packaging – all of which may include lettering.

## Plastic lettering

**2** The artwork for the lettering is reproduced as a metal or polymer plate. This can be photographically etched (*see* pp.168–70), engraved or polymer exposed. Relief lettering is made using a relief, right-reading plate, while debossed lettering is made using a relief, wrong-reading plate.

**1** A small thermoforming unit for producing blister packs, chocolate box liners and small signs. The stainless steel unit consists of a vacuum pump beneath a gauze sheet and a hinged lid containing an electrical heating element. Controls on the front of the unit vary the temperature and vacuum.

**3** The letters on this metal plate are cut with a 10-degree return to make it easier to remove the plastic once it has been moulded. The metal plate is laid square on the base gauze and the plastic sheet is clipped into the supportive frame.

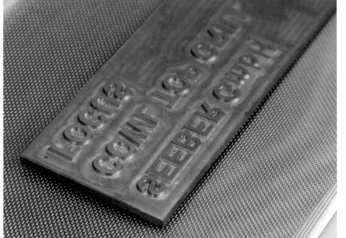

**4** The lid is lowered over the sheet, locked into position and the heating element is turned on. The temperature is set according to the type of plastic. After 90 seconds the plastic sheet becomes pliable and the vacuum pump is turned on.

**7** The completed embossed lettering, clearly defined, is removed and allowed to cool.

**5** The pump is turned off and the unit is opened. As the counters and intercharacter spaces are relatively complex in this particular example, gently stroking the warm plastic encourages it to fall into the desired spaces.

**6** The vacuum pump is used again, and the plastic is moulded tightly round the plate.

Thermoforming is suitable for shaping a wide range of plastics: acrylonitrile butadiene styrene (ABS), polyester copolymer (PETG), polystyrene (PS), polycarbonate (PC), polypropylene (PP), polyethylene (PE), polyvinyl chloride (PVC) and acrylic (PMMA). Many governments have begun to discourage the use of clear plastics in packaging as they are not easily produced using recycled plastic but are manufactured directly from hydrocarbon resources such as oil. It is likely that a combination of legislation and cost, prompted by green initiatives, will restrict the use of first-generation hydrocarbons (used in clear plastic packaging).

**Right:** Poster designed by Paul Elliman and Graphic Thought Facility (founded by Paul Neale and Andy Stevens). Four-colour lithography printing (see pp.102–05) on a 1,000-micron, matt white, plastic sheet was combined with thermoforming round an MDF mould. The poster was produced in Italy by Plasticolor.

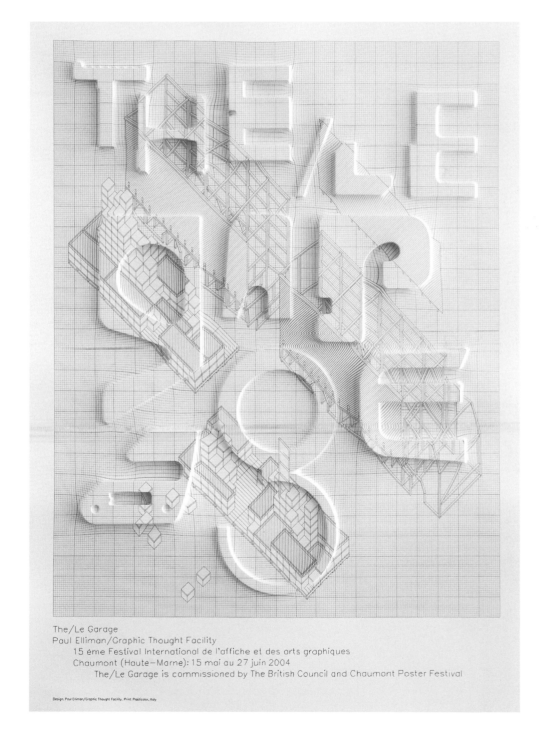

The/Le Garage
Paul Elliman/Graphic Thought Facility
15 éme Festival International de l'affiche et des arts graphiques
Chaumont (Haute—Marne): 15 mai au 27 juin 2004
The/Le Garage is commissioned by The British Council and Chaumont Poster Festival

Design: Paul Elliman/Graphic Thought Facility. Print: Plasticolor, Italy

**Right:** This 'Riot light' lampshade designed by Janne Kyttanen for Freedom of Creation makes use of rapid prototyping technology to realize three-dimensional forms and relief lettering.

Rapid prototyping is a generic term used to describe a range of techniques and processes for three-dimensional modelling. These techniques rely on digital technology, computer-aided design (CAD) drawing systems and computer-aided manufacture (CAM), which were developed during the late 1980s to prototype small, complex components used in mechanical engineering. CAD software is used by engineers, draughtspeople, and graphic and type designers to provide drawings from which skilled model- and tool-makers can produce three-dimensional prototypes, and is linked directly to CAM machinery in the form of a rapid prototype. What was originally conceived as a means of reducing product lead times by compressing the design, prototyping and toolmaking phases through the use of integrated digital technology, is now viewed by many engineers as a part of the new generation of mass production. Some technologists envision a not-too-distant future when cheap, rapid prototypes will liberate three-dimensional designers, enabling a new type of craftsperson, the digital designer-maker, and as a result anticipate a significant contraction in the number of mass manufacturers.

Three-dimensional drawing programs allow a designer to import a two-dimensional type form and make a virtual extrusion (give depth), shape any of the new form's edges and assign a textural finish to surfaces. Alternatively, the designer can construct a virtual calligraphic letterform, drawing on a graphic slate which has complex curves (surfaces that change progressively through x, y and z coordinates). Once the virtual design is completed, it must be orientated. There is no gravity in virtual space – objects float – but for three-dimensional production the object or letterform has to stand on a bed. The virtual letterform is sliced into cross-sections, which resemble contour lines on a map, one on top of another in thin layers of liquid, powder or even as a sheet, depending on the type of machine. As the shape of each cross-section can vary incrementally, and the layers are very thin, complex curved surfaces can be laid down with each successive scan.

The process is rapid in comparison to making model prototypes by hand. It may take as little as ten minutes to create a small letterform or 24 hours to rapid-prototype a full-size car body on a huge machine. Rapid prototyping has been adopted by architects and interior, exhibition, landscape, garden and graphic designers working with lettering and signage in the environment.

The rapid prototyping machine at Central Saint Martins College of Art and Design, London shown opposite, uses a liquid polymer which hardens to form the three-dimensional form. It is small scale, but works on the same principles as the larger machines used to prototype cars, boats and large-scale environmental lettering.

## Letters formed through rapid prototyping

**1** A keyline of the required letters is drawn to scale. The letterforms here have been crudely traced for speed but the quality of the ampersand curves can be improved by creating more short facets (geometric surfaces of a three-dimensional object) with shallow arcs. Compare the crude facets of the ampersand with the softer curve of the 'P'.

**2** The simple, flat orthographic drawing is extruded to the chosen depth. The three-dimensional representation can be rotated and viewed from many different angles. The fine black lines on the grey surface of the letters show the position of the internal latticework used to build up the structural triangles.

**3** Once the computer image is complete, the digital data is passed to the rapid processor (right).

**4** A brown latticework support in the shape of the letters on the base table is laid down. The support layer has a syrupy consistency but a hot fan blows warm air over it, and quickly dries and hardens it.

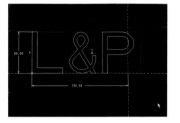

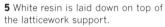

**5** White resin is laid down on top of the latticework support.

**6** Layer after layer is slowly built up and dried hard with each pass. Each layer can have a slightly different profile but here the extruded form is built up with a common profile.

**7** The letterform has square, geometric sides, and the hollow centres are strengthened by the internal, triangular latticework. A hollow form is both lighter and makes more efficient use of the resin. The top faces of the letters are sealed with a series of solid layers, which are supported by the internal latticework. The resin letters are dry and hard by the time the last profile pass is made and can be lifted from the table on the base matrix. The base matrix can be chipped away to reveal a smooth resin face. The material can then be sanded and spray painted.

**Left:** A personalized calendar produced by rapid prototyping, designed by Joe Westworth at the Royal College of Art, London. Each day is represented by a small cone with a date; the cones are arranged around a cylinder that shows the months, and are designed to be broken off with the passing of each day.

# 5.6   Coins and medals

**Above:** The pound coin (enlarged x 3) and set of British coins (reverse, actual size) designed for the Royal Mint by Matthew Dent and released in 2008. The coins are linked by the design of the shield and the royal crest.

The coin, a standardized official unit of currency rather than a found token, was first produced *c.* 600 BCE by sea-going traders in Lydia, Greece (in present-day Turkey).

Today, large electrical furnaces are used to heat the alloys of zinc, copper and nickel for silver coins and copper and tin for copper coins. Thin strips of the hot metal are drawn from the furnace and reduced to the exact thickness required for a coin by passing them through a series of tandem (top and bottom) rollers. The space between each pair of rollers diminishes progressively. Once a metal strip is the correct thickness it passes into the blanking press and enormous pressure is used to punch out 10,000 coins per minute. The blank coins must be softened and cleaned prior to pressing, processes referred to as annealing and pickling. The blanks are fed into the coining press where consistent pressure is applied to impress the obverse and reverse designs. As part of this process the edge of the coin is milled. The newest presses are capable of striking 700 coins per minute.

# 5.7 Lettering with plants

FLORAL CLOCK, WEST PRINCES STREET GARDENS, EDINBURGH (44

202923.J.V.

**Above:** A postcard showing a floral clock in Edinburgh, 1928. All the elements of the clock – text, numerals and design elements – are made of small, colourful bedding plants.

Floral and topiary lettering displays are closely associated with the beginning of the municipal parks movement in Europe in the mid-nineteenth century. From the 1880s, town gardeners began to use decorative displays of colourful bedding plants or cut specially grown box hedges to spell out a town's name. The lettering became emblematic of a town and many seaside resorts held hotly contested competitions to determine which display was the best. Ornamental crests, paintings, symbols and chess boards were often re-created in colourful bedding plants. The designs for lettering flowerbeds and floral clocks are laid out on graph paper. The gardeners work to a set scale using pegs and string to square up the bed or clock; divisions and letters are marked out with fine sand.

Topiary is the craft of growing and pruning living trees and shrubs into shapes. As a celebration of ingenuity it appealed to many Victorian gardeners, who were perhaps the first to prune trees into letterforms. An owner might dedicate an enclosed garden to a lover and have the letters of their name cut into the face of the hedge. Family crests were planted in low-growing box and tiny hedges formed the outline of the crest; the shrubs were cut into letterforms to make the Latin inscription, reinventing with words the medieval knot garden. The popularity of 'standard' trees, grown with a single stem to a specific height and with a restricted root, led to a craze for topiary standards, which included cutting the initial letter or monogram of a loved one out of the foliage. In the twentieth century, factories constructed inclined beds facing the street and planted them with hedges that were cut into factory names, brands, initials, monograms and logos. Stationmasters grew hedges behind railway platforms and cut capital letters into their top, spelling out the name of the station. Today some towns continue to cut topiary lettering, particularly on central islands at road junctions.

# 5.8 Lettering in food

The twentieth-century Dutch tradition that children receive a chocolate letter from Sinterklaas (St Nicholas) on 6 December is derived from the sixteenth-century German custom of giving children bread and pastry runic initials as symbols of good fortune.

Chocolate bars were first produced in the Netherlands in the nineteenth century as a by-product of advances in processing cocoa beans for hot drinks. Chocolate letters were first created in about 1900 by small independent shops but were not widely popular until the 1950s when major Dutch chocolate companies such as Droste, Verkade and Driessen began large-scale production. The letters are on sale in the Netherlands only from 1 October until 5 December. Any unsold initials are returned to the manufacturer and melted down to make non-seasonal bars, so preserving the special nature of Sinterklaas's visit.

**Top:** A stick of rock. The lettering that runs through the large form is retained in the small sticks, which harden when completely cool.

**Above:** Liquorice relief letters like these can be produced in two ways. The liquid liquorice can be poured into wrong-reading, female moulds, passed through a drying unit and finally turned out and bagged up. If the lettering is to be 'debossed' the mould used is a wrong-reading male form. Alternatively liquorice can be passed through a series of mechanical rollers to make it into a sheet of consistent thickness. The warmed sheet is then 'stamped' with a wrong-reading, female form and cut into small bits by a matrix of blades.

The letters are produced by melting chocolate and pouring it into metal, female moulds. They are moulded in capital Egyptian, slab serif fonts, the most popular of which is Egyptiennne. The letters are produced in several different weights. As chocolate is sold by weight and each letter size has a standard price, each character must be designed to the same weight. All the letters are the same height and depth so it is only the stroke widths that can be varied to achieve a common weight. This means 'M' and 'W' have narrow stroke widths while 'V' is very broad. Similar proportional adjustments are made to the strokes of all the characters. The letters are produced in batches. The most popular one is 'M' followed by 'S' and 'P'; most companies don't make 'Q', 'U', 'X', 'Y' or 'Z' as very few Dutch names have these initials. Though the letters are designed as gifts for children, the Netherlands, with a population of 12.6 million, produces over 40 million chocolate initials annually for home consumption.

Sticks of rock with lettering running through them have been popular seaside mementos in Britain and France since the late nineteenth century. The technique of boiling, cooling and pulling sugar, thereby creating lettering, and rolling the sticks probably began a hundred years earlier in the eighteenth century. Today, lettering in rock is made in exactly the same way as it was 250 years ago, using the simplest of equipment – a fire, a copper pan, a marble slab and sugar shears – though a rolling machine speeds up the process. Like the process, the ingredients are simple: sugar, cream of tartar, flavouring and colouring. Each of the letters is built in turn and strips of white sugar are used to fill the spaces. When all the letters are built a white roll of sugar is placed on either side of the letters and a pink sheet is wrapped around it. The whole form is rolled by hand into a huge cylinder about 45cm (18in) in diameter. It is pulled out while it is still warm and malleable, and rolled thinner. Small sections are cut off and either hand- or machine-rolled into sticks of rock.

1

2

3

**This page:**

1 The packaging for Droste chocolate letters.

2 Dutch chocolate letters in the well-known Egyptian slab serif form. As each initial must weigh the same, the letterforms are adapted: the 'F' (bottom) has an enlarged broad stroke compared with the 'A', which has other elements to make up the surface area and weight. The letters are produced by pouring liquid chocolate into wrong-reading, female moulds.

3 Mechanical piping is used to make icing decorations for birthday cakes. The liquified icing, which has a stiff consistency, is forced through a series of thin tubes arranged in the shape of a letterform. A small amount of icing is forced down each tube on to a surface where it forms a bead as it congeals and sticks to the beads surrounding it. Here the white icing of the outline was laid down first and the pink icing beads were positioned on top.

## 5.9 Sand casting metal

Sand casting is one of the oldest ways of working with metal. Its origins stretch back to the Bronze Age when weapons, utensils and brooches were made by pouring molten metal into an impression in a bed of sand. The technique is also referred to as open casting because the metal forms a visible pool within the impression, as opposed to closed casting in which the molten metal is contained within an enclosed mould or fills a void between interlocking male and female moulds. All sand casting requires an impression pattern. This was traditionally made in wood but today MDF, resin, plaster, milled nylon, vacuum-formed plastic or rapid prototyping may be used. The pattern is laid in a casting bed which is progressively backfilled with sand; the finest casting sand is packed closest to the surface of the pattern. Coarser sand is used to fill the bed to the required depth before the pattern is gently lifted away, leaving a female impression.

### Casting letters in lead

**1** The Perspex letters are cut with a 7-degree rebate which is steeper than the 10-degree angle used for letters which require vacuum forming (*see* pp.186–87). Letters shown here are in Times New Roman, sizes from 35mm (1⅜in) to 101mm (4in) are available.

**2** The sand box consists of a steel frame open at the top and bottom which sits on a smooth steel plate. The box is packed with a fine-grade foundry sand. The sand particles are all of a similar size and are bound together with an oil that gives the sand the capacity to accurately retain an impression.

**3** Sand is packed into the box and levelled. The plaque impression is made by pressing a wooden former into the sand. The letters are laid out on the surface of the sand wrong-reading, along a straight edge which serves as a baseline. They are spaced by eye in groups. If several identical signs are to be made, the letters can be temporarily glued to a pattern board.

**4** When the letters have been spaced, they are gently tapped into the sand with a light hammer. They must be hammered to the same depth so that the cast form will have a common relief height.

**8** The lead becomes molten at 375°C (707°F) but is heated to a higher temperature so that it flows freely when poured.

**9** The molten lead is lifted from the furnace in a casting ladle and poured smoothly into the sand impression, which is filled to the top.

The lead cools and solidifies quickly and can be touched within five minutes.

**10** The lead has solidified, and the sign is turned out of the sand-box.

The impression for small relief letters can be made by pressing the character pattern directly into the flattened surface of the sand, the depth of the impression determines the 'draught' (thickness) of the letters' relief on the final cast. Although the sand–casting principle is the same for all metals, the type of sand, the density of the packing and the temperature at which the metals become molten varies. Metals with high melting points require special furnaces to generate sufficient heat to change the solid ingot into a molten liquid which can be poured smoothly. For this reason many foundries tend to specialize in particular types of casting and limit the range of metals used. In the following process, lead letters are being cast as signs at Redfields English Leadwork in the same way as they were made in the 1600s.

**5** The Perspex letterforms are lifted from the sand by simply blowing along the baseline. The oil in the foundry sand prevents the edge of the impression being disturbed. Once the sand has been blown out of the impression, the letter patterns are removed as the impression is complete and ready for casting.

**6** The sand box is lifted from the bench to the levelling table, a flat surface that can be adjusted in two planes. A spirit level is used to check the box is resting flat. Molten lead forms its own level and any discrepancy would have the effect of casting a base with an irregular thickness.

**7** Molten lead is a dangerous material to work with. At a very high temperature it gives off poisonous gases. Furnace workers wear breathing apparatus and protective clothing.

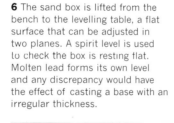

**11** The sign is brushed down with a stiff brush and wiped clean. The sand is returned to the sand bin for reuse.

**12** Lead is resistant to heat and extreme cold, expanding and contracting without distorting the original casting; it does not crack or rust; and it can easily be cleaned. Lead signs will last outside for hundreds of years but are vulnerable to vandalism because of their soft surface. They can be cold-bent on site to fit the profile of a wall or pillar.

**Right:** The new lead sign is a shiny silver. Over time it will oxidize to become the more familiar dark grey, a process that can be hastened by painting on a solution of dark (an oxidizing agent).

# 5.10 Cast-aluminium and polyurethane signs

Traditionally street signs, railway signs and fingerposts (signposts at road junctions) were manufactured from cast iron. They were both durable and robust but, left exposed to the elements, the paint was subject to water ingress, bubbling, cracking, flaking and rust staining. Many cities sought lower maintenance costs and, in some cases, cheaper alternatives to cast-iron signs. These included ceramic tiles, vitreous enamel, pressed aluminium, vinyl, cast aluminium and polyurethane. Pressed aluminium signs are not susceptible to rust staining and, providing the paint surface remains cohesive, are very durable. However, if the paint is chipped and the base metal is exposed, a fine white powder produced through oxidization quickly covers the surface and spreads across the sign, causing the paint to fall away completely.

Vinyl lettering (*see* pp.124–25) is by far the cheapest to produce and many exterior-grade vinyls are guaranteed colour- and peel-fast for ten years. This longevity, however, does not take account of vandals who cut or peel letters off in a matter of minutes,

## Casting letters

**1** Base plates for a sign are shaped out of MDF. The sign-maker has over a thousand standard shapes and sizes designed to accommodate specific cap heights and word lengths. The surface of the plate must be very smooth and is sealed with a non-stick paint. The forms are referred to as pattern blocks.

**2** The MDF can be built up in layers and glued with epoxy composites to form a very stiff pattern. The pattern block is positive – the raised edges of the final sign are raised on the block. Each raised surface will create a negative impression in the casting sand and must be cut at an angle of no less than ten degrees in order for the mould to be removed.

**3** The letters for casting are right-reading and, like the raised elements of the pattern block are cut at an angle of ten degrees. This angle can be increased to give the final cast letter a flared appearance. The letters can be in any typeface but very fine serifs are ill suited to casting. Letters are cut from thin sheets of MDF or acrylic, using a hand router.

**4** A baseline is drawn on the pattern block and the characters are arranged by eye. Groups of letters are reviewed three at a time with the negative space between them. With centred type, a centrepoint is marked on the baseline and the characters in the middle of a word are positioned first. Letters are held in place with Blu-Tack.

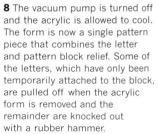

**8** The vacuum pump is turned off and the acrylic is allowed to cool. The form is now a single pattern piece that combines the letter and pattern block relief. Some of the letters, which have only been temporarily attached to the block, are pulled off when the acrylic form is removed and the remainder are knocked out with a rubber hammer.

**9** This large casting box allows many signs to be cast at the same time. The acrylic forms, or in the case of large signs MDF moulds, are laid in the bottom of the box with the lettering face-up. Casting sand, which is very fine but has a slightly oily feel, is brushed on to the form. The first layer of sand in immediate contact with the form will preserve the detail in the cast.

**10** Increasingly coarse layers of sand are added to the casting box. A board is placed over the sand and stamped down compressing the sand tightly on to the mould. A lid is secured over the box which is then suspended in a frame. The whole box is turned through 180 degrees and the upward-facing cover is removed to reveal a smooth layer of sand and the reverse of the acrylic forms or MDF moulds. When the form is removed a perfect negative impression of the lettering in the sand is revealed.

making this lettering inappropriate for pavement-level display. Also, flat vinyl lettering is not in keeping with historical, relief street signs. In the search for lower maintenance alternatives to cast-iron relief signs, some cities have reinstated repainting iron signs for specific quarters such as city centres, heritage and conservation areas. Others have removed the originals, had them sandblasted, and then used them as casting patterns for replica aluminium and polyurethane signs. These replica signs have the advantage of preserving the exact letterforms and relief depths of the originals without the associated problems of rusting and the prohibitive cost of overpainting. Aluminium- and polyurethane-cast relief signs have been widely used for the manufacture of street furniture that carries lettering, such as bollards, lamp posts, fingerposts, coats of arms and street signs. Painted polyurethane signs are indistinguishable from their cast-iron predecessors and are not subject to rust staining. They have a number of advantages as polyurethane, being inert, does not rot or oxidize and has a closed-cell structure, which accounts for the way paint adheres to it.

**7** The hot acrylic sheet is sucked down on to the pattern block as the vacuum pump removes air from

below. The plastic is drawn in tightly to the letterforms, reproducing the shapes very accurately.

**5** The layout is completed and spell-checked. There must be no tiny gaps between the letters and the pattern block as these would create an imperfection in the sand and ultimately the cast. A vacuum-formed impression is taken from the pattern block.

**6** The pattern block is carefully lifted on to the vacuum-former and a 1.5-mm (¹⁄₁₆-in) acrylic sheet is heated by electrical elements for 90 seconds until it is pliable.

**11** A two-part polyurethane is mixed and electrically warmed by machine so that it will flow as a liquid. A nozzle from the machine is used to slowly deliver the shots of liquid polyurethane into the sand impression. The polyurethane is built up in two or three layers 6-10 mm (¼-½ in) thick. Once all the impressions have been filled they are left to cure chemically and harden overnight.

**12** Both aluminium- and polyurethane-cast signs are prepared for painting by being sandblasted with fine fettling sand.

This process cleans off any residue from the casting and leaves a smooth, matt surface which paint will adhere to.

**13** The signs are base-painted with a diluted, quick-drying cellulose paint which is built up in three coats. Where the lettering is lighter in colour than the background, the characters are base-painted in a separate pale colour. The letters are painted with three or four coats of matt or gloss paint. Designers can specify whether the ten-degree bevels are matched to the base or the letter colour.

**Above:** Village signs and a pub sign made using either aluminium casting or the new polyurethane which suffers less from paint peeling. The pub sign (bottom) combines modern casting techniques for the lettering with fibreglass animals.

**Above:** Phil Baines designed lettering for a modern stainless steel memorial commemorating people who died in the London bombings in 2005. The process is very similar to lead and aluminium casting; it uses sand-casting moulds but the temperature is in excess of 1,500°C (2,732°F).

# 76

## Lettering in textiles

# 6.1 Embroidery

Embroidery is the craft of decorating a fabric by stitching threads, yarns, wire, beads, shells or semi-precious stones to its surface. Today the vast majority of embroidered lettering on high-street clothing and sportswear – logos, badges, crests, insignia, slogans, numerals and manga designs – is undertaken by automated machines driven by digital software. Some short runs for designer ranges are machine-embroidered by hand. The traditional craft skills of genuine hand embroidery are preserved in small specialist fashion houses, such as Hand & Lock, a merger of two companies who were founded in 1767 and 1898 respectively.

## Hand-embroidered letters

**1** Embroidery frames stretch the fabric evenly and are made in many different sizes and shapes. Here a large, rectangular frame rests on two trestle legs. Two large, wooden battens which run parallel to one another are joined by two large, wooden screws. The fabric to be embroidered is stitched to brass strips attached to the battens before being gently tensioned by tightening the wooden screws.

**2** When the fabric is fragile, inclined to puckering or the embroidery is heavy and complex, it is backed with stiffening (a sheet of bonded material which is ironed on to the reverse). Here the lettering is traced on to a shirt pattern in a soft pencil; as it is so small the frame has not been tightened.

**3** Almost any letterform and colour can be embroidered by hand but a set of informal conventions has been established over time. The initials on men's shirts are characteristically 1.3cm (½in) caps and clients choose the colour of thread and the lettering from two sample sheets (sans and fish tails).

**4** Embroidery is worked from either side of the fabric. Here the needle is pushed down through the fabric with the right hand and caught by the left hand below.

**5** The needle is then pushed back through the fabric with the left hand from below and caught with the right hand.

**6** The thread is pulled until the stitch is tight and the process is repeated until the initials are complete.

**7** The finished initials; they were embroidered by hand in 20 minutes.

**Left:** The embroidery store holds thousands of different cottons and threads, which have to be matched by eye to the fabric or to the customer's requirement.

1 Embroidery is a way of personalizing a garment or a pair of shoes and has long been associated with aristocratic luxury. Each monogram design is specific to an individual; even when two people share the same initials the form of the letters and the way they intertwine must be unique.

2 Existing monograms can be adapted for embroidery. Alternatively, a monogram is designed by the embroiderer and usually lasts for the lifetime of the client. The monograms are drawn life-size and stored alphabetically. Some of those stored in this wooden filing cabinet are over 60 years old and have been used as the pattern for hundreds of personalized items.

3 The decorative letterforms used for monograms have a range of sources. Some are loosely derived from medieval illuminated manuscripts; others have their origins in nineteenth-century ornamental forms or the calligraphic traditions of roundhand and copperplate. Virtually all monograms are designed with caps.

4 The monogram design is copied on to tracing paper with a pencil and is then perforated using a pin stick (literally a short stick with a pin in the end). The outline of the letterform is perforated every 2–3 mm (1⁄16–3⁄16 in) on a padded cushion.

5 The cap line and baseline are drawn in above and below the monogram, together with a centre line dividing the width. The monogram shown here is to be embroidered on to a pair of velvet slippers.

6 The monogram tracing is positioned on the centre front of the slipper pattern which has been marked out by the slipper-maker but not cut. The centre line on the tracing paper is aligned with the centre on the velvet.

7 A tailor's weight holds the pattern in place while a chalk bag is patted on to the pattern.

8 The chalk powder falls through the tiny pinholes in the pattern leaving an outline of the monogram on the surface of the velvet.

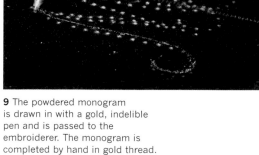

9 The powdered monogram is drawn in with a gold, indelible pen and is passed to the embroiderer. The monogram is completed by hand in gold thread. Purls may be added (see overleaf).

**Above:** A completed slipper monogram 'AH' on ruby-red velvet uses gold thread and purls showing fish tail terminals on the letters.

Embroidered lettering using thread alone stands just proud of the surface of the cloth. To produce more three-dimensional lettering and crests the embroiderer must use thicker metallic threads, beads, purls (small coils of gold threaded on to bullion thread) here shown resting on an embroiderer's cushion, and blades (short strips of metal with a hole at either end which are stitched into a pattern to lift the surface).

Purls are small springs of coiled gold wire, made in a variety of widths and used to thicken the embroidery thread.

One small gold purl is threaded on to the needle for each stitch. Here the gold purl is visible two-thirds up the needle. As the purl is wider than the hole made by the needle it will not pass through the fabric but is fixed on the front face. Stitching in the purls is referred to as couching down.

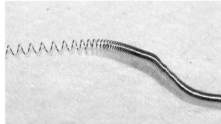

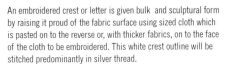

An embroidered crest or letter is given bulk and sculptural form by raising it proud of the fabric surface using sized cloth which is pasted on to the reverse or, with thicker fabrics, on to the face of the cloth to be embroidered. This white crest outline will be stitched predominantly in silver thread.

A detail of the lettering and crest shows how the stitches are arranged in a half-drop pattern like the bonds in a brick wall. The small stitches immediately above the lettering outline the ribbon and are beaded; each stitch forms a tiny gold ball.

Here the crest above the text has been bulked out on a hand-emboidered blazer badge. The sized bulking fabric is yellow as the embroidery is gold. The white tacking stitches hold the backing fabric in place and are later removed.

**Right:** A completed gold-embroidered monogram on a velvet slipper.

A monogram, RL, uses gold purls in a rope-stitch pattern.

A silver purl monogram KBF.

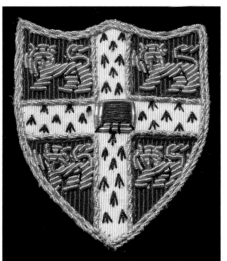

A raised crest shows a combination of coloured embroidery over-stitched with gold thread and purls.

A complex, raised monogram intertwines the letters CBH in old-gold purls.

This raised numeral is made up of white-gold thread and purls. Note how the purls twist round the bowl of the number.

Hand & Lock specialize in ceremonial embroidery for monarchs, peers, ecclesiastical robes, the diplomatic service and academic dress. It takes over 150 hours to complete the very complex embroidery on these crests for ceremonial robes, which show how the three-dimensional forms can be built up. The Latin text is embroidered in gold, and silver bullion threads are used in combination with beads, purls and blades or plates (thin strips of silver or gold) couched down with stitches. The three-dimensional forms are further enhanced by the selection of lustre finishes on the plates, which include matt, burnished and a polished mirror finish.

Right: Italian Order of St Ferdinand and of Merit. The Latin lettering reads Faith and Merit; it is in black thread on a white-gold embroidered ribbon.

Above: Order of the Thistle, Scottish chivalrous order. The Latin lettering reads No One Attacks Me with Impunity. White-gold thread is used for the lettering.

**Above:** The embroidery workshop at Newton Newton flag-makers where a collection of hand-embroidered ceremonial flags are laid out on the pattern-cutting table.

Today the words standard, banner, flag and even ensign are often used interchangeably, but historically these were the terms for artefacts constructed from a variety of materials and hung in different orientations. Flags can now be produced using five main processes: printing, painting, appliqué, and machine and hand embroidery.

Cheap printed flags and banners have been responsible for the demise of traditional flagmaking. Some printed flags are produced on large-format inkjet printers using rolls of polyester fabric and printed single-side only. Slightly more sophisticated flags and banners are screen-printed on a variety of fabrics such as silk, nylon and polyester. Waterproof banners, designed to hang from the exterior of a building or be stretched around a frame, can be screen-printed on to PVC-coated nylon, which is extremely hard-wearing and can be easily wiped clean. They can be manufactured with eyelets or a heat-welded sleeve to fit over a frame or pole. Painted flags are now rarely commissioned but provide a sophisticated alternative to appliqué and embroidery. They rely on the skill of the signwriter and artist and, up until the early twentieth century, the process was common for flags carrying complex heraldic designs, lettering and realistic pictorial elements with blended colour that is not easily achieved through embroidery.

Traditional flag-makers specialize in appliqué and embroidered flags, both of which can be used in interiors and exteriors. Flag cloth has a very open weave – tiny holes are visible between the warp (vertical thread) and weft (horizontal thread). These allow wind to pass through the fabric and enable the flag to fly. Traditional flags are two-sided so the design and lettering are visible on both sides. Some banners are single-sided only and wall-mounted. The proportions of flags vary and it is vitally important for correct presentation that they are observed in the design.

## Ceremonial flags

Examples of European ceremonial flags show the historical use of combinations of appliqué and embroidery with gold thread, which produce rich raised crests and lettering.

## Flag quality

**Appliqué**
The appliqué design for this Royal Naval Association flag is created by drawing out the crest on yellow fabric, then machine-stitching the fabric to the navy-blue flag cloth. The excess material is carefully cut away to reveal the design. The blue letters are drawn out on blue fabric and stitched on top of the yellow ribbon, and then cut round. The detail on the rope, laurels and crown is stitched through with navy-blue thread using an embroidery machine. The design of the crest is strong and graphic, but the surface is relatively flat.

**Machine embroidery**
The second method of traditional flag manufacture, known as better, is by a hand-operated embroidery machine. Each element of the design is traced on to fabric that matches or best supports the colour of the embroidery thread. Separate elements of the design are then machine-embroidered in the appropriate colours. Pieces are positioned and pinned on to the flag cloth, then machined round using a zigzag stitch. Once the embroidery is attached to the flag cloth the excess fabric can be cut away to reveal the design. The colours are very rich but the threads sit fairly flat on the cloth.

**Hand embroidery**
Hand embroidery, known as best, is the most time-consuming and therefore the most expensive form of manufacture. It is predominantly used on ceremonial flags where detail is visible. The process is similar to that of machine embroidery in that the stitching is not made directly on to the flag cloth but on separate pieces of fabric before the design is assembled. The gold and silver elements of the design are made using mylar bullion wire, which is thicker than the thread used on a machine and comes in a range of lustres and purls. Stitches must be very even but can vary in length across the design to give the impression of modelling. Because the crest and lettering detail stand proud of the surface this type of flag cannot be rolled, and must be stored flat or hung.

**1** The artwork for this relatively small commercial flag is supplied by the client as an A4 acetate sheet. This is enlarged to the correct size using a projector.

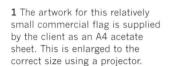

**2** A sheet of brown paper is pinned up on the wall and the projected image is traced off in pencil to form a pattern. The outline of each letter is skilfully traced by hand. Tiny deviations in the letterform are unlikely to be visible to the viewer once the flag is 9.1 m (30 ft) up on a flagpole.

**3** The flag-maker's tracing is accurate and seeks to preserve the character of the lettering; outlines are cleaned up using drawing instruments (top). The final paper pattern (bottom).

**6** The pencil outline of the letter provides a guide for the very tight zigzag stitch. The machine operator must turn the fabric carefully as it passes through the needle foot.

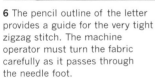

**7** When all the letters have been stitched to the front of the flag, the excess fabric can be cut away. The outside of the letter is cut away first (top) and then the counter (bottom) and the waste thrown away. Cutting away the fabric is a very skilled task as neither the flag cloth, nor the zigzag stitch that surrounds the letter, must be cut with the scissors.

**8** A detail of a finished appliquéd letter shows how close the stitching is to the edge of the letterform.

**4** Each word is traced from the paper pattern on to a separate piece of white, polyester fabric using a pencil. The strips of fabric are laid out on the flag cloth. As the lettering is white on a coloured ground, two strips have been laid down on top of each other to produce a greater colour contrast. The measurements, alignment and position are checked before they are pinned.

**5** The fabric strips are pinned to the flag shape (top). The positioning of the strips (bottom) is rechecked once they have been pinned and before the appliqué is sewn to the flag.

## Ceremonial two-sided flags combining appliqué and embroidery

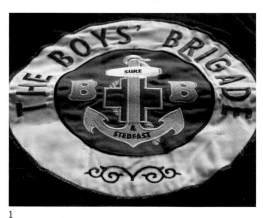

1

2

3

4

5

**Above:** Details of ceremonial flags which combine appliqué work with hand embroidery. The complex designs of each flag are not embroidered directly on the flag cloth but are made on separate pieces of the same coloured fabric and couched down in layers.

**1** The central motif of this flag is made up of four appliqué pieces: an outer white circle, a French blue circle, and a yellow anchor (with gold embroidery), which is laid over, and couched down over, a red cross.

**2** The high, elaborate crest on a flag for Newark Golf Club.

**3** This detail of the Newark flag shows how different weights of silver thread are used to define the imagery of the crest.

**4** A single-colour, hand-embroidered flag; the ribbon is appliquéd to the flag cloth.

**5** Front (above) and back (bottom) details of a crest. Two-sided ceremonial flags are made of two flag cloths so that the reverse sides are hidden.

# 6.3 Machine embroidery

Graphic designer Lizzy Finn was intrigued by the textural qualities of fabric and began to explore the relationship between digital lettering and the embroidery machine. Finn found she could 'draw' lettering 'freehand' merely by moving the fabric under the foot of the machine. She was quick to acquire a Pfaff sewing and embroidery machine which runs from a personal computer platform. The accidents, and perhaps even the odd mistake in drawing with a sewing machine gave the letterforms a vitality that would have to be deliberately constructed digitally. Finn began to use scraps of fabric as a kind of loose sketchbook to explore lettering and imagery. She leaves the embroidery threads long and enjoys the fact that they sometimes fall across the image. She talks enthusiastically of turning over the piece and how often the back is better than the front, as it is more a consequence of the process. Where more exact letters than those created by freehand drawing are required, Finn can link the personal computer to the embroidery machine and produce an embroidered font automatically. However, to give the lettering more character, she often prefers to scale letters on screen, print them out on paper and trace them on to fabric before using a machine to stitch them by hand. Finn continues to work between sewing and digital design, and often rescans her letterforms, scaling and positioning them to create a text, illustration or poster.

## Writing with a sewing machine

**1** (top) The lettering is sized digitally on screen, printed on to paper, then traced on to fabric using a pencil and put on the sewing machine. (bottom) Finn has an embroidery machine but uses a sewing machine to draw lettering by moving the fabric under the needle foot.

**2** The sewing machine is threaded with the chosen colour and the type of stitch is set.

**3** (top) The fabric is supported with a facing material that prevents surface puckering. The fabric must be carefully guided round the pencil outline; the speed of the stitches is controlled by the foot pedal. The running stitch (bottom) is ideally suited to lettering with connectives, while blanket stitch produces a broader line.

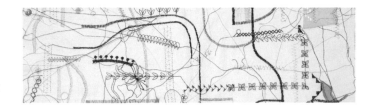

**Right:** A section of a page from Finn's sketchbook shows experiments with different types of stitch and coloured threads.

1

2

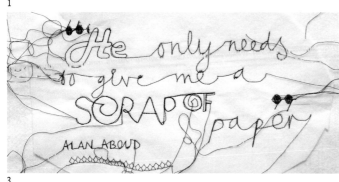

3

6

4

5

**1** and **2** Front (1) and back (2) of the same piece of embroidery. Finn embroidered a series of quotes about graphic designers, collaborating with Peter Saville in *Print* magazine. The lettering has the appearance of doodles on a page. The threads on the final lettering are left long, revealing the nature of the process.

**3** A detail shows how the process embraces accident, and the kink within the letterforms which are not perfect but are full of character. The dots of the speech marks appear to have been scribbled in.

**4** and **5** This piece, shown front (4) and back (5) combines both 'freehand' lettering and embroidery, which references typographic forms.

**6** An example of appliqué – felt lettering Finn developed for *Esquire* magazine with minimal embroidery that consists of white tacking stitches.

# 6.4 Cross stitch

**Right:** Traditional cross stitch uses an embroidery fabric or tapestry gauze as a base, but Kasikov often uses paper as her work is derived from the CMYK print production processes based on enlarging a digital dot screen from a four-colour image.

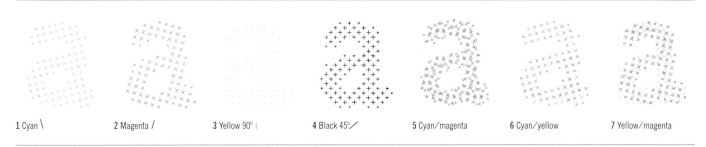

| 1 Cyan \ | 2 Magenta / | 3 Yellow 90° | | 4 Black 45° / | 5 Cyan/magenta | 6 Cyan/yellow | 7 Yellow/magenta |

**Above:** (1–4) A series of single-colour cross stitch. (5–9) Combinations of two cross-stitch colours, echoing duotone printing or some of the progressives of four-colour printing. (10–13) Three colours combined resembling three-colour printing, and finally (14) CMYK. The cross stitches were originally drawn to match the screen angles of the four-colour process: cyan 105°, magenta 75°, yellow 90° and black 45° (1–4), then angles and colours were mixed and matched.

Cross stitch is an ancient craft and has developed independently within different cultures and folk traditions. The stitch, which is literally a cross, is used in both tapestry, traditionally using wool, and embroidery, using silk or cotton.

Graphic designer Evelin Kasikov has always been interested in the physical qualities of print, in particular the impression made by letterpress, the soft, continuous tone of gravure and the dot screens of lithography. Her sensitivity to the pattern of print, coupled with a natural facility for craft skills – crochet, embroidery and cross stitch – have led her to develop lettering that is a hybrid of print and embroidery. In one of her early experiments Kasikov produced a bitmap font as a piece of crochet. The success of this piece spurred her interest in hand-made graphics, in part a reaction to the digital presentation of letterform. She realized that analogue and digital print production rely on a grid structure, and that cross stitch could be viewed as a historical precursor to the dot screens of print and the pixels of the screen – all three are the smallest element from which lettering or images can be built.

**1** Digitally coloured text made from the four process colours – cyan, magenta, yellow and black – is enlarged in Photoshop so that the dot screen is coarse. By working in either Illustrator or InDesign Kasikov is able to draw crosses that match the width of the dots in the correct positions.

**2** When each of the colours is complete, the layer holding the screen dots is removed leaving the crosses which can be printed out on to paper. The paper must be sufficiently resilient to support the stitches and is usually at least 120gsm (4¼oz).

**3** To ensure the cross stitches are accurate, a bradawl (a tool for boring holes) is used to make a hole at the end of each stitch before the needle is threaded. All the holes in one colour are made and stitched before the bradawl is used to make another set of holes for the second colour.

**4** The needle is pushed from the back of the paper, feeding it across the front and down through the hole at the end of the first stitch. The needle is then repositioned in one of the holes that make up the cross stitch, pulled through it and returned from the front to complete the cross. The process is repeated for all the stitches in one colour before the holes for the next colour are made.

**8** Yellow/black    **9** Magenta/black    **10** Cyan/magenta/yellow    **11** Cyan/magenta/black    **12** Cyan/yellow    **13** Cyan/yellow/black    **14** Cyan/magenta yellow/black

**5** Once the cyan stitching is complete, the next colour is marked out using the bradawl and the stitching process is repeated systematically. Six-ply cotton embroidery thread is used for the cross stitching. The thread can be unwound and split into two, four or six twists. Separating the threads in this way enables Kasikov to vary the weight of the cross stitch.

**6** The process is then repeated using yellow and finally black.

**Right:** The almost complete CMYK final cross stitch letter shows how the stitches of each coloured layer overlap in the same way as the dot screen for print. The length of the stitches matches the size of the dots. If the cross stitch is held at a distance, it works like a dot screen; the eye perceives a single colour rather than the four process colours.

**1**

**2**

**3**

**5**

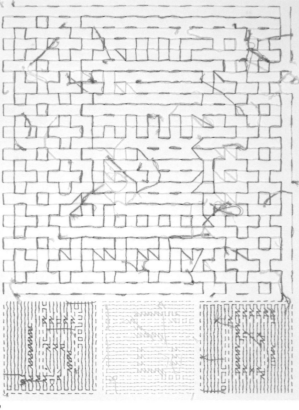

**4**

**This page:**
A series of cross-stitch experiments
by Kasikov.

**1** Cross-stitch threads sewn through a
preprinted sheet of CMYK squares. Both the
squares and the stitches are the smallest
components of the letterforms.

**2** The reverse of the sheet showing the
embroidery floats – threads linking the holes.

**3** Blocks of cross-stitched colours applied to
a linear grid.

**4** Multiple letterforms overlaid in cross stitch
of different colours.

**5** Three examples, in different colourways,
of letters formed using blocks of overlapping
cross stitch. The letterforms are cruder than
others on this page as they are made up of
fewer stitches (here the grid is 19 units tall
by 14 wide).

**202**

Lettering in textiles

# 6.5 Hand knitting

Throughout the eighteenth, nineteenth and first half of the twentieth centuries, knitting was an essential domestic craft for thousands of working-class women in farming and fishing communities, and provided a means of clothing the entire family. Unlike weaving, it required no machinery – only needles and yarn – and could therefore be taken up by the poorest of families. Hand-knitted sweaters, once the workwear of fishermen, are now highly prized luxury items. Lettering has long been a feature of the hand-knitting tradition. Fishing communities developed patterns specific to a port or coastal region, which were sometimes adapted by individual families. A man's initials were usually knitted into the pattern just above the rib. Should he fall overboard and drown, the local pattern would ensure his body was taken to the appropriate port and the initials identified the family. Here Wendy Baker, a fashion knitwear designer, shows how lettering can be knitted into a garment either as a texture or a colour.

1

2

3

**This page:**

1 A lettering pattern for hand knitting is plotted out on graph paper. Each square represents a stitch. The type of stitch or a change of colour are indicated by marks, dots and crosses. Yarn companies produce patterns for the home knitter, but it is the knitwear designer who charts out the design. Here the T has been knitted in a single colour. The stitch change defines the letter.

2 The reverse of the fabric shows how the stitches are raised and the variation in pattern. Some designers will interchange front and back to create different textures.

3 Lettering can be produced using two principal techniques: changing the colour (Fair Isle or intarsia) or changing the texture of the letters by using a different stitch. Fair Isle is used to knit small lettering patterns. The back of the knitting has floats (lengths of unlooped yarn stretching between the stitches). Intarsia has the second colour twisted into the knit and is used for larger letters.

# 6.6 Machine knitting

**Above:** The 'Shima Seiki' knitting machine has multiple needle beds that stretch along its length and a rolling carriage that moves horizontally across the beds to create a row of stitches. The yarn is drawn off the cone through a series of wire guides, then through the feeder to the carriage. The fabric construction of knitwear based on stitches provides elasticity which is referred to as tension, this can be adjusted on the machine. Here Wilson checks the needle beds and the fabric tension.

The first domestic knitting machines were popular in the 1970s and enabled home knitters to produce knitted fabrics over 90cm (3ft) wide. These relatively inexpensive machines require the operator to push a carriage across the needle bed. The technological advances in industrial knitting machines, particularly in Japan and Switzerland, have now enabled fabrics several metres (up to 7ft) wide to be knitted.

The word 'knitting' often conjures up images of cardigans and pullovers, but the inherent stretch of a knitted fabric – absent in most woven fabrics without the addition of Lycra – is a property that can be widely exploited. Hundreds of stretch fabrics for fashion and furnishing textiles are knitted and are collectively referred to as Jersey wear. This includes T-shirts, hosiery, underwear, skirts, dresses and sportswear. Industrial machines can produce fully-fashioned garments in which the sleeves and body are knitted in the round, between two needle beds. Stitches can also be increased or decreased to shape a garment to fit the body. Knitting machines have grown increasingly complex as manufacturers attempt to replicate the number of variations made possible by hand knitting – needle size, gauge, tension, stitch type, double-sided knitting, intarsia (where a separate length or ball of yarn is used for each area of colour), jacquard (figured and brocaded fabric) – while continually trying to speed up the production process and minimize the set-up time.

Here Rodney Wilson shows how an older Shima Seiki machine can reproduce a letter in a knitted structure.

**Right:** A computer command controls the carriage's movement across the needle beds. A detail of the carriage shows the dials that read the number of rows and the fabric tension.

**Far right:** Jacquard patterns or letterforms are knitted by alternating the colour of the yarn between the figure and the ground, producing two-sided reversible knitting. Letters are reproduced in a reverse colour way on the back of the fabric, shown here in red and green.

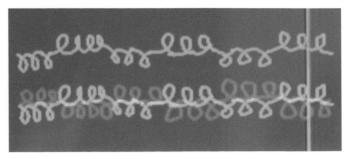

## Machine-knitted lettering

**1** The letter design is drawn on paper prior to being visualized on screen. An image can be scanned and imported on to the Shima Seiki software before being traced over to create a digital pattern. Here, a grid 24 units wide by 30 units deep is drawn over a News Gothic lower-case 'a'. Each square on the grid represents a knitted stitch.

**2** The Shima Seiki machine has a bed of 360 needles, so any design must fit within 360 stitches. A specialist graphics tablet and pen designed by Shimo Siki provide the interface between designer and machine.

A starting point for the design is selected and the first stitch is filled in. By carefully following the coordinates on paper and matching them on screen, the designer redraws the letter into the digital grid.

**3** With the basic letter drawn, adjustments can be made to the shape by adding or removing stitches. The larger the knitted letter, the more faithfully its curves are reproduced. The letterform can be copied and repeated to produce a pattern or a new letter can be systematically drawn on the digital grid.

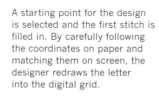

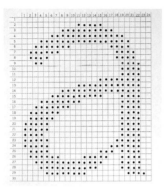

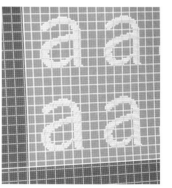

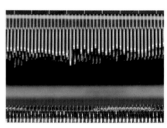

**4** The designer instructs the machine how the piece is to be knitted. His decisions are realized by setting up the machine commands, which are designated by a series of colours. The machine shown here has 128 different commands but newer versions have many more.

**5** The Shima Seiki has two needle beds, and Jacquard is knitted on both of them. The letter will appear right-reading on one side of the fabric and reverse-reading in the reverse colourway on the other. The commands break the letter into two rows of stitches in a process known as jacquard separation. The red rows represent the stitches on the front bed of needles, while the green rows represent those on the back bed.

**6** The computer commands are stored on a disk which is inserted into a reader on the knitting machine. The commands control the movement of the carriage across the needle beds. Commands for each row and stitch appear at the base of the screen.

**7** The commands control the integration of front and back needle beds for the jacquard knit. This detail shows the arrangement of the needle beds one above another. Each needle picks up the yarn, makes a stitch as the carriage passes over the bed, and releases it before the process is repeated as the carriage returns. Knitting is made in rows as the carriage moves across the needles.

**Right:** The knitted fabric with the repeated News Gothic letterform appears as a continuous roll at the base of the knitting machine.

# 6.7 Rugmaking

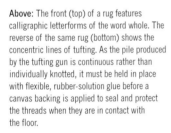

**Above:** The front (top) of a rug features calligraphic letterforms of the word whole. The reverse of the same rug (bottom) shows the concentric lines of tufting. As the pile produced by the tufting gun is continuous rather than individually knotted, it must be held in place with flexible, rubber-solution glue before a canvas backing is applied to seal and protect the threads when they are in contact with the floor.

**Above right:** Carol Kemp draws with a tufting gun in her rugmaking studio.

Rug and carpet weaving was a handcraft practised in Assyria in the eighth century BCE and has strong traditions stretching back over two millennia in Arabia, Persia, Afghanistan, India, China and Tibet. The process involves a hand loom consisting of a slightly inclined standing wooden frame, with the warp (vertical thread) and weft (horizontal thread) loosely interwoven between upper and lower beams. The pile or tufting is threaded through the open weave with a rug hook looped around a warp pulled back on itself before being tied in a knot. Ancient carpets were characteristically patterned and the fashion for putting lettering into a design only gained popularity in Europe and the United States in the nineteenth century when a monogrammed rug was seen as a status symbol. Today most domestic rugs and carpets are machine tufted. Hand-crafted rugs continue to be made but there are two discrete schools: the traditional, Middle-Eastern and Asian patterns and a more modern, Western painterly approach. With the invention of the mechanical tufting gun, artists and designers could draw directly on the loom, pull the wool away if they made a mistake and draw again. The tufting gun changed the craft of rugmaking from a design and make process resembling tapestry or cross stitch, to an iterative process, like painting or drawing. Carol Kemp, a lettering artist realized that the freedom offered by the tufting gun resembled that of the calligrapher.

## Writing with a tufting gun

**1** The base fabric for a rug is an open-weave canvas stretched over tiny pins protruding from the edge of a wooden frame. The lettering is either painted directly on to the canvas or enlarged from an artwork using an epidiascope (an enlarging projector). The pile is long on the front of the rug (top) and tight on the reverse (bottom).

**2** The tufting gun that Kemp uses here was designed and made by Ian Heron to fit on to an electric power drill. The rotating chuck of the drill links to a cam which pushes the needle through, and back out of, the canvas.

**3** Two details of the needle show the tubular sleeve with the needle recessed (top) and with the needle extended (bottom) as it penetrates the canvas before being pulled back to form a looped tuft of yarn.

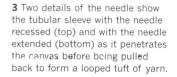

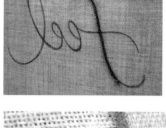

**4** The yarn, made up of 80 per cent wool and 20 per cent polyester, is automatically drawn into the tufting gun by the rotating chuck and is bound into the warp and weft of the canvas as it is moved across the surface. The depth of the pile can be set by adjusting how far the needle penetrates through the canvas before being pulled back.

**5** (right) The letters must be drawn from their lowest descender up towards the canvas. Pulling the gun down will cause the thread to snag.

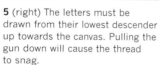

**6** The pile can be left in its looped form or sheared (the thread of each loop is cut at the top). It can be cut using scissors (above)

or mechanical shears (above) like those used to cut the fleece from a sheep.

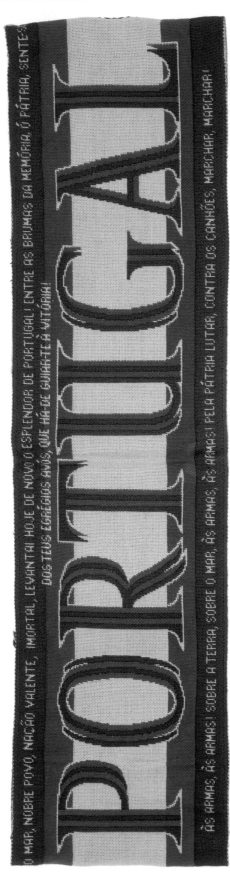

**Right:** Lettering can only be produced on a jacquard loom, which creates a double thickness of fabric. On the front (right) and back (far right) of this woven football scarf colour has been reversed in the weaving process. Note yellow and green reversed as the keyline around the 'P', while red and yellow, green and red alternate along the stroke. This form of reversal is similar to that produced on a knitting machine (*see* pp.204–05).

# 7

## Illumination, animation and motion graphics

# 7.1 Fireworks

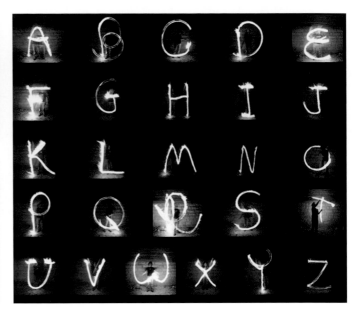

**Above:** Individual fireworks burning simultaneously on a softwood trellis frame (here just visible) create points of light which combine to make letterforms.

**Top:** In places the individual lights merge to create complete letterforms.

**Above right:** A very simple alphabet created by drawing with light.

Fireworks have existed since the third century BCE when gunpowder was invented in China. They were perhaps the first illuminated and animated imagery, and perhaps the first illuminated lettering. No one can be sure when the first fire lettering was developed but there are accounts of nineteenth-century circuses, fairs and buildings being opened with illuminated signs. Today specialist registered firms produce highly choreographed firework displays controlled remotely by computer and often accompanied with live or recorded music. These sequences may include large, illuminated lettering panels in which messages and logos appear, change colour and are even animated.

Lettering or fire-writing signs are generally constructed by hand. The lettering display or logo is designed as an artwork, often on screen. The artwork is then printed out full size as a keyline and laid on a bench. A support frame or trellis is constructed using softwood or flexible willows. The support and lettering are then armed, the fireworks used for this purpose are described as lances and the process of attaching them to the wicker letters as lance work.

Lances are made in many different colours and sizes, and have different levels of luminosity and burn time. As lettering involves many hundreds of fireworks illuminating simultaneously in a relatively small space, a lot of smoke is produced very quickly and fire lettering is best viewed on an evening when there is a slight breeze. To alleviate this problem, and for indoor displays, some firework companies have developed smokeless lances. The lances must be taped to the trellis in an even pattern and the designer must make a decision as to the effect that is required. Placing lances very close together produces a solid, burning letterform, while spacing them evenly produces individual points of light which collectively make up a letterform. The designer can infill letters with different colours, and create outlines or changes of colour. These decisions affect the position of the lances on the support.

Above: Spectacular large-scale lettering using armed lances on a softwood trellis raised above the ground on posts.

## Arming the lettering

Above: The painstaking task of taping the lances to the trellis. At the display venue the trellis is clamped or screwed to wooden posts or metal scaffolding (seen here behind the lance worker) and covered with waterproof sheeting. The main fuses are electrically fired by commands from a computer and are linked to the trellis tapes. Large displays are generally automated, with the venue manager and safety officer overseeing rather than controlling the automated programme.

Above right: In order to ignite the lances they must all be linked to one another by a fuse. This is done with a reel of pyrotechnic tape. The fuse tape is connected to every lance on the display trellis. The lay of the fuses – the order in which the letters, or parts of a letter, are linked – determines the order in which the lances are ignited and how they will burn in the final display. The designer has great control over this order and through developing different lays (fusing patterns) can make the same

words burn in many different ways. (The gunpowder is clearly visible on the surface of the tape linking the two lances.) When the fusing is complete the display panel must be boxed for short-term storage and transport to the venue.

212

# 7.2 Illuminated metal and Perspex lettering

Three-dimensional illuminated letters are fabricated from metal sheets. Today the letterform pattern is usually machine-routed, although in the past it was often cut out by hand. The outline of the letter forms the base around which a raised skirt is folded and welded. Like illuminated light boxes (*see* pp.214–17) the letter can be open fronted, in this case the bulbs are visible but recessed below the height of the skirt or enclosed in a Perspex sheet cut to match the shape of the letterforms' metal tray. The base letterform can be illuminated with tungsten bulbs, fluorescent strip lights or neon tubes. The inside of the tray is characteristically painted white or silver to reflect the light from the bulbs but highly polished mirror or chrome finishes were popular in the 1950s and, more recently, corporate colours have been used. Today letters are generally constructed individually and then aligned on a building's fascia or rooftop. However, during the 1950s the interest of American and Italian industrial designers in brush scripts, was reflected in three-dimensional illuminated signs that featured a complete word constructed as a single

## Hand-routed lettering

**1** Routed Perspex letters weigh much less than the equivalent metal letters. They are not cut completely through the sheet; a tiny sliver remains, just enough to hold the letters in place.

**2** The remaining sliver of Perspex is cut by hand and the letter, together with its protective scratchproof paper, is removed from the sheet.

**3** The depth of the letter is determined by a metal skirt which must be fabricated to fit the Perspex front face. Note the flange on the Perspex letterface, which will form a footing for the skirt to sit on.

**4** A strip of metal which will form the skirt of the letter is shaped in a folding press.

**5** A section of the skirt fabricated to fit the Perspex letterface.

**6** A fabricated letter 'S' sits on top of a pile of letters which will be moved to the paint shop. The Perspex letterface is temporarily taped to each letterform.

element – the bulbs illuminated letter strokes and connectives. Motel, Diner, Casino and Vespa are examples of this form of sign. During the day the letterform stands proud of the shop fascia, defined by its colour and its three-dimensional nature, and casting shadows on to its supporting fascia board. At night the light from the illuminated bulbs is reflected back off the interior paint, making the letterform glow with a suffused halo, words appearing to hover above a building. In mainland Europe, the United States, India, Korea, Japan, Hong Kong and Australia, huge letterforms were often situated on the top of hotels, theatres and department stores supported by metal frames or scaffolding. The silhouette of the entire building featured its name and purpose: Astoria Hotel, The Grand Theatre and even huge trade names such as Amstel and Heineken. In cities such as Las Vegas, Monte Carlo and Hong Kong, where this form of sign is permitted, the night skyline becomes an illuminated surrealist poem with architecture serving as a pedestal for hundreds of glaring but disconnected words.

## Spray painting and heat drying

1 These letters designed for exterior architectural use must withstand the elements and considerable variations in temperature. To ensure they are highly durable the paint is baked in an infrared oven. Both Perspex and metal-faced letters are spray-painted. The Perspex face is removed prior to spraying.

2 The Perspex letterface is temporarily removed and the metal letters are sprayed both inside and out with a matt grey undercoat which is allowed to air dry.

3 The front face of a set of metal letters sprayed with a final corporate colour. Note the spray paint covers nearly half the skirt.

The letters are allowed to air dry before the skirt is sprayed – in this case with a second colour.

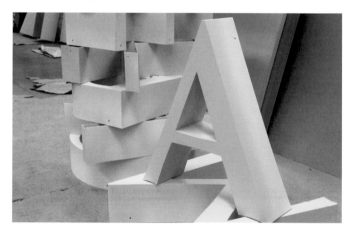

4 The painted front face of the letter is covered with a mask of adhesive paper while the skirt is sprayed. The paper is cut to the exact shape of the letter by hand. In this example the skirt has been sprayed dark green and the masking paper is being removed before the letters are baked.

5 The letters hang from a conveyor belt and pass through the 'oven', an open-ended chamber with banks of infrared heaters.

6 Once the painting is completed, the letters are allowed to cool. The finish is matt on the front face and silk on the skirt. Both are very hard-wearing, as they are chip-proof and scratch-resistant.

# 7.3 Light boxes

**Above:** Commercial signs vie for attention, each trying to outdo each other with the power of their brand. They cling to shop fascia, hang out over the street on gantries and rise up the sides of gables and multi-storey buildings.

Light box sign is the term used to describe three styles of illuminated sign. The first is characteristically used on shop fascia and consists of a metal-faced box from which letterforms have been cut out and in-filled with Perspex. The letterforms are illuminated from the reverse by fluorescent tubes. The second style is described as open fronted or tray. In this the metal box form is fabricated with a back to support the fluorescent tubes, and four sides but no front. The front is made of a Perspex sheet with plastic routed letters stuck to it. An alternative form of this type of light box is used by advertisers and is referred to as an illuminated billboard. A metal tray containing the fluorescent tubes is faced with white, opaque Perspex over which a paper sheet with a lithographically printed image, or a large-format printout is hung. Direct-to-media printing on Perspex is a more recent development. The paper sheets are held in place with a clear sheet of Perspex and are easily changed without requiring the traditional stripping and pasting of billboards. The third style is hot-moulded light boxes, which work on similar principles to the open-fronted or tray style but a Perspex or plastic sheet is moulded into a relief form before being attached to the metal tray containing the fluorescent tubes.

The light box sign has become an integral part of branded retail identities the world over and specialist companies, such as Active Signs, produce thousands of window and shop fascia, providing a full installation and maintenance service. The signs are built to exacting standards, and are developed in response to a brand consultant's brief by specialist design groups. These groups ensure the consistent presentation of the overall corporate identity by controlling the logo, typeface, colour and illumination levels, while also adapting the design's dimensions to the site proportions of individual stores.

**1** Hot moulding is a process used for the production of many illuminated signs. Different types of acrylic and plastic can be moulded into three-dimensional forms and internally illuminated. The large moulding press sits alongside the oven used for heating the acrylic or plastic sheets.

**2** Two forms – male sitting on the bed of the press and female suspended above – are used to mould a sheet into shape. Both forms are built out of MDF.

**3** Acrylic, which has a relatively low melting point, becomes pliable when heated in the oven. The hot acrylic sheet is placed in the press between the forms and pneumatic pressure of several tons is applied. The acrylic cools quickly, the pressure is reduced and the moulded shape can be removed.

**4** The waste is cut away with a bandsaw (a saw consisting of an endless moving steel belt with a serrated edge). Lettering on the acrylic form is machine-routed from the reverse as this allows the form to sit flat on the routing bed. As with most machine-routed acrylic, the cut does not pass completely through the sheet. Here the form has been moved to a bench where the letters will be cut free by hand.

**5** A detail of the letters on the reverse of the sign awaiting hand cutting.

**6** The same sign with all the routed letters removed.

## Routed Perspex light box lettering

**1** The centre section of an internally illuminated double-sided sign is fabricated in the metal workshop. Here the supporting flange is spot-welded to the base plate. This metal plate will support all the electrical tubes.

**2** The Perspex letters used for the light box must fit the letter shapes routed in the acrylic sign. This is achieved by cutting a second set of letters on the router. These are glued to a sheet of acrylic to make a guide for hand-routing. By undertaking the task in this way machine time is freed up.

**3** The hand router is used to make copies of the letters required for the sign. The yellow acrylic sheet is placed over the blue guide letter. The router bit has a cutting edge lifted above the surface supported by a pin. The operator moves the sheet round the cutting edge, controlled by the pin which runs up against the edge of the guide letter.

 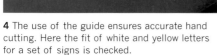  

**4** The use of the guide ensures accurate hand cutting. Here the fit of white and yellow letters for a set of signs is checked.

**5** The letters fit almost perfectly into the form and are glued from the back with an ethylene-based resin which seeps down between the two acrylic surfaces, creating a watertight chemical weld.

**6** The front of the sign shows how the letters sit flush with the surface.

**Right:** A pair of illuminated signs – a downlit version (left) and an internally illuminated version (right) – produced through hot moulding Perspex and routed Perspex lettering.

## Metal illuminated light box

**1** This metal light box has been fabricated from a single large sheet of 4mm (³⁄₁₆in) galvanized steel. The lettering has been machine-routed. Note the letter counters have been removed.

**2** The light box has been spray-painted and baked in an infrared oven. Small pins (short metal rods with a screw thread) have been spot-welded to the back of the light box around the letters. A button washer and a nut are placed over each pin and screwed tight. The button washer extends over the edge of the Perspex, clamping the letter in place.

**3** The reverse of another light box, this time using nylon washers to secure the letters to the pins. The light box must be completely waterproof. To ensure this the joint between the metal box and the Perspex letter is smeared with a thick coat of silicon gel.

**4** (top) The completed back of the sign with all the letters in position, before it is passed to the electrician who will install the lighting tubes. (bottom) The front of the same sign with all the letters fixed in position.

**5** Fluorescent tubes are fitted to the reverse of the sign. Each tube is retained by small clips which are riveted to the sign's internal supports. Connections, transformers and wiring must be waterproof. The number of tubes per sign, and the distance between the reverse of the letterform and the tube, determine how evenly the lettering on the front of the light box is illuminated.

**6** (top) Another long, external light box fitted with legs designed to be mounted on a roof. (bottom) Smaller signs which stand at 90 degrees to the shop façade have a Perspex colour-infilled top and bottom, throwing light on to the wall and street, creating a glow around the sign.

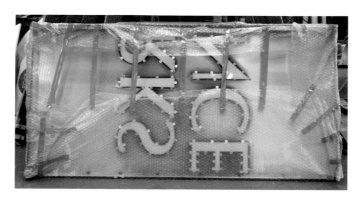

**Left:** A section of a large light box sign packed for delivery to site where it will be installed in front of wall-mounted strip lights.

**Top:** Illuminated bulb letters were popular on fairgrounds before the uptake of neon signs in the 1920s.

**Above:** An American neon sign from the 1950s. The letters in the word store have been encased in open-faced and painted fabricated forms. This form of lettering gives intense, well-defined characters.

**Above right:** The Santa Fe sign featured opposite. Some of the colours have been achieved by sheathing a white neon tube in coloured plastic.

The glow of a neon sign is caused by an electrical current passing through gas trapped in a thin glass tube. Today neon signs seem synonymous with American culture. But it was a Frenchman, George Claude (1870–1960) who, basing his invention on the principles of vapour lamps, first filled glass tubes with neon. Neon literally means new gas, from the Greek *neos* meaning new. Claude developed an illuminated sign in 1902 by bending a neon-filled glass tube into letterforms. The first public neon sign is thought to have been a huge white Cinzano which Claude erected in Paris.

After the First World War, neon signs encapsulated the zeitgeist in the United States, symbolizing the country's hedonistic exuberance. As the 1920s drew to a close, however, the American economy stalled and then collapsed. Thousands of unemployed farm labourers fled to the slums of the big cities where their distractions were the newly illuminated bars, risqué theatres and illegal strip joints. As a consequence neon, most visible at night, gained a salacious reputation.

Following the Second World War, Las Vegas became famous for legalized gambling. Casino and hotel owners commissioned outrageous neon signs which were mimicked by smaller businesses, roadside restaurants, drive-ins and motels, transforming the city to such an extent that tourists came not merely to gamble but to see the spectacle of Las Vegas at night. Eventually the proliferation of neon signs in towns and cities in America was curtailed by civic and highway authorities. This policy, together with large hotel chains buying out small independent diners, motels and gas stations, and the decline in cinemas, saw the demise of neon in the late 1970s. Neon signs deteriorated through lack of upkeep and it was not until the late 1990s that many historic examples were repaired or reinstated. Today Las Vegas once again has amazing neon and bulb illuminations, and there are many private collectors of neon signs and several museums dedicated to their preservation. Neon is also used as a medium by artists such as Jenny Holzer who incorporate lettering in their work.

Electro Signs Ltd was established in 1952 and was responsible for the first neon sign to be erected in London at Paul Raymond's Revue Bar in Soho, London. The company services hundreds of old signs across Britain, many of which it built originally. It produces new neon signs in over 150 colours for a wide range of multinational companies, retailers, theatres and hotels, and has a special workshop for film and television props.

## Letters made from glass tubes

**1** A base board is not always used to support the neon tube, which can be attached directly to the façade of a building. In this case the lettering used on the base board forms a guide for shaping the tube. White lettering has been prepainted by a signwriter.

**2** A single, continuous piece of glass minimizes the number of electrical contacts. Some letters or words may have to be produced by butting tubes close to one another. The longest tubes are generally 3m (10ft). Any longer and they are vulnerable to breakage. Here opaque, black rubber sheaths over the tube create the impression of a break between letters when the tube is illuminated.

**3** A waterproof transformer must be wired either to the building façade or to the reverse of the base board.

**4** Small, plastic supports are screwed to the base or, on location, directly to the façade. They are clear so that they do not create unsightly shadows when the tube is illuminated, and sprung to allow the tube to flex in high winds or during cleaning. They are positioned at least every 30.5cm (12in) along the length of the tube and closer together when complex bends must be secured.

**5** Neon strips are laid out on their respective supports and positioned in relation to the base-board lettering and imagery.

**6** Very thin soft wire is used to secure the tubes to the plastic supports.

**7** Excess wire is cut away.

**8** The electrons protruding from the end of the neon tube are wired to the flex leading to the transformer and covered with a waterproof, silicon sleeve.

**Left:** A fitter works on the Santa Fe sign in the workshop at Electro Signs surrounded by a veritable treasure trove of neon lettering.

**Top:** Coloured neon is produced by varying the amount of gas and the electrical charge.

**Above:** A range of colours produced with neon and argon.

# 7.5 Variable message space

Variable message space (VMS) is the generic term for signs on which the text, symbols or image can be changed. These signs are frequently used on undergrounds, railways, bus routes and motorways to inform travellers of departure times, and road conditions and hazards. VMS signs can be used anywhere a potential audience needs to be guided, informed or persuaded to read information which is transient in nature. Today they are common in public spaces such as sport stadiums, museums, libraries, theatres, cinemas and banks.

Earlier mechanical VMS signs include cinema signs in which the name of the current film is spelt out on a clip system using individual letters. The cinema principle of small Perspex or moulded plastic letters which clipped into tracks on felt-faced boards is still used in hotel lobbies and conference centres. Old-fashioned mechanical cash registers made use of keys which raised little numbered price flags behind a glass window to show the tally to be paid. The revolving drums on petrol pumps showed a succession of digits for the quantity and cost of the petrol in two separate windows. The front and back of trams and buses had windows to display route numbers and destinations painted on separate canvas scrolls which the driver rotated by turning a handle. Railway destination boards consisted of a series of thin plastic strips on which were printed the names of the stations on a line. The strips were clipped to a drum with a release mechanism that allowed them to fall forward until the correct destination and platform were revealed.

In the mid 1980s developments in circuit boards and light-emitting diodes (LEDs) enabled the remote control of bulbs that are evenly spaced vertically and horizontally in a matrix. By turning some bulbs off and others on, patterns are visualized which form letters, numerals and simple symbols. The letterforms created vary in visual refinement depending on the number of bulbs used to visualize them. Simple matrix arrangements may be as crude as seven bulbs tall by four bulbs wide, giving a total of 28 bulbs to visualize each character of the alphabet.

Letterforms designed for print and screen were unsuitable for variable message space systems. Type designers realized that the problem of creating letters using a simple, pixel-based grid had been addressed by embroidery (*see* pp.198–202) and knitwear designers (*see* pp.203–05) and looked to these letterforms as a source of inspiration. As a consequence of the limited number of pixels, many fonts for visual message space systems are designed to be displayed only as upper or lower case, others have either lower-case descenders or amputated ascenders.

Manufacturers of signs quickly realized that the LED matrix could be used not only to change a message but also to animate a sign, which in a busy urban environment was more likely to attract the reader's attention. The lettering on a sign can be moved in any direction by retaining the character's pixel pattern but by moving it to another row or column. As the LED matrix can be turned on and off in fractions of a second, a word or text appears to move across the screen. The movement is most easily read when the text moves in opposition to the reading direction, from right to left.

**Top:** A pharmacist's sign in the shape of an illuminated cross uses single-colour green LEDs. A temperature sensor on the sign automatically controls the VMS display. The complexity of modular letterforms in VMS systems varies. Here the single-colour numerals are 14 modules high and the strokes two modules wide.

**Middle:** An illuminated VMS sign for petrol prices. The large numerals at the top 103.9 use red LEDs and are 34 modules tall with a stroke width of four modules, while the smaller numerals are 22 modules tall with a stroke width of three units.

**Above:** A detail from a railway train information sign that uses simple illuminated discs with a coarse grid pattern only eight modules tall. The ascenders are two modules tall, the x height is five and the descender only one, while the stroke is a single dot wide.

1

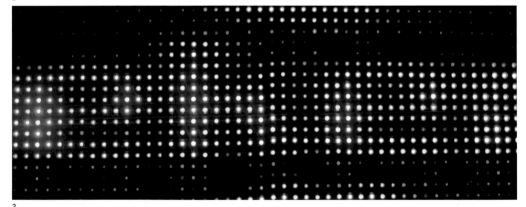

2

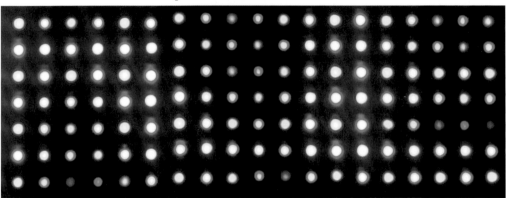

3

4

**This page:**
Multicoloured VMS systems can be built up into banks to form enormous displays. The matrix is finer than on displays used in transport (smaller dots more closely grouped than single colour signs) and each of the points can display up to 256 colours, giving the same effect as enormous televisions. The inputs can be motion graphics or video and the screens are often used at pop concerts, sport stadia, and outdoor festivals.

**1** Metre-square (10¼-ft²) units rest on a trolley before being built up and linked together to form a stage backdrop.

**2** A detail shows the illuminated pattern of RGB (red, green, blue) lights that make up the lettering.

**3** The letters become increasingly visible when the dot matrix is viewed from a distance.

**4** The screen at an exhibition shows a promotion video. The scale of the giant screen 4m (13ft) high and 6m (19¼ft) wide can be seen in relation to the lamp post (right) and is made up of 24 screen units.

# 7.6 Hand-drawn animation

All animation, together with live-action film and video, relies on deceiving the eye. A succession of still images in which the positions of elements change marginally within the frame must pass before the eye faster than 13 frames per second, giving the impression of continuous movement. If the frame rate of presentation is slower than 13 frames per second the brain perceives the objects moving in a succession of tiny jumps. Increasing the number of drawings above 24 frames per second for film, or 25 frames per second for digital, can be used to present slow motion, where objects appear to move more slowly than the viewer would anticipate in real time. Animating hand-drawn lettering can be realized in a traditional manner by drawing on paper or acetate cells

## Hand-drawn digital animation

**1** The initial drawing for the lettering is made on an animation light box, an opaque, circular Perspex sheet, backlit and housed in a wooden frame. The light box is inclined and the Perspex sheet can be rotated to enable the animator to turn the drawing.

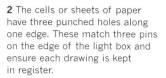

**2** The cells or sheets of paper have three punched holes along one edge. These match three pins on the edge of the light box and ensure each drawing is kept in register.

**6** The paper line drawings are digitally scanned individually. The flat-bed scanner has a three-pin peg bar at one edge, which ensures that all the sheets are positioned in the same place on the bed and are therefore in register.

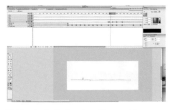

**7** The key frames are imported into Flash and are traced or the line quality is tidied up. Some animators work to a very tight storyboard (sequence of drawings) which defines the movement within each sequence. Others use key frames as stages between which sequences are developed. The progressive development of in-between frames and the overall sequence can be as clear as it is in the following sequence of frames.

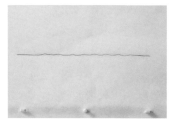

**8** Most digital animation software, has a score (see top of image). It enables the animator to control the sequence of individual frames and the transitions between sequences which links image to sound. The score reads from left to right. A symbol representing the key frame is positioned on the score. Vertical divisions of the score grid represent seconds and the increments one twenty-fifth of a second. Positioning key frames along the score determines the length of the sequence.

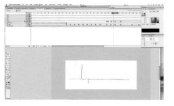

**9** With digital software the animator can try different approaches to a sequence. It can be played back, reviewed, copied and amended a sequence or a new sequence can be begun and frames copied between versions. On film, every frame would have to be hand-drawn and line tested before the sequence could be reviewed.

(plastic sheets on which animators draw single frames) and shooting on a rostrum camera (a camera mounted above an animation table), or by making use of digital software. Today, many commercial animators have developed working methods that maximize the benefits of both processes.

Digital animation software has enabled illustrators and graphic designers, as well as animators, to collapse many of the time-consuming hand-drawing production processes on to Apple Macintosh software. Not only has digital software made animation more accessible, but digital formats capable of supporting animation sequences are growing exponentially.

Here Kimberley Alexander, who works at 12 foot 6 Animation, London shows how a simple hand-drawn lettering sequence can be animated digitally.

**3** The first drawing is made (top) by hand in pencil. This drawing is often referred to as a key frame. A second sheet of paper (bottom) is placed over the first and another drawing is made for the final frame in the sequence.

**4** The third (top) and fourth (bottom) intermediate stages are drawn by hand between the beginning and end of the sequence of movement.

**5** By putting all the drawings on to a peg bar the animator can flick between sheets to see movement developing from one drawing to the next, amend previous drawings or develop movement in a new way. In-between frames are usually produced by importing images into

digital software. The lettering moves up and down on a flat picture plane, but the principles of establishing key frames at the beginning and end of a sequence of movement hold good where lettering is drawn in perspective.

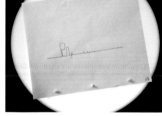

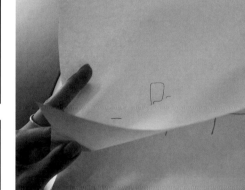

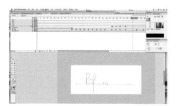

**10** When the position of the key frames on the score has been established, the animator is able to consider how the movement will be visualized in time. To make the lettering grow at a constant speed he or she measures the distance between the letters in the first key frame and the last key frame, then counts the number of intermediate frames.

**11** To create pace within an animation, objects must change the speed at which they move. The rise and fall of the lettering can be adjusted by altering the distance between each frame. To make the lettering appear to accelerate as it rises, the distance must increase frame by frame.

**12** Reversing the order of movement in the sequence will create the impression of deceleration. Some animators work out acceleration/deceleration curves by drawing an arc on graph paper between the highest and lowest positions, and plotting the distance for each frame along the graph lines. Here the lettering appears to sink back into the line.

**13** Prerecorded sound can be linked to the movement of the letters via the score. The order of development between sound and image depends on the nature of the project. When lettering is developed to visualize a conversation on screen, the sound is generally edited first and determines the sequence length, the number of frames and the speed at which the lettering within them changes. The sound forms a signature to which the images are matched.

Until the beginning of the twentieth century virtually all processes of reproducing lettering were static – permanently locking characters into a predetermined space. The calligrapher's pen, the letter-cutter's chisel and the printer's impression, all left an indelible, fixed mark on vellum, stone or paper. The invention of film, the cinematic camera and television liberated lettering, enabling it to move across the screen. Where print had permanently reproduced type in register, film projected light, animated and fluid lettering. The first silent films of the early twentieth century made use of words that appeared and disappeared within the frame, yet the lettering itself was static, presenting the spoken dialogue as text. The words were reproduced as white type on a blackboard and spliced into the live action. When technology advanced sufficiently to match sound and image, lettering really began to move on screen. In the 1930s, early credit rolls (as they were called at the time) borrowed their form from the printed music hall and theatre bills of the nineteenth century. They listed producer, director, lead actor (with their name above the title), film title, and finally the supporting cast.

The credit roll, with its list of smoothly ascending names falling over a static illustration or long shot, was gradually replaced by the use of imagery for the title sequence in which the names of actors and live action were faded in and out, or shots dissolved into one another. In the 1930s, directors began to consider the framing and composition of location shots to support the integration of lettering at post-production. The images were supported by lettering styles developed by in-house studio artists, originally trained in book and magazine illustration, who were responsible for promotional posters and advertising. These commercial artists often transposed the lettering styles associated with print genres to the title of a film: Westerns made use of saloon-bar slab serifs; horror films appropriated blackletter or broken script, 'dripping blood' characters or scratched 'screaming' letters from comic books; while comedies and cartoon shorts frequently made use of brush scripts. Hollywood studios of the early 1930s were quick to recognize the commercial advantages of using the same lettering as the title sequence for the printed advertising and promotional material. Artists began to customize lettering and type styles for a specific title, adjusting the letter shapes and spacing of words to produce a unique logo-type – a visual branding strategy retained for the large budget blockbusters of today.

The rivalry between studios intensified as each attempted to outdo the other in all areas of film production. The simple credit roll format of the pre-war era was challenged by directors who began to commission art directors, designers and cinematographers specifically to develop the title sequences for major films. The remit of the title sequence was subject to a paradigm shift; a film's introduction became a portent of the narrative yet to be revealed. Title sequences were influenced by short films made in continental Europe. Art directors storyboarded visual allegories and metaphors, which were often shot by a separate crew in a very different style from the subsequent live action. Alfred Hitchcock (1899-1980) was so impressed by the ground-breaking title sequence and supporting advertising posters for the film *The Man with the Golden Arm* (1955), devised by the American graphic designer Saul Bass (1920-96), that he commissioned him to create visual introductions to his suspense thrillers *Vertigo* (1958) and *North by Northwest* (1959). Bass used the title sequences to obliquely reference or condense a film plot and playfully teased the viewer with visual ambiguity, while developing his now famous kinetic typography – monumental letterforms which rolled across the screen, accompanied by memorable signature soundtracks.

# Creating a title sequence

**1–4** A title sequence for film is often conceived and storyboarded before the shooting schedule or while it is being drawn up. This enables a director to consider how narrative and titles are combined and assess the location shots required. Television titles are often commissioned during or even after a shoot has been completed and during editing. The music often precedes the visual as it sets the

tempo for the sequence. For a title sequence for *The Bill*, a police drama series set in London, senior designer Roisin began by creating a series of indicative images. She made use of found pictures scanned, collaged and colour-adjusted in Photoshop. Stills were printed out and ordered as indicative key frames, and discussed with the director and programme producer.

**5** The images illustrate a treatment for each part of the sequence here (top) visualizing the camera zooming in on the grid and a street name. The colour palette and mood for the sequence are illustrated by the key frame storyboard (bottom). Here the red, chaotic movement of a street incident at night with revolving beams of flashing light and the sound of police sirens.

**6** The storyboard anticipates the use of stills (top) and live-action footage (bottom). As the drama was still in the process of being shot while the title sequence was being made, Roisin went on set to art direct a series of shots. Stills from these form a shot guide of the live action to be incorporated into the sequence.

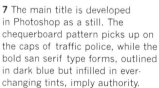

**7** The main title is developed in Photoshop as a still. The chequerboard pattern picks up on the caps of traffic police, while the bold san serif type forms, outlined in dark blue but infilled in ever-changing tints, imply authority.

**8** The Photoshop stills are recreated in Smoke software in the editing suite, which consists of three screens and a graphics tablet. The central screen is the workspace that displays the software capable of editing HD

television pictures, though Roisin works sections of the sequence in Flame or AfterEffects. The right-hand screen is perfectly colour-balanced and shows the frame being worked on. It is used to play back the edited sequence.

**9** Master tapes are stored in a central library (top). Roisin is able to call up any tape she requires and it is installed by an operator (bottom) in a remote room. Once she has completed her work and the sequence is agreed it is passed on to the telecine suite where colour is refined, balanced and prepared for different formats.

# 7.8 Motion graphics: bumpers and stings

**Above:** AFTER EFFECTS is an uncompromising short film that deals with the effect a death caused by knife crime has on not only a family but also the surrounding community. This film challenges the audience to look at their own attitudes towards gun and knife crime. The shattering text is designed to reflect how lives can be shattered by crime. Rushes MGFX Studio developed the shattering effect using software of the same name: After Effects. The text was painstakingly animated by Matt Lawrence and Brad Le Riche using a combination of fractal noise, shatter maps and stock footage of dust and debris exploding.

Lettering tops and tails most screen-based imagery and is the servant of thousands of messages which take many forms. Channel idents, stings, bumpers, promos, title sequences, credits, subtitles, in-programme graphics and advertising are all imbedded within the broadcast, while news listings, navigational guides, channel selection menus, interactive television access, software guides and search engines help the viewer organize information and edit the stream of pictures.

The simple credit roll of early cinema titles has grown into a huge motion graphics industry. Film, television and games producers have retained in-house design departments but a host of independent specialist companies have grown up facilitated by digital technology. Rushes is one of the world's leading post-production facility houses, offering an enormous range of services to clients dealing with any form of motion graphics. Roisin has worked on many title sequences for film, television, broadcast idents, promos, music videos and motion graphics for commercials. Title sequences for films may be as long as three or five minutes, particularly if the sequence includes introductory scenes from the narrative, whereas television titles take a short form, usually no more than 30 seconds and operate on a different premise. Film titles introduce a single event, while television titles serve to separate individual programmes within a broadcast schedule and tend to work in series. For this reason the television titles are less likely to include narrative elements and have fewer credits. The main emphasis is placed on the name of the programme, while the sequence must reveal the nature of the content. The music forms a familiar signature with a strong hook.

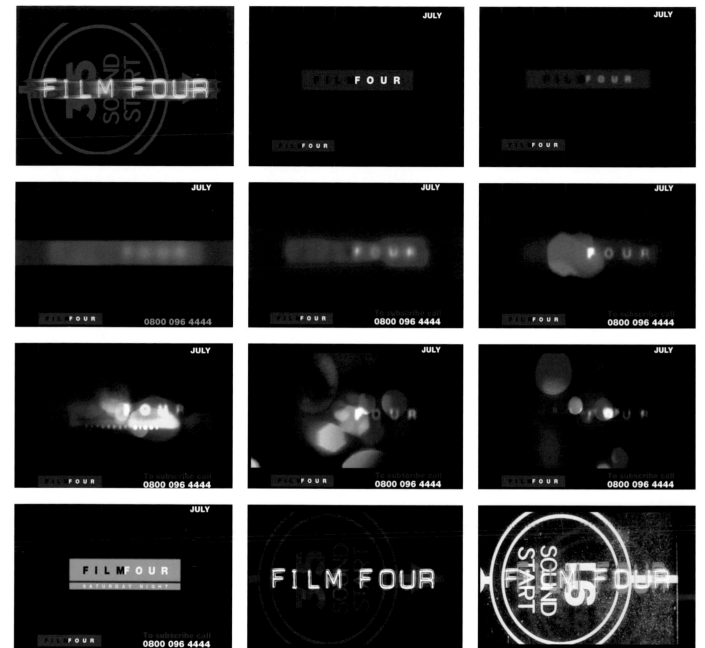

**Above:** Stills from a bumper sequence used to head and tail a commercial break. The initial lettering for the sequence has been embossed into plastic tape with a simple DYMO printer which has a very clear visual signature. The colour grading ensures beautifully rich colour saturation, while Smoke software has been used to make the out-of-focus, hexagonal lens reflections, mimicking a film camera.

Resources...

# Further reading

## 1 Hand-drawn and painted lettering

### Calligraphy
Michelle P. Brown & Patricia Lovett, *The Historical Source Book for Scribes*, London, The British Library, 1999.
Edward Catich, *The Origin of the Serif*, Davenport Iowa, St. Ambrose University 1968.
Ewan Clayton, Edward Johnston: *Lettering & Life*, Ditchling, Ditchling Museum, 2007.
Albert Kapr, *The Art of Lettering*, Munich, K G Saner, 1983.
David Harris, *The Calligrapher's Bible, 100 Complete Alphabets and How to Draw Them*, London, A&C Black, 2004.
Edward Johnston, *Writing and Illuminating and Lettering*, London, Hogg, later Pitman, A&C Black, 1994.
Edward Johnston, (ed.) Heather Child. *Formal Penmanship & Other Papers*, London, Lund Humphries, 1971.
John R. Nash, *English Brush Lettering, the Workshop of William Sharpington*, London, The Scribe no. 45, spring 1989.
Banksy, *Existencilism*, London, 2001.
Banksy, *Banging Your Head Against a Brick Wall*, London, 2001.

### Tattooed lettering
Ina Saltz, *Body Type: Intimate Messages Etched in Flesh*, New York, Abrams, 2006.

### Signwriting
A. J. Lewery, *Signwritten Art*, David & Charles, Newton Abbot, 1989.
Alan Bartram, *Fascia Lettering in the British Isles*, Lund Humphries, 1978.
British Institute of Industrial Art, *The Art of Lettering and Its Uses in Divers Crafts and Trades*, Committee Report, Oxford University Press, 1931.
L. C. Evetts, *Roman Lettering*, London, Pitman, 1938.
Harry Carter, *A View of Early Typography Up to About 1600*, Oxford, Oxford University Press, 1969, reprinted Hyphen Press, 2002.
Nicolete Gray, *A History of Lettering, Creative Experiment & Letter Identity*, Oxford, Phaidon, 1986.
Sir Ambrose Heal, *The English Writing Masters & Their Copybooks 1570–1800*, London, Pitman, 1938.
John Lancaster, *Lettering Techniques*, London, B.T. Batsford, 1951.
Bob & Roberta Smith, *Art U Need, My Part in the Public Art Revolution*, London, Black Dog Publishing, 2007.

### Fairground painting
Anna Carter & Adrian G Shaw, *Carters The Royal Berkshire Steam Fair*, Maidenhead, undated.
Geoff Weedon & Richard Ward, *Fairground Art*, London White Mouse Editions, 1981.

### Signwriting and Canal boat painting
A. J. Lewery, *The Art of the Narrow Boat Painters*, Newton Abbot, David & Charles, 1974.
Tony Lewery, *Flowers Afloat, Folk Artists of the Canals*, Newton Abbot, David & Charles, 1996.
James Hornell *Water Transport*, Newton Abbot, David & Charles, reprinted 1970.
Robert Wilson, *The Number Ones*, Kettering, 1972.

### Road lettering and markings
*The Traffic Signs Regulations and General Directions*, London, HMSO Stationery Office, 1994.

### Painted stained glass
David Beaty, *Light Perpetual, Aviators' Memorial*, Shrewsbury, Airlife, 1995.

## 2 Type casting, composition and design

### Letterpress
R. C. Elliot, *The Monotype from Infancy to Maturity, Monotype Recorder*, vol. 31 no. 243, 1932.
Fred Smeijers, *Counterpunch: Making Type in the Sixteenth Century, Designing Typefaces Now*, London, Hyphen Press, 1996.

### Hand-casting metal type and Hot metal composition
Lawrence Wallis, *A Concise Chronology of Typesetting Developments, 1886–1986*, London, Wynkyn de Worde & Lund Humphries, 1988.
*The Book of Information, the Monotype Corporation Limited*, London, 1970.

### Book finishing
Arthur W. Johnson, *The Manual of Bookbinding*, London, Thames & Hudson 1978.
Kōjirō Ikegami, *Japanese Book Binding: Instructions From a Master Craftsman*. Original text 1979 translated into English adapted by Barbra B. Stephan, first English edition, New York, Weatherhill, 1986.

### Stencil lettering
Tristan Manco, *Stencil Graffiti*, London, Thames & Hudson, 2002.

### Braille
Michael Evamy and Lucienne Roberts, *Insight: a Guide to Design with Low Vision in Mind*, Hove, Rotovision, 2004.

### Transfer lettering
Dave Farey, Colin Brignall et al., *Letraset and Stencil Cutting*, New York, International Typeface Corporation, St Bride & London Printing Library.

### Ishihara colour deficiency lettering
S. Ishihara, *Tests for Colour-blindness*, Tokyo, Kanehara Shuppa Company Limited, 1964.

### Designing type
John D. Berry (ed.) *Language Culture Type: International Type Design in the Age of Unicode*, Association Typographic Internationale, New York, Graphis, 2002.
Michael Harvey, *Lettering Design*, London & New York 1975, The Bodley Head.
Ron Eason & Sarah Rookledge, Phil Baines & Gordon Rookledge (ed.), *Rookledge's International Handbook of Type Design*, Carshalton Beeches, Surrey, Sarema Press, 1991.
Peter Karow, *Digital Formats for Typefaces*, Hamburg, URW Verlag, 1987.
Gerrit Noordzij, *Letterletter, An Inconsistent Collection of Tentative Theories That Do Not Claim Any Other Authority Than That of Common Sense*, Vancouver, Hartley & Marks, 2000.
John W Seybold, *The World of Digital Typesetting*, London, Seybold, 1984.
Hermann Zapf, *About Alphabets, Some Marginal Notes on Type Design*, New York, The Typophiles, 1960.

## 3 Printing

### Woodblock printing
Walter Chamberlain, *The Thames & Hudson Manual of Wood Engraving*, London, Thames & Hudson, 1978.
John O'Conner, *The Technique of Wood Engraving*, London, Batsford, New York Watson-Guptill, 1971.

### Letterpress composition
Glen U. Cleeton & Charles W. Pitkin, *General Printing*, Illinois, McKnight & McKnight, 1941.
Christopher Perfect & Gordon Rookledge, revised by Phil Baines, *Rookledge's International Typefinder*, Carshalton Beeches, Surrey, Sarema Press, 1990.
Southward's, *Modern Printing*, first published 1900, seventh edition edited by Harry Whetton, Leicester, De Montfort Press.
Geoffrey Dowding, *Finer Points in the Spacing & Arrangement of Type*, Hartley & Marks, 1995.

### Thermography and hot foil blocking
John Drefus, *Into Print, Selected Writings on Printing History, Typography and Book Production*, London, British Library, 1994.

### Lithographic printing
Alastair Campbell, *The New Designer's Handbook*, Quarto, 1993.
David Carey, *How it Works, Printing Processes*, Loughborough, Ladybird, 1971.
Alan Pipes, *Production for Graphic Designers*, third edition, London, Laurence King, 2001.
Michael Twyan, *Printing 1770–1970*, Eyre & Spottiswoode Limited, 1970, reprinted Reading, The British Library, Oak Knoll Press and Reading University Press, 1998.

### Screenprinting
Brian Elliot, *Silk-screen Printing*, Oxford, Oxford University Press, 1971.
Tim Mara, *The Manual of Screen Printing*, London, Thames & Hudson, 1979.
Hans G. Scheer, *Graphic Screen Printing*, Zurich, Silk Bolting Cloth Company Limited, 1968.

### Vitreous enamel signs
Justin Howes, *Johnston's Underground Type*, London, Capital Transport, 2000.
Phillip Attwood, *Badges*, London, The British Museum, 2004.
Melissa Schrift, *Biography of a Chairman Mao Badge: the Creation and Mass Consumption of a Personality Cult*, New Jersey, 2001.
Frank R. Setchfield, *The Official Badge Collector's Guide: from the 1890's to the 1980's*, Harlow, 1986.

### Rubber stamps
Alexander Nesbitt, *The History and Technique of Lettering*, New York, Dover Publications, 1957.

### Tin plate printing
Graziella Buccellati (ed.) *Biscuits*, Milan, Franco Maria, 1982.
Hyla Clark, *The Tin Can Book*, New York, New American Library, 1977.

Robert Opie, *The Art of the Label*, Brookvale, NSW, 1987.

**Gravure printing**
Harry Whetton, *Practical Printing and Binding: A Complete Guide to the Latest Developments in All Branches of the Printer's Craft*, London, Odhams Press, 1946.

**Banknotes and security printing**
David Standish, *The Art of Money, the History and Design of Paper Currency from Around the World*, San Francisco, Chronicle Books, 2000.

## 4 Cut, engraved and etched three-dimensional lettering

**Letter-cutting in wood**
S. Harvard, *Ornamental Initials: the Woodcut Initials of Christopher Plantin*, New York, The American Friends of Plantin, 1974.
Michael Harvey, *Carving Letters in Stone and Wood*, London, The Bodley Head, 1987.
John Howard Benson & Graham Carey, *Elements of Lettering*, Newport, 1940.

**Lettercutting stone**
Alan Bartram, *Tombstone Lettering in the British Isles*, London, 1978.
Brenda Berman & Annet Stirling, *Heavens Above, Incisive Letterwork, Exhilarating and Imaginative Letter Carving in Stone and Slate*, Fowey, Ian Grant Publishing, 2005.
Ruth Crib & Joe Crib, *Eric Gill & Ditchling: The Workshop Tradition*, Ditchling, Ditchling Museum, 2007.
Michael Harvey, *Creative Lettering Today*, London, A&C Black, 1996.
David Kindersley & Lida Lopes Cardozo, *Letters Slate Cut, Workshop Philosophy and Practice in the Making of Letters*, Cardozo Kindersley Editions, Cambridge 1990.
Montague Shaw, *David Kindersley, His Work and Workshop*, Cambridge, Cardozo Kindersley Editions & Uitgeverij de Buitenkant, 1989.
W. A. D. Wiggins, *The Shapes of Roman Letters*, New York, The Typofiles, 1947.

**Sandblasting lettering in glass**
Klans F Schmidt, *Signs of the Times*, New York, Watson-Guptill Press, 1996.

**Hand and machine engraving**
John Buckland-Wright, *Etching & Engraving*, London, Studio, 1953.

**Glass-engraving**
Peter Dreiser & Jonathan Matcham, *The Techniques of Glass Engraving*, London, 2006.
Charmian Mocatta, *Lettering on Glass*, London, 2001.
David Pearce, *Glass Engraving, Lettering and Design*, London, Batsford, 1985.

## 5 Moulded and cast three-dimensional lettering

**Rendered lettering**
Nicolete Gray, *Lettering on Buildings*, London, Architectural Press, 1960.

**Lettering in paper**
J. B. Green, *Paper Making By Hand*, Maidstone, Hayley Mill, 1967.
*Paper, Art & Technology*, San Francisco, World Print Council, 1979.
*Paper Making, A General Account of Its History, Process and Applications*, London, The Technical Section of the Paper Makers Association, 1949.

**Rapid prototyping**
C. K. Chua, K. F. Leong, C. S. Lin, *Rapid Prototyping Principles and Applications*, Singapore, World Scientific, 2003.

## 6 Lettering in textiles

**Embroidery**
*English Embroidery 2, Cross Stitch a Handbook*, London, Embroidery Society, 1931.
H M Hands, *Church Needlework, a Manual of Practical Instruction*, London, 1961.
Elizabeth Laird, *The Needlework Library, a Modern Manual*, London, Mathisen, 1949.

**Cross stitch**
Thérèse de Dillmont, *Encyclopedia of Needlework*, Paris, Mulhouse, 1924.
Maria Foris, *Charted Folk Designs for Cross-stitch Embroidery*, New York, Dover, 1975.
Goodey's Lady's Book, *Victorian Alphabets, Monographs and Names for Needleworkers*, New York, Dover, 1974.
Jane Greenoff, *The Cross-stitcher's Bible*, London, David & Charles, 2007.
Jana Hauschild, *Treasury of Charted Designs*, Weldon's Practical Needlework, London, Weldon's Limited, 1947.

**Hand knitting and Machine knitting**
Sarah Barnes, *Manual of Knitting and Crocheting*, Philadelphia, 1936.
James Norbury, *The Penguin Knitting Book*, Harmondsworth, Middlesex, 1957.
Marjory Tillotson, *The Complete Knitting Book*, London, Pitman & Sons, 1947.
Barbara G. Walker, *A Treasury of Knitting Patterns*, New York, Charles Scribner's & Sons, 1968.
Barbara G. Walker, *A Second Treasury of Knitting Patterns*, New York, Charles Scribner's & Sons, 1970.

**Rug making**
Jane Olson, *The Rug Hooker's Bible*, New York, 2005.

## 7 Illumination, animation and motion graphics

**Neon signs**
Len Davidson, *Vintage Neon*, New York, Schiffer Reference, 1999.
J Natal, *Neon Boneyard*, Las Vegas, 2006
Wayne Strattman (ed.), *Neon Techniques, The Handbook of Neon Signs and Cold-cathode Lighting*, New York, 1947.
D J Sprengnagel, *Neon World*, New York, 1997

**Motion graphics**
Jeff Bellantoni & Matt Woolman *Type in Motion, Innovations in Digital Graphics*, London, Thames & Hudson, 1999.

# Glossary

**Acid etching** Dissolving either the surface of a metal plate or cutting through the plate with acid. Letterforms can be produced right-reading to be read from the plate or wrong-reading to be printed from the plate.

**Appliqué** Decorative work that involves cutting out one piece of fabric and stitching it to the face of another.

**Ascender** The stroke of a lower-case letter which projects above the x height.

**Baseline** Invisible line upon which letters appear to sit.

**Bastard size** A metal type size that does not fit into the conventional size scale of 6, 7, 8, 9, 10, 12, 14, 18, 24pt, e.g. 13½pt; or a type cast on a body larger or smaller than that for which it is cut.

**Block line plate** An etched or engraved (wrong-reading) aluminium, copper, magnesium or zinc plate which is mounted on a type-high block of wood for printing.

**Block printing** Printing from a wood-engraved or metal-etched line or half-tone block. The block sits face-up on a press bed and a sheet of paper is rolled over it on a rotary press or forced down on the block on a platen press.

**Blocking press** A press on which the metal line block is electrically heated to stamp debossed lettering and designs on to a hardback book cover.

**Bowl** The rounded forms in letters, e.g. the lower half of the lower-case b.

**Broken script** Calligraphic letterforms drawn with a broad-edged, square pen.

**Brush script** Calligraphic letterforms written with a pointed or square-cut brush.

**Bubble jet** Type of digital printer that releases ink on to the page by bursting a tiny ink bubble at the end of a very fine nozzle.

**CAD** Computer-aided design. Any computer software programme that enables design, or type design (e.g. FontLab, FontStudio), or typesetting layout for graphic design (e.g. Quark Express, InDesign).

**Calligrapher** A person who has been trained to make hand-drawn lettering.

**CAM** Computer-aided manufacture. Any software program that can be linked to a machine to enable the automated or semi-automated manufacture of an object, product or letterform.

**Cap height** An invisible line that determines the height above the baseline in a font. The term is also used in calligraphy, though here greater freedom allows some capitals to be terminated above or below the line.

**Case (type case)** A wooden case with small compartments for storing letterpress characters. Each case holds letters of the same font and point size, and each compartment within the case is dedicated to a separate character, e.g. all Bembo 14pt characters are stored together. Cases of the same font and size are often stored in pairs, e.g. the upper case for majuscules, the lower case for minuscules.

**Casting** Pouring or injecting any liquid material into a mould so that it solidifies into a solid form, e.g. bronze or chocolate letters. Hand-type-casting is the type-manufacturing process invented by Gutenberg and involves pouring molten lead into a matrix (female letter mould). Monotype, Linotype and Ludlow machines mechanize the casting process.

**Centred** Symmetrically aligned text.

**Character** An individual letterform.

**CMYK** The four process colours cyan, magenta, yellow and key (the printer's term for black).

**Colour separation** The process of separating a full-colour photographic image into the four process colours CMYK.

**Composition** The process of setting type by hand, mechanically or digitally.

**Compositor** A highly trained specialist in letterpress printing who sets type either by hand or machine.

**Connectives** Forms that link letters in a word, derived from calligraphy, but found in engraving, e.g. copperplate.

**CRC** Camera-ready-copy. Artwork prepared for print reproduction.

**Deboss** A letter or design that is pressed beneath the surface of the paper, leather binding or book cloth.

**Descender** Stroke of a minuscule or lower-case letterform that descends below the baseline e.g. g, j, p.

**Die-form** A metal tool that determines the shape of a letter or design.

**Die cutting** Process where paper or card is cut into a shape or letterform by a blade mounted in a block of wood.

**Digital type** Type which is drawn on screen in a software program and linked to a QWERTY keyboard, a word-processing program or type composition software.

**Direct-to-media** A type of inkjet printer that can print on to the smooth surface of virtually any substrate, e.g. wood, metal, glass, ceramic, plastic or paper.

**Dry proof** A generic term for proofing which does not use water or lithography, but makes use of dyes, light-sensitive powders, or laser, photographic or digital exposures.

**Dye-sublimation** The process of transferring dye from one substrate to another through heat and pressure.

**Emboss** A raised design or letterform which stands proud of the surface of the paper, leather binding or book cloth. The plate may be pressed from the reverse.

**Fascia** The board or stone surface which sits under a shopfront cornice. It is used to display the shop sign and was traditionally signwritten.

**Foil blocking** The process of debossing metallic foil into a book cover or printed packaging using a heated block and mechanical pressure.

**Font/Fount** Set of characters in a specific typeface of one size and style. Used to describe a single weight or style.

**Foundry type** Metal type which is cast in a harder lead alloy so as to be more durable.

**Finishing** A group of processes in the final stages of producing a case-bound book, such as cover titling, spine lettering, gouge work, embossing, gilding and decorative linework.

**Freehand** Lettering drawn by hand without a mechanical aid, e.g. calligraphy, signwriting or from a digital slate; or a software program that enables free drawing.

**French curves** Set of drawing tools used in formal drawing with logarithmic curves that can be drawn around.

**Galleys** Three-sided metal trays of varying width in which letterpress type forms are tied up with string and stored.

**Galley proof** Printed impression of letterpress type taken to check for, and correct, errors prior to the type being imposed on the stone.

**Gouache** Form of water-based paint.

**Gouge work** Designs or lettering on the cover and spine of a book which use curved gouges to form the letters.

**Graffiti** Scratching, drawing, writing or painting on walls or other surfaces; in modern times often with Magic Markers or spray paint.

**Gravure** An intaglio print process in which the ink is held in tiny engraved pits below the surface of a metal plate. It is used for high-quality security printing, such as stamps and some banknotes.

**Ground** Visual surface on which a letterform sits. Commonly a black figure, e.g. type, sits on a white ground paper or screen.

**Half-tone** Process by which continuous tone is reproduced in print by a series of dots which vary in size.

**Hand** A style of lettering in calligraphy e.g. copperplate, roundhand.

**Hand-tooled** Lettering on book covers that is worked by hand rather than machine.

**Hinting** Refining the appearance of curves within digital type forms so that they best delineate the outline of the desired letterform within a square pixel grid. This information is then embedded within the font to control its on-screen appearance at different sizes or resolutions.

**Hot foil blocking/printing** Debossing lettering into a book cover using metallic foil and a heated platen press.

**Hot metal composition** Mechanized metal setting in which the molten lead is automatically injected into the matrix (see Monotype, Linotype).

**Impression (letterpress)** The slight debossing or indentation in the paper where the letterform is forced down on the sheet (visible from the reverse).

**Inkjet** A form of digital printer where the ink is released through a nozzle under pressure.

**Interpolation** Intermediate weights of a type family created between the extreme tolerances; forms adapted visually for different sizes of the same weight.

**Italic** Calligraphic term for lettering inclined at an angle, adopted to describe similar typographic forms which were originally developed to fit more words on to a line.

**Justified** A column of text where the left- and right-hand edges are even; each line is the same length and the spacing between words is not identical.

**Kern** The part of a metal letterform that

projects beyond its body.

**Kerning** In metal type, adjusting the space between characters positively; in digital type, adjusting the space between characters positively or negatively.

**Keyline** Outline of a design or letterform which a hand or mechanical cutter follows to shape the letter.

**Letter-cutting** Incising letters in wood, stone or metal.

**Letterface** The surface area of a metal letter which is pressed on to the paper to make an impression.

**Letterform** The shape of a calligraphic or typographic letter.

**Letterpress** A method of relief printing where the ink is transferred under pressure directly from the face of the letter to the paper.

**Ligature** Letters combined to form a single character, e.g. æ.

**Linotype** A hot metal casting and composition machine that sets one line of type at a time.

**Lithography** A planographic print process in which the ink sits on the dry surface of the plate but not on the wet or greasy areas. In offset lithography the image is set off on to a blanket roller, and the plate does not come into direct contact with the paper.

**Logotype** A bespoke symbol that uses a word or letterform to communicate an idea.

**Lower case** Small, typographic letters, of uneven height derived from hand-written miniscules.

**Majuscule** Calligraphic term for capital letters.

**Matrix (type)** A copper (hand casting) or brass (machine casting) slug containing a wrong-reading female letterform that forms the mould for casting metal type.

**Measure** The line length in a column of type.

**Minuscule** Calligraphic term for small or lower-case letters.

**Monotype** A hot metal casting and composition machine that sets a single character at a time.

**Motion graphics** Generic term for lettering in animated, film or television title sequences.

**Pantograph** System of mechanical levers, arranged in a diamond shape, which enable a letterform or design to be copied actual size, enlarged or reduced. Used in mechanical engraving and stone cutting.

**Pantone** A trade name for an extensive set of printing inks with over 1,000 colours (which can be viewed on screen and specified digitally), that can be matched to CMYK-equivalent colours. The system includes pastels, metallics, dyes and marker pens.

**Pixel** The smallest digital unit which can carry tone and colour to make up an image or letterform. The greater the number of pixels, the higher the screen resolution.

**Photographic etching** Acid etching in which the resist is screen-printed onto the surface of the metal from a photographically generated stencil.

**Photo polymer** A light-sensitive solution which changes or solidifies when exposed to light.

**Plate** A sheet of aluminium, plastic or paper which carries an image, lettering and/or type in one colour or one of the process colours for lithographic printing.

**Platen** A flat, heavy metal plate used on some forms of printing press to create the impression through the application of pressure. The platen on foil blocking and dye-sublimation machines is electrically heated.

**Production** Mechanized processes for reproducing letterforms.

**Proofing** Generic term for reproducing a limited number of prints for the purpose of checking and correcting the design, layout and type on a sheet before moving to the final run.

**Pull** Making a single printed impression.

**Punch** A steel rod which is shaped into a wrong-reading letterform before being hammered into a copper matrix.

**Punch cutter** Highly skilled craftsperson who uses files to shape the end of a steel rod into a wrong-reading letterform, thus creating punches and counter punches.

**Punch press** A very powerful press which forces a male die-form into a female form, cutting a metal strip between the two. Used in stencil cutting.

**QWERTY keyboard** Keyboard layout used on all standard computers, named after the first six letters of the keyboard's alphabet.

**Rapid prototyping** A generic term for a group of technologies that create solid models of three-dimensional objects, products or letterforms prior to production, without the expense of tooling.

**Refreshable display (Braille)** A series of six or eight pins arranged in a Braille cell, which rise and fall to create Braille lettering and enable a Braille user to check what they have typed.

**Registration** The correct positioning of one print colour in relation to another on a printed sheet.

**Relief** A letterform that stands proud of a surface.

**Rendered lettering** Large relief lettering created in the sand and lime mortar used to face buildings.

**Right-reading** Lettering designed to be read from left to right; all the forms are presented with the correct orientation.

**Roman** Upright letterforms, not italic; the 'normal' weight of a font not bold or condensed; or a serifed font as opposed to a sanserif font.

**Sandblasting** The process of firing small particles of garnet or sand through a tiny nozzle using pressurized air to produce a profile-cut or incised surface in wood, stone or glass. A rubber stencil is used as a resist to create the letterforms. A sandblasted glass surface will appear opaque.

**Sand casting** A traditional type of open metal casting. A male mould is placed in a casting box and packed with a combination of very fine sand and oil. The mould is removed and molten metal poured into the impression to create a solidified object or letter when the metal has cooled.

**Sanserif** A typeface without serifs.

**Screen printing** A process in which ink is squeezed through a stencil resist supported by a fabric mesh on to the paper, where it sits proud of the paper.

**Separation** A layer of artwork which is reproduced in one colour, e.g. cyan from a four-colour process.

**Serif** The small, tapering stroke at the terminal of the broader vertical stroke, derived from Roman capital forms. Also used to describe a font with these strokes.

**Setting** The process of composing or arranging letters and words into the order determined by an author's manuscript, or arranged to a designer's specification.

**Signature** Section of a book made up from a folded sheet to create pages when guillotined. Signatures are built up in 2, 4, 8, 16, 32, or 64 pages. Two- and four-page signatures are now generally referred to as 'tip-ins'.

**Slab serif** A square stroke termination.

**Slate-and-stylus method (Braille)** The slate consists of a surface with six or eight small, dish-shaped impressions arranged in Braille cells. A sheet of paper is placed over the cells. A short stick with a soft-pointed tip (the stylus) is used to press the paper into the impressions. The process is repeated to form the raised dot patterns that represent letters and words.

**Tag** Hand-drawn, decorative signature of an individual graffiti artist.

**Thermoforming** The process of bending plastics between male and female forms using heat and pressure applied in a forming press.

**Thermography** A process which produces glossy or metallic raised lettering or imagery in letterpress type. Resin crystals impregnated with pigment are sprinkled over the wet ink, which expands and hardens when dried under an infrared, red or ultraviolet light.

**Typeface** The surface of the relief type which is inked to form the impression.

**Typo** A spelling or font selection error made by the compositor.

**Typography** The mechanical notation and arrangement of language.

**Uncial** Inch-high calligraphic letters which are rounded with a vertical axis, and have short ascenders and descenders.

**Upper case** Capital letters or majuscule, letterpress type stored in the top of a pair of cases.

**Variable message space (VMS)** Generic term for signs, either electronic or analogue in which the message can be altered remotely.

**Wet proof** Proof printed lithographically or gravure using the same process as the final run.

**Woodblock** Solid wooden block, often of close-grained fruit wood, e.g. pear is used for engraving.

**Wrong-reading** Lettering which has been flipped horizontally so that each letterform is presented in reverse. Wrong-reading forms are used in many production processes in print and casting.

# Index

# Acknowledgements

The author would like to thank the following, designers, craftspeople, researchers, academics, manufacturers and companies for their help in the making of this book. So many people were extraordinarily generous with their time: providing access, enabling us to photograph, giving permissions, samples, contacts, suggesting alternative or related processes, setting up interviews and answering technical questions in person, by telephone and e-mail. I have grouped together by chapter the names of all those who were so helpful and hope these acknowledgments will be of service to those readers interested in a particular group of processes or section of the book. Some contributors are identified as individuals whilst my thanks are extended to others as groups or companies. I have made every effort to ensure the contact details listed are correct at the time of going to press.

## 1 Hand-drawn and painted lettering

**Calligraphy**
Rachel Yallop, calligrapher, UK
www.rachelyallop.co.uk
Carol Kemp, calligrapher, UK
www.carolkemp.com
Lettering on p.20 designed for the
BBC programme of the same name:
*The Swagger Portrait* (1992)
**Digital calligraphy**
Carol Kemp, as before
**Graffiti**
Bates, graffiti artist, Sweden
*Killing Scraps*, Copenhagen
www.greatbates.com
Eine, stencil/graffiti artist, UK,
*Vandalism*, Shoreditch London
Einsamkeit, graffiti artist, Spain
*I wake up from a nightmare and I am scared of going back to sleep and dreaming of the second half*, Nov 2008
www.fotolog.com/madrizeinsamkeit
Nylon, graffiti artist, UK
*Chairman*, September 2004
*Toon Town*, July 2009, legal wall,
Newcastle, UK
Siner LTS, graffiti artist, US
www.sinergraf.com
Stayhigh149, graffiti artist, US
Media requests, Chris Pape
www.stayhigh149.com
**Tattooed lettering**
Tom Blank and Wizard Tattoo, London, UK
tel: 020 8 544 0045
**Signwriting**
Crich Tramway Village
The National Tramway Museum, Matlock, UK
www.tramway.co.uk
**Fairground painting**
Joby Carter, Carter's Entertainment,
Maidenhead, UK
e-mail: info@cartersentertainment.com
Peter Tate, signwriter and fairground artist,
Tate Decor, Derbyshire, UK
tel: 01332 883 388
**Canal boat painting**
David Moore, Brierly Hill, UK
tel: 01384 571 204
e-mail: davemoore4@tinyworld.co.uk
**Road lettering and markings**
HELIOS Domzale, d.d, producers of paints and resins, Slovenia
www.helios.si/eng
The Stationery Office, UK
*The Traffic Signs and General Directions, 1994*
www.tso.co.uk
**Painted stained glass**
Joseph Nuttgens, Stained-glass artist
The Stained Glass Studio, High Wycombe, UK
www.josephnuttgens.co.uk
St Mary's Cathedral, Newcastle upon Tyne, UK
www.stmaryscathedral.org.uk
Nick Goonan, photographer, UK
Scenic Photos Ltd
www.scenicphotos.com
**Mosaic lettering**
Stuart Whatling, photographer, UK
Travel Photography
www.flat3.co.uk
Baines, P. and Dixon, C.
*Signs: Lettering in the Environment*,
Laurence King, 2008

## 2 Type casting, composition and design

**Letterpress**
Museum Plantin-Moretus Pretenkabinet,
Antwerp UNESCO World Heritage
www.museumplantinmoretus.be
**Hand-casting metal type**
Nigel Roche, St Bride Library of Printing,
London, UK
www.stbride.org
**Hand composition**
Phil Able, Hand & Eye Press, London, UK
e-mail: print@handandeye.co.uk
**Hot metal composition**
Stan Lane, Gloucester Typesetting, UK
tel: 0145 382 5623
The Monotype Corporation Limited, UK
www.monotypefonts.com
**Book finishing**
John Goss & Derek Reid, Shepherds Book
Binding, London UK
www.bookbinding.co.uk
**Punch-press stencils**
Mr P. Gardner, AT Brown precision engravers,
signmakers, stencil cutters and rubber
stamp suppliers, Brentwood, UK
www.atbrown.com
David Ottley, graphic design, art direction
& Typography
www.davidottley.co.uk
me@davidottley.co.uk
**Typewriters**
The Martin Howard Collection, Canada
www.antiquetypewriters.com
Chestnut Ridge Typewriter Museum
Herman J. Price, Fairmont, US
www.hpricecpa.com/typewriters.html
**Braille**
Royal National Institute for Blind People
(RNIB), UK
www.rnib.org
ClearVision Project
www.clearvisionproject.org
**Transfer lettering**
Paul Pinyot, Tube Radio Restoration,
Pittsburgh, US
www.ppinyot.com
Letraset Limited
Kingsnorth Industrial Estate, Ashford, UK
e-mail: info@letraset.com
www.letraset.com

Central Lettering Record,
Central Saint Martins College of
Art & Design, London UK
**Snellen eyesight test**
1862–1875, published by Van der Weijer,
Utrecht Collection
University Museum Utrecht,
the Netherlands
www.hetfotoatelier.nl
**Ishihara's colour deficiency lettering**
Ishihara's Test for Colour Deficiency
copyright of Isshinkai Foundation,
Tokyo, Japan
**Designing type**
Jeremy Tankard Typography Limited
e-mail: info@typography.net
*Construction*: Clayton Dixon
*Identity*: Alec Bathgate
of Strategy Design & Advertising, NZ
www.strategy.co.nz
**Creating digital type**
András Benedek, Fine Fonts, UK
www.finefonts.com

## 3 Printing

**Woodblock printing**
Bjørn Ortmann, graphic designer/art director,
DADDY, Copenhagen, Denmark
www.daddy-studio.com
Ilse Buchert Nesbitt,
The Third & Elm Press
Rhode Island, US
www.thirdandelm.com
Alexander Nesbitt, photographer
www.alexandernesbitt.com
www.nesbittphoto.com
**Letterpress printing**
Phil Able, Hand & Eye Press, London, UK
e-mail: phil@handandeye.co.uk
Michele Jannuzzi, Jannuzzi Smith Design
Consultancy, London UK
www.jannuzzismith.com
Martin Z. Schröder, printer, Berlin, Germany
www.druckerey.de
David Jury, editor *TypoGraphic*, Head of Graphic
Design, Colchester Institute, UK
Scott Williams & Henrik Kubel, A2/SW/HK
Design Studio, London, UK
www.a2swhk.co.uk
Stan Lane, Gloucester Typesetting, UK
tel: 0145 382 5623
Vince Frost, Frost* Design, Australia/London
www.frostdesign.com.au
Typeset: The House of Naylor
**Lithography**
Studio Dumbar for Holland Festival,
Rotterdam, the Netherlands
www.studiodumbar.com
**Screen printing**
Signscope (Previously Active Signs)
Blaze Group incorporating Blaze
Maintenance and Signscope, UK
Tel: 01843 850 800
www.signscope.com
Becky Redman, London, UK
www.beckyredman.com
**Vitreous enamel signs**
David Gatrell, A. J. Wells & Sons Vitreous
Enamellers, Newport, Isle of Wight, UK
e-mail: enamel@ajwells.co.uk
National Motor Museum, Beaulieu,
Hampshire, UK

www.nationalmotormuseum.org.uk

**Rubber stamps**
Polydiam Industries Limited, London, UK
e-mail: info@polydiam.com
www.polydiam.com

**Tin plate printing**
Bob Christmas, Causeway Trading Estate,
Bristol, UK
tel: 0117 958 6888
Peter & Ben Luff, Cyril Luff Limited
(Metal decorators), Cwmbran,
South Wales
e-mail: info@cyrilluff,co.uk
Andrew S. Cahan, author of *Chinese Label Art
1900–1976*, US: Schiffer Publications, 2006

**Dye-sublimation**
Larry Hickmott, photographer, British Cycling
new.britishcycling.org.uk
Stylo Graphics Limited, Hertfordshire, UK
tel: 01923 800 666
www.stylographics.co.uk

**Vinyl lettering**
Nat McBride, photographer
www.grandprixpixltd.moonfruit.com
Stylo Graphics Limited, as before

**Inkjet printing**
Stylo Graphics Limited, as before

**Direct-to-media printing**
Stylo Graphics Limited, as before

## 4 Cut, engraved and etched three-dimensional lettering

**Letter cutting in wood**
Caroline Webb, lettercutter (wood), Wiltshire, UK
www.carolinewebblettering.com

**Letter cutting (stone) by hand**
Michael Harvey, photographer and
typographer, UK
www.finefonts.com
*Stone* created by Andrew Whittle,
Photographed by Michael Harvey
for the book *Letter Carver*
The Cardozo Kindersley Workshop,
Cambridge, UK
www.kindersleyworkshop.co.uk
John Neilson, Stone carver
Text from *Duino Elegies* by R. M. Rilke,
translated from the German by
Stephen Mitchell
Fergus Wessel, Oxfordshire UK
www.stoneletters.com

**Letter cutting stone by machine**
Elfes Monumental Masons, London, UK
headstoneslondon.com
The Commonwealth War Graves Commission,
Maidenhead, UK
www.cwgc.org
Andrew Grassby, Computer-controlled, machine-
cut letters in stone & sand blasting stone,
Dorchester, UK
tel: 01305 269 678

**Sandblasting**
Lesley Pyke, glass engraver, Suffolk, UK
www.lesleypyke.com

**Machine-routed letters**
Signscope (Previously Active Signs) as before

**Water-cut letters**
Aqua Cut UK Limited, Northfleet, Kent UK
e-mail: aquacutltd@AOL.com

**Hot-wire cutting**
Samuel Oswick, designer
www.indigobronze.com

Graphic Workshop, Wembley, Middlesex, UK
tel: 020 8 903 0490
www.thegraphicworkshop.co.uk

**Laser cutting and etching**
Central Saint Martins College of Art
& Design, London UK

**Pop-up and paper lettering**
Celia Kilner, calligrapher and stone carver
West Yorkshire, UK
e-mail: info@celiakilner.co.uk
Alida Sayer, artist
alidarosie.blogspot.com

**Hand and machine engraving**
Keith Raes, engraver, Canterbury, Kent, UK
example on page 160 based upon
that of Charles Demengeot,
a Parisian engraver born 1881
tel: 01227 710 533
www.keithraesengraver.co.uk
Department of Typography & Graphic
Communication and Teaching Archive,
University of Reading UK
www.reading.ac.uk/special-
collections/collections/archives/sc-
publishers

**Glass-engraving**
Lesley Pyke, glass engraver, as before

**Acid-etching glass**
Keith Jenkins, Nero Signs (glass/designs),
London, UK
e-mail: sales@nerodesigns.co.uk
Stuart Bourne, artist
*We have only come to look*, 2003, located
at Hannah Peschar Sculpture Garden in
Ockley, Surrey, UK

**Photographic etching**
Photofabrication Limited, St Neots,
Cambridgeshire, UK
tel: 01480 475 831
e-mail: sales@photofab.co.uk
Autechre 'Quaristice' steel album cover,
special edition CD
Design: The Designers Republic
Production: Warp Records
Released: 3rd March 2008

## 5 Moulded and cast three-dimensional lettering

**Rendered lettering**
Valentin Mandache, historian
*Historic Houses of Romania*,
www.historo.wordpress.com

**Lettering in paper**
Justin Hobson, Fenner Fine Paper
St Cuthberts Paper Mill, Wells, Somerset UK
tel: 01749 672 015
www.inveresk.co.uk
Benwell Sebard Embossing
www.benwells.co.uk

**Polystyrene moulding**
Dow Europe GmbH, Switzerland
Hampshire Insulation Products, Marwell
Winchester, UK
tel: 01962 777730
www.hampshireinsulations.co.uk

**Vacuum-forming and thermoforming**
Polydiam Industries Limited, as before
Graphic Thought Facility and Paul Elliman,
The/Le Garage exhibition
GTF Design Consultancy, London UK
info@graphicthoughtfacility.com

**Rapid prototyping**

Janne Kyttanen for Freedom Of Creation,
the Netherlands
www.freedomofcreation.com
Central Saint Martins College of Art & Design,
as before
Joe Wentworth, Rapid Manufacturing
Personalised Calendar, London, UK
www.joewentworth.co.uk

**Coins and medals**
The Royal Mint
www.royalmint.com

**Lettering with plants**
Peter Stubbs, Scotland
www.edinphoto.org.uk

**Lettering in food**
Droste chocolate letters
www.droste.nl

**Sand casting metal**
Redfields English Leadwork Limited,
Hampshire, UK
e-mail: sales@redfields.co.uk

**Cast-aluminium and polyurethane signs**
Signs of the Times, Tebworth,
Bedfordshire, UK
tel: 01525 874 185
e-mail: enquires@sott.co.uk
Phil Baines
Central Lettering Record, Central Saint
Martins College of Art & Design, as before

## 6 Lettering in textiles

**Embroidery**
Piers D.R. Macleod, Hand & Lock Embroidery,
London, UK
tel: 020 7 580 7488
e-mail: enquiries@handembroidery.co.uk

**Flag making**
Newton Newton, The Bishop Tozer's Chapel,
Burgh-Le-Marsh,
Lincolnshire, UK
e-mail: mail@newtonnewtonflags.com

**Machine embroidery**
Lizzie Finn, Illustrator (machine embroidery)
c/o Bianca Redgrave & Co
www.biancaredgrave.com
p.199, *Print Magazine* stitched lettering,
art directed by Kristina De Matteo

**Cross stitch**
Evelin Kasikov, graphic designer (cross stitch)
London, UK
www.evelinkasikov.com

**Hand knitting**
Wendy Baker & Sue McLaughlin,
Queene & Country, Berkhamsted,
Hertfordshire, UK
e-mail: wendy.baker@queeneandcountry.co.uk
sue.mclaughlin@queeneandcountry.co.uk
Susan G. Feltman Sweater Designs
LLC, t/a Custom Design Sweater Studio, US
www.customsweaters.com

**Machine knitting**
Rodney Wilson
Central Saint Martins College of Art
& Design, as before

**Rugmaking**
Carol Kemp, as before

## Acknowledgements *continued*

### 7 Illumination, animation and motion graphics

**Fireworks**
Blackcat Fireworks Limited, Huddersfield, UK
www.blackcatfireworks.co.uk
Nir Tober, graphic designer, Israel
www.nirtober.com
Karmelo Bermejo, artist
*The Grand Finale*. Bank Loan Granted to an
Art Gallery Used to Pay a Firework Display
at the Closing Ceremony of Art Basel Miami
Beach 2009
Maisterravalbuena Gallery
www.karmelobermejo.com
**Illuminated metal and Perspex lettering**
Signscope (Previously Active Signs), as before
**Light boxes**
Signscope (Previously Active Signs), as before
**Neon signs**
Mr & Mrs Brophy, Electro Signs Limited,
London UK
www.signbuyer.co.uk
**Variable message space**
Euro Display, LED screens and LED display
manufacturer, Italy
www.EuroDisplay.com
**Hand-drawn animation**
Kimberley Alexander, animator
12foot6 Animation, UK
www.12foot6.com
**Motion graphics: title sequences**
Rushes Post Production Limited,
London, UK
www.rushes.co.uk
with thanks to TalkbackThames &
FremantleMedia
**Motion graphics: bumpers and stings**
Mark One, Designer & Director
London
www.markone.tv
with additional thanks to Natasha Preville
Production Traffic Manager, Red Bee Media

## Picture credits

The location photographs for this book
were taken by Daniel Alexander and art
directed by Andrew Haslam.
The author and Laurence King Publishing
Limited would like to thank the following owners
of the following photographs for granting
permission to reproduce them in this book.
Every effort has been made to contact all
copyright holders, but should there be any
errors or omissions the publishers would
be pleased to insert the appropriate
acknowledgement in any subsequent
printing of this publication.

Numbers refer to pages; numbers in brackets
refer to caption number from main page.

Martin Andrews, University of Reading: 161
Phil Baines & Catherine Dixon: 50 (2,6,7); 188 r
Bates: 26 cb
Karmelo Bermejo: 211 t
Stuart Bourne: 167
British Cycling (Larry Hickmott): 122
The British Library: 14 © The British
    Library Board: MS Harley 2793,
    folio. 33, lines 5 and 6
Andrew S. Cahan, Nov 2009: 117 (2,3,4)
ClearVision: 75 tr
The Designers Republic/ Warp Records: 170 t
Anthony Dickenson: 106, 107, 111, 112, 113,
    143, 144, 145
Eine: 26 tl, ml, bl
Einsamkeit: 27 (4)
Euro Display: 220 t, c; 221 t
Susan G Feltman: 203 (3)
Freedom Of Creation: 178
Vince Frost, Frost* Design: 98 (3)
Goodland Collection108 from Goodland
    Collection, Commonwealth War Graves
    Commission: 141 t
Nick Goonan, Scenic Photos Ltd: 48
Graphic Thought Facility and Paul Elliman: 177 cr
Hampshire Insulation: 175 (3)
Michael Harvey: 136 c
Andrew Haslam: 32, 33 t, 34, 35, 50 (3,4,5),
    71 (3), 100, 140, 141 b, 156 (1,3), 165,
    166 br, 170 (2,3,4), 175 (2,4), 220 bl,
    221 (2,3,4)
www.hetfotoatelier.nl Utrecht (1862–1875,
    published by Van der Weijer, Utrecht
    Collection): 82
Martin Howard: 72, 73 t
Guy Hutsebaut: 53
IBM Archives: 73 bl, br
Michele Jannuzzi: 97 (3)
Stefan Jansson: 136 l
David Jury: 98 (1,2)
Evelin Kasikov: 200, 201, 202
Ilan Kelman: 214
Celia Kilner: 156 (2)
Kindersley Archives: 137 (1)
K Kremerskothen: 110 l
Letraset: 81 b
Nat McBride: 124, 125 br
Valentin Mandache: 172
Tim Marshall: 56, 57, 81 t, 203 (1,2)
MMP Photographic: 137 (2)
Kevin Moores: 33 b 1–6
Kai Hofmann, Museum für Druckkunst
    Leipzig: 96 bl
John Neilson: 137 (3)
Alexander Nesbitt: 91 (b 1–4)

Vinnie Nylon: 27 (1, 2)
Samuel Oswick, Buttress Font: 152
Pagoda Red, Chicago: 133 (5)
Chris Pape: 27 (9)
Lex van Pieterson, 1988: 103
Paul Pinyot: 80
Sascha Pohfepp: 179 b
Herman Price, Chestnut Ridge Typewriter
    Museum: 73 c
Lesley Pyke: 162 (3)
Becky Redman: 108, 109
Réunion des Musées Nationaux 195 t
RNIB: 74 c, 75 b
Rushes: 224-5, 227
Royal Mint: 180
St Cuthberts Paper Mill: 174 (2, 3)
Tvrtko Sauerborn: 42
Martin Z. Schröder, Drucker: 97 (4, 5); 99 (4, 5)
Siner LTS: 27 (8)
Standard Fireworks : 210 tl, bl; 211 bl, br
David Stewart for TBWA/Brussels/2007: 128 t
Strategy Design & Advertising: 84 (10, 11)
Peter Stubbs: 181
Styron Division of the Dow Chemical Company:
    175 (1)
Swiss National Bank: 121
Peter Tate: 39
Nir Tober: 210 r
Chris Vu aka GenkiGenki: 27 (5)
Mark Walters 226
Fergus Wessel: 139 (2,3)
Stuart Whatling: 50 (1)

## Additional thanks

There are a great many people who have
contributed informally to the content and
offered support in the making of this book,
Wendy Baker, students and staff, both past
and present from the MA Communication
Design Course at Central Saint Martins College
of Art & Design and the London College of
Communication. Particular thanks goes to: our
former acting Course Director Geoff Fowle, the
staff team, Andrew Foster, David Moore, Sadhna
Jain, Associate lecturing staff supporting the
Graphics route, Paulus Driebholtz, Maria de
Gandra, Annegeret Mølhave, Ros Streeton,
Rathna Ramanathan, and from BA Graphic
Design Phil Baines and Catherine Dixon. It
is also important to thank those who have
afforded me the time to undertake this project
while at CSM, Jonathan Barratt, Dean of School
of Graphic & Industrial Design, Martin Wolley,
former Head of Research, and Dani Salvadori at
the Innovations Centre CSM for commissioning
the title which I originally proposed over a
decade ago. There are also those who have
performed very specific roles in the making of
this book: Annegeret Mølhave, initial location
research; Suzanne Doolin, picture research and
permissions; Jo Lightfoot, commissioning
editor; Melanie Walker, copy editor; and
particularly Peter Jones senior editor for all
his hard work and support during the writing,
editing and design phases of this book.

## Dedication

*To the memory of Albert and Violet Baker,
my parents-in-law, and to James Alexander,
Daniel's father, all of whom died while this book
was being written.*